ORGANIZING FREEDOM

Black Emancipation Activism in the Civil War Midwest

ORGANIZING FREEDOM

Jennifer R. Harbour

Southern Illinois University Press
Carbondale

Southern Illinois University Press
www.siupress.com

Cover illustration: Alfred Jackson Tyler, *John Jones and His Wife Aid a Fugitive*, oil on canvas, 45 × 35 inches. Illinois Legacy Collection, Illinois State Museum, transfer from the State Historical Library; photographer, Dannyl Dolder.

Library of Congress Cataloging-in-Publication Data
Names: Harbour, Jennifer R., 1971– author.
Title: Organizing Freedom : Black Emancipation Activism in the
    Civil War Midwest / Jennifer R. Harbour.
Description: Carbondale : Southern Illinois University Press, 2020.
    | Includes bibliographical references and index.
Identifiers: LCCN 2019033235 (print) | LCCN 2019033236 (ebook)
    | ISBN 9780809337699 (paperback) | ISBN 9780809337705 (ebook)
Subjects: LCSH: African American abolitionists—Middle West—
    History—19th century. | African American abolitionists—Middle
    West—Biography. | Antislavery movements—Middle West—
    History—19th century. | Free blacks—Middle West—History—
    19th century. | United States—History—Civil War, 1861–1865—
    Middle West.
Classification: LCC E185.915 .H37 2020 (print) | LCC E185.915
    (ebook) | DDC 973.7/114—dc23
LC record available at https://lccn.loc.gov/2019033235
LC ebook record available at https://lccn.loc.gov/2019033236

Printed on recycled paper ♻

This paper meets the requirements of ANSI/NISO Z39.48-1992
    (Permanence of Paper). ∞

For Charles Harbour, who has cheerfully carried my books in and out of time zones, zip codes, apartments, dorm rooms, houses, basements, offices, hospitals, libraries, museums, galleries, cars, trains, airports, airplanes, churches, schools, universities, stores, and even castles.

I think I probably love you as much as I love my books.

You have been paid for. Each of you, Black, White, Brown, Yellow, Red—whatever pigment you use to describe yourselves—has been paid for. But for the sacrifices made by some of your ancestors, you would not be here; they have paid for you. So, when you enter a challenging situation, bring them on the stage with you; let their distant voices add timbre and strength to your words. For it is your job to pay for those who are yet to come.

—*Maya Angelou*

Contents

Illustrations

Acknowledgments

"We don't carry black women here." This was the bad news given to me by an archivist one oppressively hot summer day when I was a graduate student. The records at this large state-sponsored institution should have been impressive. After all, the state had allowed slavery, and I had done my research prior to making the trip. My inner monologue: "Black women lived here. Thousands of them were enslaved. They must be here somewhere!" Imagine my joy when, a few hours and several folders later, I found a letter written by a black woman. What the archivist probably meant to say was this: "Go ahead and look, but we generally arrange Civil War materials according to battles, white male leaders, and presidents. Black women aren't our priority."

Thus began five long years of research for this book, my attempt to give a voice to people who no longer have one. It is true that to unearth the daily lives of African American women and tell their story properly, one must place her faith in a combination of serendipity, mind-numbing detective skills, and pixie dust. Actually the last ingredient was delivered entirely through the good humor and endless grace of a cadre of mentors with whom I was blessed. In high school, Jack Howard found me, the kid who was bullied so mercilessly, and helped me learn that I was a valuable person. After he finished knocking some sense into me, he made me read everything from Charlotte Brontë to Michel Foucault to Albert Camus to the *New Yorker* to Shakespeare. When I told him that I didn't understand one book he'd bought for me, he simply said, "Read it again." Jack took me (and Kitty) to New York City to see plays and museums, to the movies to see *Thelma and Louise* and foreign-language films, and he told us to be feminists. When I wasn't sure what that meant, he told me to read *A Room of One's Own* and *The Second Sex*. Jack took us many times to Canada to attend the Stratford Festival, and the entire world opened up before my eyes. When I was done with high school, and the other kids tried to get me removed from the "top ten" because they said I wasn't smart enough, Jack helped me fill out my college applications and sent me on my way.

When I got to university, I met Sandra Seaton, playwright, author, and lover of all things poetic. I wasn't a particularly good writer, but Sandra took me under her wing and told me to "write what you know." I did. I wrote about my grandparents, and she helped me understand the person I was becoming. Sandra introduced me to Alice Walker, Zora Neale Hurston, Audra Lorde, Octavia Butler, Lorraine Hansberry, bell hooks, Toni Morrison, and Maya Angelou. Each day after class, I would follow Sandra to her office, where she'd find another play or book of poems for me to read. At the same university, I studied history with Dr. Patricia Ranft, who taught me to love primary sources and English history. If it weren't for these women, I would not have had the courage to go to Britain and study at a university there. I've never stopped going back to Britain, actually.

When I moved to Washington, DC, to earn a master's degree at George Washington University, I took my first black history class with the late James Horton, who was the grand purveyor of the *real* American history. Jim took me to the National Archives (where he got me a summer internship), the Library of Congress, and all of the Smithsonian museums and buildings. Every single one. I followed Jim through DC the same way I followed my papa when I was a little girl. I was in awe of him then, and I still am now. At GW, I met Linda Grant DePauw, yet another scholar of women. The nation's capital wasn't an easy place for me to live, but Linda took me to Maryland and introduced me to the shoreline, crabs, and how to make space in one's head to write. Linda's specialty was women and war, and she introduced me to history that was never meant to be uncovered, lest it upset the storytellers of the white male hetero-patriarchy. Linda also had a scriptorium, and she told me that I could have one someday, too. It's where I write now. Linda actually encouraged me to leave DC and move to Iowa because she thought I would benefit from studying with other scholars of women's history.

I met my mentor, Leslie Schwalm, at the University of Iowa. Leslie made it possible for me to pursue a crazy hobby (parenthood) while I was in graduate school, and in the many years of taking classes, teaching, writing, and job hunting, she never once told me that I should limit myself or my ambitions. Leslie has such an abundant supply of grace, jubilance, and downright technical skill that she made being a real historian and writer look easy. Only later did I realize it was because she is the Conqueror of all Things Historical. Truly, Leslie taught me how to engage with ghosts whose voices might have otherwise been lost to history. I am still trying to do it well, even though I still feel like a little girl standing on a stool watching her make brownies.

My goodies might always come out a little burned, but the sheer pleasure of cooking alongside Leslie has been one of the greatest joys of my life. I am forever your obedient servant.

My other muse at Iowa, Johanna Schoen, is the most authentic feminist scholar I know. She constantly raises the bar for vigorous scholarship and inquiry, and I am so lucky to have labored in her light. Johanna is tough, funny, and incisive. She spent hours and hours with my prose and the jumbles in my head, helping me to work out what I was really trying to say. To this day her work—in history and in philanthropy—inspires me to be a better human being.

Several institutions provided me with research scholarships. They include the Graduate College and the Department of History at the University of Iowa, the College of Arts and Sciences at the University of Nebraska Omaha, and the Illinois State Historical Society. Dr. Roy Finkenbine at the University of Detroit Mercy offered stellar search guidance for the Black Abolitionist Archive, long before these records were digitized and made available online. At the University of Exeter in England, Dr. Anne Duffin taught me how to pose proper historiographical questions and to work efficiently not only in the archives but in the cemeteries and cathedrals, too! At Oxford University, during the International Human Rights Law Programme, I was lucky enough to work with Radhika Coomaraswamy, who was United Nations special rapporteur on violence against women. Professor Coomaraswamy taught me how to apply the principles of human rights to my teaching and activism and never to back down from a strong feminist stance.

There is a long list of fine individuals I must thank for their advice, counsel, and friendship: Jean Aikin, Janet Ashley, Ned Bertz, Bob Bionaz, Loren Blake, Dave Boocker, Karen Christianson, Catherine Denial, Michael Gaudreau, Heather Godley, Nat Godley, Pat Goodwin, Sarah Hanley, Elizabeth Heineman, John Jackson, Karen Johns, Courtney Donald Kimble, Lionel Kimble, Rick Klagstad, Tim Moon, Annie Peacock, Rebecca Pulju, Jacki Rand, Jennifer Russo, Karen Ruzzin, Sue Stanfield, Doris Stormoen, Mary Strottman, TiShara Wardlow, Ron Warren, and Maryse Zekpa. Drs. Bruce Fehn, Tikia Hamilton, John McKerley, and Kevin Mumford provided substantive comments and helpful criticism. Dr. Joseph Stothert and his team of trauma surgeons at the University of Nebraska Medical Center saved my husband's life and repaired him countless times after that. I also had the good fortune to study with Dr. Robert Jefferson while he was still at Iowa.

The faculty of the Department of Black Studies at the University of Nebraska Omaha deserve special mention because they did a crazy thing and hired a little white girl from Detroit to be their historian. My work and career have benefited from the good counsel of Drs. Nikitah Imani and Cynthia Robinson. Peggy Jones is my soul sister in all things rockstar-teacher-scholar. Peggy has been a mentor to me since day one and has the distinction of being the only person who took the time to cheer me up on that warm day in November 2016 when Hillary Clinton *didn't* become president. Peggy always reminds me that my choices are honorable, thoughtful, and singularly my own. She is the embodiment of black radical feminism, and I hope we will be friends for a very long time.

I also owe sincere thanks to Sylvia Frank Rodrigue, my editor. Syl has spent countless hours reading my work, sending my work to readers, and helping me make this rambling text into something resembling a real book. Her kindness and patience over the past several years have been nothing short of astounding, and I hope this book does you proud. I also had the good fortune to have three anonymous readers who spent a great deal of their precious time reading the manuscript and offering suggestions. I would not have been able to publish this book without their sage advice, and I am so appreciative of the goodwill it took to hang in there with me.

It seems that I have always been going to school, and my family has never wavered in their constant support. My grandmother taught me to love history, and my grandfather taught me to work hard at it. Were it not for them, I would not have been able to leave home and get a "fancy" education. My grandparents were uncomplicated people, and they were the ones who made sure that I was "paid for," as Maya Angelou wrote. My beloved Papa Buster was functionally illiterate but was the most emotionally intelligent person I have ever known. He taught me to be grateful for everything I have, especially the earth, labor unions, and my health. My grandmother, Mae Dell Thompson Williams, insisted that I write long, descriptive letters to all of her friends and relatives "down south." At her knee, I learned to write with love, longing, and kindness. My grandparents modeled integrity, generosity, and plain old sweat equity, and those are the qualities that allowed me to persevere. My father-in-law, the late Charles E. Harbour Sr., always took the time to ask me about graduate school and tease me about my pursuit of a doctorate. My mother-in-law, Rose Anker Harbour, took care of my children for me while I went on long research trips. My sister, Lisa Jensen, accompanied me on several research trips and arranged all manner of celebrations (wedding shower, baby showers, graduation parties) while I was busy going to school.

"It was the laundry." People ask me why it took me so long to write this book. Part of the answer is that it bears little resemblance to my dissertation. The other part of the answer is that laundry for five people is among the most time-consuming tasks on the planet. I was lucky to have a partner who changed diapers, rocked babies, and read bedtime stories, but no person can take over for you when you are pregnant, nursing, or learning to become a good mother. Were it not for the loving care provided to my babies at the West Branch Community Day Care Center, I could not have had a career at all. I often felt guilty, but considering that my "side job" included three beautiful human beings called Olivia Grace, Will, and Henry, I think I paced the work perfectly. Who would want to write a book instead of going to concerts, plays, movies, swimming pools, restaurants, theme parks, and even the dentist with these Harbour children? They also understand that I hate the zoo and am not particularly good at having fun anywhere that isn't a museum or library, so they cheerfully waved goodbye while leaving with Daddy to do normal kid things. They explain superhero subplots to me over and over, they cuddle with me when I require it, and they allow me to get takeout rather than make them a proper supper. They have never expected me to be a normal cookie-baking momma, and for that I am eternally grateful. These little humans have filled my heart in inestimable ways, and they lived with this book for longer than was reasonable. Through late nights, long trips, and sixteen-hour teaching days, they have greeted me with hugs and kisses and cheered me on. My scriptorium is covered with their photographs, art, and notes. They might not realize it, but they have been here with me the whole time.

It's difficult to describe the people who make your life possible, but in this space I can attempt to express my gratitude for two people who have enabled me to fulfill my lifelong dream of being a professor and scholar. First, since I left home some thirty years ago, my mother has driven thousands of miles to reach me and my babies. When she lived in Michigan, she drove back and forth at least three times each year. She came, at her own expense, when I needed to go do research, teach classes, or simply take a nap. Now that she lives with us, she has taken over even more of my reproductive labor so that I can go to work. Any person who understands the weight of the responsibilities that come with a house, a partner, and three kids knows what a heavy burden it can be. Simply put, there aren't enough hours in the day for everything I want to do, but she makes it possible. She has experienced more loss and cruelty than any person I know, yet she happily stands in for me and still manages to mother me all at the same time. I love you, Momma.

Finally, to my partner, who has battled angry library dragons for me on countless occasions. This guy, who is much smarter than I am, gave up his own education so he could pay for mine. He has read this manuscript too many times to count and has also purchased a bigger computer monitor every year following my vision exam. If I asked him for the moon, he would go and fetch it for me, along with something blingy or sparkly. Chip has had unwavering faith in me all along and has been my finest cheerleader. He has been the calm to my storm, my nervousness, and my instability when I couldn't see, much less reach, the shore. I still get a shiver when he walks into a room. What a lucky woman I am.

ORGANIZING FREEDOM

Introduction

In October 1851, Sarah Ann Lucas stood before justice of the peace Jared C. Jocelyn to attest to her "proof of freedom." Born free in Ohio, Sarah had immigrated to Indiana some twenty years earlier. Her white male witnesses, Benjamin Connor and Andrew Israel, further authenticated her state citizenship by swearing that they had known her to be "a free person of colour" for ten years.[1] A year later, in August 1852, Sarah returned to the same Floyd County Courthouse to register as a black resident, which Indiana law required of all African Americans. In late 1853, Sarah helped another black woman, an enslaved runaway called "Amanda," to cross the Ohio River into New Albany, Indiana. Ostensibly, Sarah provided Amanda with legal advice, because Amanda presented herself as a free person in the Floyd County Courthouse in early December 1853, albeit with a fake name. On January 7, 1854, in Louisville, Kentucky, police arrested Sarah for "enticing [the] slave" Amanda, known property of Benjamin J. Adams, a resident of Kentucky. Judge Joyes threw out the felony charges and gave Sarah bail, set at six hundred dollars, as long as she demonstrated "good behavior" for a year.[2]

Sarah and Amanda's story illustrates the complicated and dynamic nature of freedom in the antebellum and wartime Midwest, where African Americans resolutely claimed free states as locations for emancipated communities. This book analyzes black community activism in antebellum and wartime Illinois and Indiana, places that would become tremendously important sites of contest. These states shared similar circumstances: they were geographically close to slave and border states, they had a history of similarly functioning black codes and other repressive laws, they protected the rights of slaveowners whenever enslaved people were brought in, and they were home to some of the most virulent proslavery racists in the region, especially in their southern sections. An analysis of the black activism in these states reveals an obscene truth in African American history—freedom was not granted by any one law or slaveowner or politician or state constitution or even a civil war; it had to be made into something tangible by blacks themselves. Indiana earned statehood in 1816, and Illinois followed suit in 1818. Both state constitutions, representing the supposed demands of the white constituency, disallowed slavery.[3] Those same voters, however, would do everything in their power to stop blacks from coming into their states. Scholars have engaged in the crucial task of posing what seems to be an elementary question: How did slaves transition from cradle-to-grave, race-based, labor-intense servitude into a condition of personhood called freedom? Somehow we have managed to teach schoolchildren that crossing a river like the Ohio—with slavery on one side and freedom on the other—might have been arduous, but touching a foot or hand to "free" soil equaled the end of a thousand brutalities wrought by slavery. America, we are told, is a place where one can judge how much terrorism, dehumanization, and degradation was meted out just by knowing whether a place was a "slave state" or not.

Mid-nineteenth-century Indiana and Illinois amplify the neglected history of the black experience by highlighting the inadequacy of this argument. In America, there was no "good" place to have black or brown skin, and to be a woman with black or brown skin was even worse. By studying the Midwest, we can see emancipation for what it really was: sluggish, protracted, and filled with its own barbarities. But we can also see the raw humanity in the people who sought it: aggressive, tenacious, and anxious to engage with the most powerful institutions in America. In common parlance, *slavery* and *freedom* are used to describe seemingly opposite states of birth and of being. In fact, American slavery was sui generis, incomparable in world history for its self-propagation.[4] The Northwest Ordinance forbade slavery in Indiana and Illinois, but the rights of slaveowners to transfer, detain, hunt, and secure their property was stunningly well protected both de jure and de facto. Race-based slavery also meant that nonwhite people could be caught, bought, and sold at any time, regardless of their free status. As a result, the institution of slavery—and sweeping national respect for it—created a closed society in which black people were neither slaves nor masters, nor entirely free. As such, the precarity of midwestern African Americans defies the usual historical categorization, and the only way to truly understand their approach to emancipation is to retrace their steps leading up to it.

Free blacks' vision of emancipation included ideals of self-determinism, citizenship rights, and the ability to control their own families and domiciles. In the 1840s and 1850s, long before anyone could have predicted the Civil War, activists sought jobs and began to build schools and churches in their free black neighborhoods. Indiana and Illinois legislators discouraged and blocked black settlement with fines, bounties, and rigorous legal requirements, such as those encountered by Sarah Ann Lucas. Still, blacks entreated the local white power structure to extend some degree of formalized state citizenship to them, despite the threat of violent backlash. In the 1860s, this activism was mature enough for blacks to demand equal treatment as Union soldiers and families. Black people insisted that the destruction of slavery was crucial to their emancipation everywhere, including the Midwest. Men and women alike sought to define and secure their freedoms by becoming activists within local and state settings. Emancipation activism sought the acquisition of rights and responsibilities for blacks as groups and as individual citizens.

This book makes a pointed delineation between the study of *Reconstruction* and *emancipation*. While the study of presidential and radical Reconstruction, especially the Reconstruction amendments, has been useful to historians when analyzing a wide range of wartime topics, emancipation as part of the black experience has yet to be fully explored. Thus, my choice to focus on emancipation rather than Reconstruction is a deliberate one. Although Foner's impressive and legendary *Reconstruction: America's Unfinished Revolution, 1863–1877* indicted the Dunning School for its description of blacks as childlike and simpleminded, scholarship in general was slow to revise its one-dimensional portrait of blacks as a victimized, blighted population with nearly no agency.[5] Studies of Reconstruction have generally approached it as a period of Union occupation of the South, which ended in 1877. In these traditional histories, African Americans played mostly minor roles. More recently, historians have demonstrated the relationships among black suffrage, labor, and politics as they pertain to the end of the war and the rebuilding of the South.[6] Civil War historiography may be an overcrowded field but not for the cause of black women as historical agents—this literature is pitifully small when compared with the prodigious volumes describing the lives of soldiers, presidents, and military leaders, not to mention the details of regional and local histories, battles and skirmishes, medical practices, legislative and legal occurrences, and even historical memorialization.[7]

This book offers a narrative of emancipation as a gradual, incremental process. It also emphasizes the contributions of black women as central to that narrative, rather than just peripheral.[8] In this endeavor, I hope to repair some of the astoundingly reductionist historiography of gender, race, and slavery. Emancipation was an activist enterprise designed, managed, modified, and implemented by blacks themselves. Emancipation was not conferred, granted, or even gifted. Yes, an enslaved human being could be bought, sold, emancipated, manumitted, willed, stolen, kidnapped, deeded, mortgaged, jailed, seized as an asset, transferred, or simply let go, but that is the language of the oppressor and the purview of the white gaze.[9] Emancipation in its purest form was self-empowerment, either for groups or individuals, and it was the stated goal of black communities everywhere.

Many Americans still believe that emancipation was something bestowed on blacks—whether through antislavery or abolitionist efforts—by benevolent whites, beginning with Lincoln himself.[10] Because this interpretation has done little to suffuse the history of African Americans with tangible evidence of agency and self-determination, the first goal of this book is to enlarge the definition of the term *emancipation*. This word is used by many historians to mean "the destruction of slavery," but this book reveals the hidden dimensions of black activists who sought emancipation from outside the South—in this case, in two free midwestern states. African Americans often found themselves (and their families) stuck in a liminal space between legal slavery and freedom but squarely in the capitalistic marketplace.[11] Enslaved men and women were often "hired out" by their owners to earn money for the planter's coffers or occasionally allowed to keep the money themselves. The contractual vagaries of slavery meant that enslaved persons could legally be owned by infants and children, people who lived abroad, and even the long dead.[12] In the nineteenth century, to be black meant that freedom was never a given, no matter where one lived. In short, emancipation for all—which included the destruction of slavery—required the commitment of the larger black community.

The second goal of this book, then, is to direct the historian's gaze north and west, and toward women and gender roles.[13] Historical treatments of emancipation have heretofore focused almost exclusively on the Northeast and the South, and mostly concern men. This book also offers a fresh approach to the study of the Civil War, emancipation, and African American life by expanding the focus to include free black women, their spouses and families, and their communities.[14] In American historiography, black women's raced, gendered, and sexualized lives have only recently attracted sophisticated analyses.[15] Even when black women do appear in secondary sources, the analysis of their lives is overly focused on their oppression, their roles as mothers and wives, or their position at the very bottom of the racial caste system.[16] By capitalizing on local activist opportunities, black women promoted the construction of educational, civic, and occupational opportunities for women in American society.[17] By centering themselves squarely in community activity, they also created opportunities for protest discourse, racial self-expression, and freedoms defined by their own conceptions of gender.[18]

Furthermore, this book enlarges the current historiographical conversation by describing and analyzing the legal and socioeconomic situation for blacks in the Midwest. One would be pressed to find a better example of a landscape so susceptible to constant transformation. Despite the expansion of the historiography in recent years, the African American struggle for existence and adaptation beyond the Mississippi and Missouri Rivers has only begun to be fully examined by historians.[19] Emancipation activism occurred in all parts of the country, wherever black people lived, but especially as they escaped slavery and sought refuge. American society in the nineteenth century was culturally, economically, socially, and legally shaped by the institution of slavery, but the dichotomy of slave/free is no longer particularly useful as we struggle to understand the subtleties and nuances of the history of race relations in this country.[20] Because the justification of slavery emphasized the supposed natural inferiority of blacks, free African Americans naturally suffered under the sister system of white supremacy.

Another objective of this study couples the traditional study of war's totalizing nature with an interrogation of how black communities functioned during the conflict. Many historians have chosen to focus on individual black military participation as the chief method by which blacks sought citizenship rights, but that method was limited to men. Additionally, the case for male soldiering as *the* exclusive method for black entry into the civic arena has been overstated: "Military service had given Chicago blacks their first opportunity to participate in any sort of community activity."[21] Military participation was certainly a conspicuous political act, but it was not a decision that men made alone, nor was it something they alone experienced. Because the Civil War was one of the world's first forays into what scholars term *total warfare*, it would be a mistake of great proportions to interpret combatants independently of their wives, children, families, and communities, not to mention the fact that slavery as an institution played a colossal role in the war.[22] Using the voices of the women themselves, this book aims to provide sharper treatment of the sacrifice, economic stress, and civic turmoil that the war brought to black families and communities.[23] If we are to understand the black experience as something more than just a one-dimensional portrayal of a people grateful for white paternalism and the end of slavery, then we must be more incisive as we examine the real risks and outcomes of black enlistment, and we must do so with a sophisticated gender and race analysis.[24]

The third goal of this book is to describe and analyze midwestern black organizational activity, which accelerated in the two decades before the Civil War. By analyzing how black activists wrapped up their meanings of emancipation in the politics of institution building, we can better understand both their battle to survive as well as their place in nineteenth-century politics. I refer to this organizing as *emancipation activism*, a theme that runs throughout the book and encompasses foundation building, legal battles, regional geopolitics, and wartime participation. By tracing change over time, this analysis offers a new perspective on the story of local black communities. Older narratives about pre-emancipation society focused on white abolitionists rather than black ones. Traditional approaches to the history of black communal activism have also focused mostly on men, because they identify leaders who participated in the political process through local male-centered organizations, state constitutional conventions, the ministry, and, later, through the ballot itself.[25] This study analyzes the kind of solid structural foundations that members of burgeoning black communities created to sustain their emancipation activism.[26] Additionally, antebellum protests and organizing help us understand the two most important loci of communal growth—education and religion.

Chapter 1 maps out the genesis and evolution of local black communities. Illinois and Indiana were terrifically important sites of geopolitical debate and conflict from 1840 to 1865, and this study chronicles the maturation of the black community in those years. African Americans living in the Midwest were supposedly free, but they were hardly at liberty to do whatever they wanted. Inspired by C. Vann Woodward, historians have understood the fin de siècle Jim Crow era as the "nadir" of African American history, but white racists crafted restrictions to black emancipation in the antebellum Midwest with the same frightening precision. Black codes were critical to white governance and so severe that they limited free blacks' engagement with civil society in every possible way.

As chapter 2 illustrates, black activists initially planned full-scale resistance to the black codes in the 1840s, only to be confronted by the horrifying realities of the 1850 Fugitive Slave Law (FSL). Since it had the effect of making slavery national—by relaxing slavery's boundaries in the South—black midwestern organizational thought and planning flourished following this catastrophic event. Although the methodology used here examines black activists in a study of mostly small communities, this book aims to enlarge the conversation about emancipation to include the Midwest, while analyzing the complicated nature of gender, race, and citizenship.

Most white midwesterners supported a segregated, racist idea of governance with such force as to create unfailingly onerous living conditions for Illinois and Indiana blacks.[27] Whether they were proslavery or not, Republican or Democrat, lawmakers repeatedly considered and passed laws characterized by staunch proprietorship over Indiana and Illinois. As has been the case throughout much of American history, white inhabitants assumed an offensive stance, claiming that black immigrants would steal their labor opportunities and upset the local economic and civic status quo. Whites also wanted complete control of social space and would insist on strict racial segregation when immigrants did appear. Indeed, many whites believed that blacks might take over white towns altogether. What is ironic, of course, is that blacks were in no position to appropriate much of anything. Nevertheless, they longed for self-sufficiency and independence, and they continued their active fight against legislation designed to curtail their freedoms.[28]

Midwestern blacks were dedicated to creating havens for themselves, their extended families, and their enslaved brethren.[29] As chapter 2 demonstrates, the church was the physical, emotional, spiritual, and intellectual core of each black community. Since its inception, the African Methodist Episcopal (AME) Church in particular placed heavy emphasis on solving problems within the black community, which included political and social as well as religious concerns. AME's founder, Richard Allen, maintained that the church should pay special attention to the problems of individuals. Thus, the mission of the AME Church included development of the mind and racial uplift, as gained through education, temperance, and good personal habits. In order to fulfill this mission, black activists concentrated on building church edifices, membership rolls, coffers, schools, and ministry services. The philosophy of race unity translated directly into a process of mutual aid and self-help for emancipation activism.

Chapter 3 shows how, as regional activists persevered, they remained committed to free communities that included emancipation in all areas of civic life. Emancipation, for these activists, went way beyond the destruction of slavery. This chapter traces the trajectory of midwestern black activism as the sectional crisis developed. Much of what was happening on a national scale was mirrored in the small settlements of Indiana and Illinois where black Americans sought to define the pace and tone of emancipation on their own terms. For blacks who chose to remain in these emerging places, emancipation needed to occur on a local and regional level as well. Activists had no choice but to react to oppressive measures like the FSL, but they also continued to build churches and schools and campaign against the black codes.

Chapter 4 examines women's philanthropic work and men's participation in the Union army (as well as the effects of both types of labor on kinship ties) to understand how free communities interpreted the war. Furthermore, by offering an analysis of how citizenship roles were adopted and played out in African American communities, my study broadens the work of scholars who have concluded that blacks turned the war into a crusade to eradicate not only slavery but other forms of injustice enacted against them.[30] An analysis of the gendered nature of black soldiering as part of the broader social context of servicemen and their families illuminates the ways in which soldiers and their families have been negligently examined as separate entities. Each black man who served on the battlefield, in the camps, and in the trenches represented a whole family and an entire community rather than just one individual. In terms of gender roles, there is much to be learned from participation in total warfare. Black men reported feeling emasculated, for instance, because they could not provide protection for their wives. And in the course of military service, black manhood underwent a transformation that would have lasting effects on women's lives as well. When the war came, responsibilities back home became so burdensome that women longed for their male helpmates—not because of the dictates of gender but because the conditions of war created a welter of choices, emotions, and tasks that were overwhelming for one person to manage who cared for an extended family.

Chapter 5 further complicates this narrative by exploring clusters of free black women who, despite these hindrances, offered service to the Union in myriad ways. The achievements of this wartime labor, or warwork, created an elaborate web of meanings for black women. Surely these women felt some degree of patriotism and desire to be included in the franchise, yet they understood all too well the hegemonic forces that were constantly at work to suppress them. Free African American women fought their own internal (individual/personal) and external (civic/communal) war, and this chapter illustrates some of the ways they constructed their identities in a hugely fragmented society. This chapter also shows how the activism of free blacks involved complex constructions of gender roles and how the process of emancipation mediated those roles. Activism affected ideologies of black womanhood and manhood as free people sought religious, educational, political, military, and social-service roles. Black women's traditional reproductive labor grew exponentially when the community's resources were so stretched. To be sure, women probably would have liked to relinquish some of their duties, but they instead added more tasks to their laboring lives. In turn, that labor shaped ideals of emancipation and citizenship for both individuals and communities.

In all, this book aims to identify and analyze the type of political culture sown and reaped by African American activists. With each step in the emancipation process, they were met with new horrors: black codes, exclusionary laws, the FSL, and, later, the war itself. I join other historians who desire a better understanding of the claims black people laid on themselves as well as their government. In the continuing search for security, dignity, and freedom, black identity evolved over time—but it was not simply a matter of victimhood. Discussions about race and gender intertwined as blacks tried to understand how each man, woman, and child would take his or her place in the "new" country, free of white control and blossoming with opportunities for self-determination. Democracy for black Americans meant that slavery would be abolished so that all people could take part in an egalitarian society. Citizenship, and the freedoms it promised, brought complex and often competing roles to its bearers, especially for black women. This story of free black people shows how the ideal of equality often competed with reality in an ever-shifting and imperfect growing nation. Faced with a horrifying set of circumstances that understandably compelled thousands of others to flee to Canada, midwestern activists appropriated the legal threats against them to bolster their groups and sustain their goals. Black people in the region participated in the Underground Railroad, formed neighborhood police forces and watches, raised money during prayer vigils and church fairs, and continued to argue in public and in print that oppressive laws barred them from enjoying the full citizenship they deserved as free persons.[31] In doing so, they created a unique regional identity anchored to a wider range of opportunities for black life in a new space.

1. Free Black Communities and Black Codes

African Americans immigrated to Illinois and Indiana because they wanted religious, educational, and occupational opportunities. Collective resistance to black codes encouraged the development of sophisticated self-conscious communities that fostered a political culture dedicated to challenging laws.[1] Although emancipation proceeded sluggishly, black emigrants choose Indiana and Illinois because the region was a geographically ideal place to put down "deep roots" at a reasonable distance from slave states.[2] Traveling anywhere in the nation was risky for black people because the color of their skin alone brought risks ranging from baseless accusations, denial of services, demands to produce freedom papers or pay bounties, beatings, theft, lynching, sexual assault, and sale into slavery.[3] Added to that was race-based segregation in the public sphere. Even blacks who had been born free in America could be wrested from their loved ones and sent south to be sold.

Black settlers who arrived in the Midwest were unsurprised to discover that the so-called free territory owed its republican political and legal infrastructure to white hostility and racism. Nevertheless, for those black people who had escaped cruel masters and barbarous conditions, settling in a place where legislation banned slavery still put them one step closer to freedom.[4] Scholars have recently engaged in the significant work of probing myriad nuances and subtleties of racialized freedom in border and free states, but we have yet to fully humanize the very people who experienced it.[5] African American activists were relentless—they simultaneously established and supported organizations in the Midwest, fought black codes, advocated for the destruction of slavery, and pursued plans for their own emancipation.[6]

Emancipation activists identified their opponents, sought to influence public opinion, and created a specific collective identity intimately linked to social protest. As social movement theorists suggest, African Americans possessed a profound desire to overcome instability and disorder in their lives, and they sought to construct a new viable social order. For the midwestern black community's emancipation activism, the key to success was thoughtful organization and community building. Schools, churches, and protest rallies often served as avenues for disruption and agency for both men and women.[7] Newspapers, pamphlets, sermons, state conventions, and speeches became the essential tools by which activists could voice their beliefs about the true scope of emancipation. In churches, schools, courtrooms, conventions, and public-speaking spaces, their commitment to the abolition of slavery would remain unchanged, even though their methods and means sometimes did change.[8]

While most whites viewed the presumed black incapacity for proper citizenship to be a major obstacle to emancipation, African Americans refused to accept the notion that they would be dependent on whites in their new circumstances, but they puzzled over their best community-building strategies.[9] Black women in particular envisioned access to financial and occupational success and the eventual creation of permanent cultural fixtures such as Christian churches and schools.[10] Once activists decided on their priorities in achieving emancipation, they could then focus on the preparation and process of their design, which required local interaction and cooperation.[11] The answer lay in their ability to organize themselves in structured and meaningful ways. African Americans reveal themselves in the historical record as people who understood themselves as a planned, self-conscious community.[12]

* * *

Conditions of autonomy and self-determination were so constrained for blacks in the Midwest that it is difficult to discern the distinction between slavery and freedom.[13] Slavery and involuntary servitude were forbidden by the Northwest Ordinance, but there was no provision for enforcement, which allowed whites to bring slaves into the area with an alarming degree of ease and frequency.[14] A majority of whites who lived in the five states created by the Northwest Ordinance either had little sympathy for slaves or were proslavery.[15] White residents had a vested interest in maintaining the subordinate position of blacks so that they might fully benefit from a race-based caste hierarchy.[16] The Northwest Ordinance protected the rights of resident slaveholders who already owned slaves. Indiana's 1816 state constitution was so ambiguous as to ban both slavery and indenture but allow for "limited slave" labor in places like salt mines. Hoosiers also insisted that slaveholders' rights were grandfathered, thereby making it easier for masters to bring enslaved people into Indiana, Illinois, and Ohio and simply refer to them as "indentured servants."[17] Illinois allowed such indentures until 1820, and in the antebellum Midwest it was unclear whether a black person could quit his indenture without incurring criminal charges.[18] Escaped and manumitted slaves did immigrate to the Midwest, but it is difficult to estimate the number of slaves who resided there in the late 1840s and early 1850s.[19] The census of 1840, which did enumerate slaves, estimated a total of 350 slaves, most of whom were listed as residing in the river counties of southern Illinois.[20] Not until 1820 and 1848 would slavery be explicitly outlawed by the state constitutions of Indiana and Illinois.[21] In short, systems of labor (whether free, paid, indentured, or chattel slavery) did not always reflect the written laws of a state or territory and were purposely indeterminate so that African Americans were constantly confused, although this did not deter them from bringing freedom suits to local and state courts.[22]

African American settlers soon discovered that white legislators and their constituents were doing everything in their power to keep black immigrants out of their state.[23] Many of these whites were southern transplants themselves, so they brought ideas about race-based slavery with them to the Midwest. To claim that whites discouraged the creation of free black communities would be an understatement. In 1819, a year after Illinois was admitted to the Union, legislators passed a set of exclusionary rules called "black laws," now commonly referred to as black codes.[24] Provisions for Illinois blacks included the following: denial of education, military service, the right to vote, and recognizance by the court system; flogging of lazy or insolent blacks; fining and whipping for one African American who "harbored" another; and removal to indentured service for those who could not pay fines.[25] Black people were also required to post a one-thousand-dollar bond as security against becoming dependents.[26] Additionally, freedpeople entering the state were required to provide a "certificate of freedom," along with descriptions of family members who could potentially be forcibly removed, if the family proved poor enough to be a burden to the state. In worst-case scenarios, escaped slaves and even freedpeople could be sold back into slavery. In Golconda, Illinois, for instance, it was common knowledge among the townspeople that a man called William Bedford earned cash by apprehending black people. Bedford "kept a favorite blood-hound for this purpose, and was often seen upon the highway, on horseback with [a dog] sitting in his lap."[27]

The goals of black codes were not dissimilar to some of the strategies used by slaveowners to exert control over enslaved people. Segregationists effectively terrorized black people by allowing for constant threats, harassment, and the promise of forced removal. Indiana's Article XIII, which warned that "no negro or mulatto shall come into or settle in the state," was haphazardly enforced but still depended on the impulses of the dominant culture that demanded exclusion. White midwesterners claimed that black settlers might "Africanize" their state.[28] White supremacists also sent a clear message that black existence was entirely dependent on white tolerance and permissiveness.[29] African Americans could only remain in the Midwest if white residents were absolutely convinced that there would be no disruption to their own lives. The real value of this cruel system lay in the emotional, social, and psychological effects suffered by all blacks who were made to feel beholden to white society for their right to settle somewhere new. Yet whites had no concrete way to keep freedpeople from seeking sanctuary in the Midwest, North, or West. The situation would always be preferable to living in the South.[30] Ironically, the problem of where free, freed, and enslaved people would live was a cause of the Civil War, but what measures imposed could ever have effectively deterred slaves from running away from southern farms and plantations? As the historical record shows, African Americans would never be dissuaded from attempting to rejoin their loved ones and reunite their families following long periods of separation.

Whites in Indiana used a two-pronged approach to discourage African American settlement: they championed schemes whereby American black people would colonize Liberia, and they passed their own set of black codes. Not long after Indiana was admitted to the Union as a state, legislators began to debate how to prevent fugitive slaves from entering their state. In 1829, Governor James B. Ray noted in his address to the Indiana General Assembly that Indianans should beware of southern states' laws that required enslaved people to leave the state immediately upon manumission. Ray warned against "emigration into the state from known paupers" and suggested that such "[black] foreigners" be "thrown back to the state from whence they came."[31] The following year, a Posey County resident warned his fellow Indianans against black immigrants: "The dregs of offscourings of the slave states are most likely to change residence, and they are too incurably affected with that horrible gangrene of morals which slavery engenders, to be welcomed among a virtuous and intelligent people."[32] Of course, freedpeople understood that they were unwanted, but it was still several hundred thousand steps away from plantations and paddy rollers.

If African Americans settlers had any hope that whites might be hospitable to immigrants, white supremacy soon disabused them of that notion. Nevertheless, for thousands of blacks, the decision to leave the South was a forgone conclusion—slavery was unabashedly legal there.[33] Moreover, laws in most southern states required newly freed blacks to leave. And racial attitudes in the Northeast were acrimonious enough to cause black emigrants to look westward in the hope that the situation there might be better.[34] It was not unlikely that African American emigrants on the move would find themselves stopped by random whites and asked to pay bounties or provide proof of freedom.[35] Black people who deliberately chose to settle in the Midwest rather than the Northeast faced direct individual and institutional threats from a hostile society. As Carter G. Woodson noted ninety years ago, "Many of the [white] Northerners who sympathized with oppressed blacks in the South never dreamt of having them as their neighbors."[36] The same could be said of midwestern whites who sought to create a container culture that would keep their towns and cities segregated. In fact, early histories of the region often note the extreme nature of white supremacy in the region.[37]

In the Midwest, cooperation among blacks and whites was complicated at best, violent at worst. There were few interracial abolitionist groups, and although a small group of abolitionists supported the destruction of slavery, they were often negrophobic. Many white people objected to slavery or its expansion on moral or religious grounds, but they still understood their world according to white hegemonic dictates. The majority of whites feared the repercussions of emancipation, imagining hordes of blacks taking jobs that "belonged" to whites. The thought of emancipation provoked fearful questions: Where would black people live? Where would they work? Would they seek revenge on white society? Would they want to have relationships with whites? As a result of this fear, nineteenth-century black codes in the Midwest dictated much of the movement of free blacks. Midwestern whites, like most other whites in the nineteenth century, thought that African American people needed to be controlled and monitored in a variety of ways.[38]

Free and enslaved people often settled just north of the Ohio River, where they sought to create new lives outside the South. Since the river was also a waterway for the Underground Railroad, enslaved people often found themselves stranded in southern Illinois or Indiana. (Sometimes they had their hearts set on areas farther north where their loved ones might be waiting or were believed to be living.) Though Chicago was a terminus of the Underground Railroad, escaped slaves often did not make it that far north. For white Americans who lived in Indiana or Illinois, the encroachment was most unwelcome. Though many of these whites claimed that they disapproved of slavery, they did not espouse equality for blacks. A fair number of these whites even voiced approval of slavery (some had previously owned slaves themselves), and this caused a great deal of conflict among white groups, especially once many Free-Soilers became full-fledged Republicans as the war drew near.[39] Whites in southern Indiana and Illinois were both geographically and ideologically close to the slaveholding South. This translated into undiminished support for the black codes.[40] As a result, the issue of blacks' rights took on a bitter sectional and partisan tone in the Midwest.

* * *

Illinois was admitted to the Union in 1818 with some forty thousand settlers reportedly living there.[41] Illinois was already home to many proslavery settlers who had immigrated there from the South, but abolitionist groups also managed to grow their membership in the antebellum period. Abolitionism, however, was primarily concerned with the destruction of slavery, not with racial equality. People who claimed to be antislavery often failed to support any attempt to secure multiple freedoms for their African American neighbors. For the black people of Illinois, the freedom to form autonomous and self-sufficient communities was an entire operation unto itself.

Free black populations were concentrated in a few midwestern locations in the antebellum period and would not constitute any significant population until well after the Civil War. In Indiana, the free black population numbered 7,000 in 1840 and 11,428 in 1860, making African Americans less than 1 percent of the total population.[42] These populations were concentrated largely in the areas near the Ohio River and the lower Wabash River. Blacks also settled in abolitionist areas in the eastern part of the state. In Illinois, there were approximately 7,500 African Americans in 1860, most of whom lived either in Chicago or in counties along the Ohio or Mississippi River.[43] But for some whites, even the smallest population of African Americans constituted a menace.

Black midwestern history is full of extraordinary tales of heroism in life-and-death circumstances, especially on the Underground Railroad.[44] Stephen Vincent's study of the Roberts and Beech settlements revealed a popular tale, which he referred to as a legend. As the story is still told, a group of African Americans traveling by carriage and on foot to Indiana in the 1830s was met by a band of hostile whites. The whites demanded that the blacks stop and show their free papers, and when the travelers refused, the white men stuck fence rails between the spokes of the wagons' wheels so the party could not proceed. The blacks were saved only by the smart thinking of a light-skinned black woman called Martha Walden, who told the white men that she was leading the group across the frontier and then demanded that they be allowed to pass.[45] This story illustrates how black people confronted danger as they sought to preserve their freedom in an undeniably hostile environment.

Although the sheer number of racist incidents must have been disheartening to blacks, some whites did wish to see emancipation succeed, or at least to appear to have offered help when they were feeling generous. A few immigrants even received money from whites as they moved into the area and sought housing and employment. According to his obituary, a black man called George Fisher immigrated to Fort Wayne, Indiana, in 1846 when he was only nineteen years old. Fisher possessed such a "keen intellect" that a white man called Sam Hanna decided first to give Fisher a plot of land and then to help him start his own plastering business. This indicates how some friendly whites and stalwart blacks were able to find their way to one another and form relationships, however traumatic the process. African Americans must have known that these types of relationships were a rarity in the North, and nearly impossible in the South. Few sources suggest that midwestern whites "warmed" to black settlement. When a new state constitution was put to a vote in 1851, more Indianans voted for the passage of Article XIII, which forbade "negro or mulatto" settlement, than for the whole constitution itself. For a few lucky local people of color, some safer havens actually did exist.[46] Randolph County, which contained the largest black population in the state prior to the war, was one of four counties where a majority of citizens voted against Article XIII. This was due in large part to the prominent population of antislavery Quakers who resided in the area, many of whom had set out to convince people of other denominations (usually Baptists) to join the abolitionist cause. At any rate, concern for African Americans fell mostly within the purview of a constituency of Quakers, not the Republican Party.[47]

Midwestern African Americans did have some history of cohesiveness with white communities, especially when white women pursued antislavery activism themselves.[48] In 1843, a white mob rioted to prevent William T. Allan from forming a local abolition society. The local newspaper reported that the group of detained activists was unusual because it contained several white women.[49] Both Peoria and Galesburg had active white women's antislavery groups, and in 1844 they joined to form the Illinois Female Anti-Slavery Society. Forty-five women attended the convention, whereupon they decided that the new organization should dedicate itself to the education of black children "at Galesburg or any other place where opportunity may offer."[50] The society held regular local and statewide meetings, and in 1847 the members assembled for the special task of creating a petition against the black codes of their state.[51] They elected Mary A. Blanchard (whose husband was president of Knox College) and Mary Davis to lead the petition drive. They were disappointed when they secured only six hundred signatures.[52] Nonetheless, women leaders continued to write columns for the *Western Citizen*, offering their support for black emancipation. This newspaper, published from 1842 to 1853, was the official publication of the La Salle County and Illinois Anti-Slavery Societies. Its editor, Zebina Eastman, an antislavery activist and writer from Lowell, Massachusetts, had originally moved to Illinois to assist Benjamin Lundy with the publication of the *Genius of Universal Emancipation*, an abolitionist paper and forerunner to the Liberty Party, a branch of the antislavery political party founded in 1839, whose members included a host of Chicago's prominent activists, all of whom professed loyalty to the Constitution and to the Union.[53] Its circulation included readers primarily in Indiana, Illinois, Iowa, and Wisconsin. Mary Davis compared the treatment of blacks in Galesburg and in Peoria, arguing that African Americans in the former city fared much better as a result of white paternalism. In fact, she noted, there were six black sisters living in Galesburg who, after having received a "good English education," had purchased land, built a home and barn, and acquired a pew in the local church.[54] Some of these same activists later allied themselves with the women's suffrage movement. In 1849, Mary Davis asked Illinoisans if there "could not be some reform with regard to the right of woman?"[55] There is some evidence that white women grew to be better neighbors to blacks in their towns than some other white inhabitants.[56] In the late 1850s, a white woman named Sarah Curtis from Evansville, Indiana, attempted to procure a small room in the community in order to establish a school for black children. Curtis was ostracized so thoroughly by the other white women in the community that she gave up her teaching "in utter disgust" after only a few months and returned home.[57]

* * *

The story of one couple's migration and subsequent activism perfectly illustrates the ways in which black men and women constructed their lives as they fought for emancipation.[58] In 1838, Mary Jones (née Richardson) decided that Memphis, Tennessee, had lost its allure, as slaveholding was popular in the state. Mary had fared better than many other African American women in the city, but she was still a member of a highly marginalized group.[59] Growing up near the shores of the Mississippi, Mary was geographically close to the river that carried blacks to freedom, but she was still perilously close to the violence and brutality that were a matter of daily life in the South.[60] Tennessee imposed too many restrictions on a young African American woman such as her. So, at the age of eighteen, Mary became determined (along with her parents) to leave Memphis. Mary's father was a skilled blacksmith, and the Richardson family made the decision to move north, where free blacks might have greater occupational and legal freedoms.[61] Like so many other black families in antebellum America, they sought a place that would allow them access to a richer economic, political, intellectual, and social life.

The Richardsons chose Alton, Illinois, as their destination, aware that the growing town just north of St. Louis offered both advantageous proximity to the Mississippi River and dangerous nearness to the slave state of Missouri.[62] Although Mary had recently fallen in love with a Memphis resident named John Jones, she packed her bags and left nonetheless.[63] Tennessee, a border state with slavery, was hardly a land of great promise for African Americans who had either been born free or had escaped slavery.[64] Though the FSL and black codes gave slavery and white supremacy legal protection in the Midwest, the region had several conditions that a young woman like Mary would have found attractive: a growing emancipation network; a bustling Underground Railroad with both black and white activists; and an abundance of land for businesses, homes, schools, and especially churches.[65]

Mary preceded John in her decision to seek a more egalitarian society. When she moved to Alton, he followed. Though John must have known that his move brought a higher probability for social and economic growth, it seems that one of John's motivations for the trip was Mary's hand in marriage. Mary believed that wedlock and eventual motherhood would be better in the Midwest, but she was also willing to bet that unforeseen circumstances could prevent John's arrival entirely. In other words, Mary did not put marriage first—this is one of the first acts of agency that her historical record reveals to us. Though she undoubtedly loved her future husband, she made plans to improve her own life condition prior to marriage. Mary would wait for John for three years, and in that time, she no doubt carefully considered the options available to a free black woman. Luckily, Mary's father was a skilled tradesperson, and the Richardson family never faced the kind of destitute poverty that other black people suffered.[66]

Tracing the story of the Joneses' migration allows historians to infer some of the circumstances that other blacks faced in the region. John went west for love, as did countless other African Americans who wanted to rejoin their loved ones. John also wanted better labor opportunities and would later become one of Chicago's preeminent black activists, but he had been born in 1816 on a slave plantation in Greene County, North Carolina. His mother was a free light-skinned black of mixed parentage and his father a German with the surname Bromfield. Luckily for John, his mother's free status made him technically free, too. John's mother probably knew, however, that it could be difficult for her son's white relatives to resist the urge to enslave the small boy, so she sent him away to be apprenticed to a man named Sheppard.[67] After John moved to Tennessee, Sheppard bound the youngster over to a tailor named Richard Clere, who taught John his trade. Once John was old enough and experienced enough to work on his own, Clere hired him out to another tailor in Memphis.[68] In the course of his work with other free black tradespeople in Memphis, John had met and fallen in love with Mary. John had to remain in Memphis to finish his term of service, but he planned to follow Mary and her family to Illinois as soon as possible.[69]

For a free black person in the early part of the nineteenth century, making the decision to move to another state was complicated by socioeconomic issues. Despite his good intentions and years of hard work learning a trade, John's livelihood and person were not considered to be his own. Clere was near death, and John was still an indentured servant with a contract to fulfill. Clere's heirs were preparing to claim John as their property and sell him into slavery, most likely in Texas. Upon learning of this plot, John immediately petitioned Clere (who knew of but did not approve of the plan to sell him) for permission to travel to North Carolina to obtain proof of his free status. After having traveled to the coast in a matter of days, John filed a petition in January 1838 in the Eleventh Judicial District with Judge V. D. Barry.[70] His petition described his early life, his apprenticeship, and his travels with Clere, who had hired John out to another tailor in 1836 and 1837.[71] John argued that Clere had actually forfeited his right to custody of his person during the hiring-out process. On these grounds, John requested that he be allowed to testify in court and be discharged on a writ of habeas corpus. On January 16, 1838, the judge ordered John to be released. He was, once again, a free man—free to follow Mary to Illinois.[72]

But like other African Americans who migrated north and west, John had another problem: he needed money to make the trip and to set up housekeeping once he arrived, especially if he wanted to marry. In order to save money, he remained in Memphis for another three years, honing his talents as a tradesman.[73] Finally, in 1841, with one hundred dollars in his pocket, John made his way to Alton and formally proposed to Mary, whom her contemporaries described as a "fair octoroon whose queenly beauty was legendary."[74] Mary and John were married shortly after arriving in Illinois, but like other blacks, their stay in Alton was only temporary. The Joneses immediately became involved in black community activities, including the formation of antislavery societies, the organization of the Liberty Party, and participation in the Underground Railroad.[75] Alton was in fact a starting point on one part of the Underground Railroad that ran from Alton to Jacksonville, La Salle, Ottawa, and Chicago.[76] Apparently through their service to escaped people, the newlyweds learned about the growing antislavery atmosphere in Chicago.[77] Drawn to a locale that might offer them more opportunity for activism, John and Mary packed up their luggage, certificates of freedom, and infant daughter, Lavinia.[78] For seven days, they traveled north by stagecoach and canal watercraft to reach Chicago, arriving on March 11, 1845.[79]

For the Jones family and others, Chicago offered a chance to become involved in a growing midwestern marketplace with the promise of a better life. Indiana and Illinois had towns with open space for new buildings, land where absolutely nothing stood. This was promising space where blacks set their sights for building their communities.[80] Following their arrival in Chicago, the family rented a small one-room cottage, and John leased a small shop for his tailor's business. What was left of their cash—three dollars and fifty cents—Mary used to purchase furnishings for their small home. John pawned his watch to buy two stoves, one for the business and one for their cottage. O. G. Hanson, an African American grocer, allowed the Joneses two dollars of store credit.[81] Once settled in Chicago, Mary and John had greater opportunity to ally themselves with like-minded individuals and to make a qualitative difference for black communities. John and Mary would later become members of Quinn Chapel, as did hundreds of other black Chicagoans, in part because they were attracted to its activist ministry.

Like other African Americans who emigrated from the South, John and Mary were constantly looking back. Almost immediately, they undertook a range of emancipation activities. John made fast friends with an abolitionist named L. C. Paine Freer, who encouraged John to learn to read and write. As the Joneses' business, marriage, and emancipation activism prospered, John did indeed guide himself to literacy. Mary and John used their home as a depot on the Underground Railroad, and hundreds of fugitive slaves passed through on their way to Canada. John befriended another prominent abolitionist, George DeBaptiste, and together they arranged for more safe depots in an array of black homes and churches.[82]

Certificates of freedom for John Jones and Mary Jones (née Mary Jane Richardson), Circuit Court of Madison County, Edwardsville, Illinois, dated November 28, 1847, and signed by William Brown, clerk. Chicago History Museum, ICHi-031975.

In an age in which gender roles were strictly dichotomized, black women like Mary played important roles in both secular and sacred areas of community building.[83] In Terre Haute, Indiana, Mrs. Sylvia Artis, a black woman, signed a 1837 petition for the city's charter, along with her sons, John and Isom. Two of the five founders of Terre Haute's Allen Chapel AME were women, including Polly Bass and Mary Elizabeth Johnson.[84] Black women also kept boarders at their homes, something many nineteenth-century women did to earn money. Later, Mary Ann Shadd Cary mentioned in her discussion of black Chicagoans' advancements that women "boarding house keepers" were undoubtedly key in harboring and protecting runaway slaves and their families.[85]

Women who did perform overtly political acts (normally assigned to men) did so because the local politics of race and activism dictated it. The hostilities blacks faced were threatening enough to the whole community such that they had no choice but to loosen the rules governing gendered behavior. White lawmakers, for instance, attempted to police black women's behavior through miscegenation and marriage laws. Of course, those same women had to cope with coverture as well. Consensual relationships among black and white people were considered especially offensive. In 1840, Indiana attempted to prohibit interracial marriages completely by passing the Act to Prohibit the Amalgamation of Whites and Blacks, which assigned strict penalties to couples who dared to seek legal matrimony, as well as those who aided them in their quest to do so.[86] The wedded couple faced fines of up to five thousand dollars, along with prison terms ranging from ten to twenty years, while an officiant could be fined up to ten thousand dollars.[87]

Black women's emancipation work also sprouted from membership in fraternal orders in which spousal cooperation was essential. Moses Dickson, founder of the International Order of Twelve (of the Knights and Daughters of Tabor), was born in Cincinnati, Ohio, in 1824. He and Mary Elizabeth Butcher were married in 1848, and together they traveled widely in the Midwest as abolitionists, settling in St. Louis. Moses traveled across the Midwest in 1844, interviewing formerly enslaved and free black people in Iowa, Illinois, and Wisconsin. Mary Elizabeth helped Moses organize the national order in St. Louis and a chapter in Galena, Illinois, in 1856.[88] He earned his living as a barber until he became an ordained minister. He served in the Union army during the war and helped to create the Missouri Equal Rights League in 1865. He and Mary Elizabeth focused their brand of activism on escaped slaves, especially after the war. Her commitment to the order and the AME Church was so strong that national members bestowed on Mary Elizabeth the lifetime honor and title of Mother of All Knights and Daughters of Tabor.[89] At Mary Elizabeth's funeral, Reverend R. L. Beale called her "a faithful and zealous worker in the church . . . full of fire, and one of God's greatest women." He also noted that Mary Elizabeth not only "encouraged and kept up Moses' spirit" but was the true "hidden force" driving his activism.[90]

Mary Elizabeth's eulogy also reveals how the African American community might have viewed women as partners in a working marriage: "If certain qualities appeared more prominent in him . . . she was the refiner of these forces; his nature was the more rugged, hers was the more gentle. He, the impetuous commander, at times became discouraged at the gigantic undertaking of building up a society that should have a national reputation. She was the patient, steady plodder, who encouraged and kept up his spirit."[91] The fact that Moses and Mary were referred as "equal to the other" is somewhat astounding, given the usual tone of prescriptive nineteenth literature on the relative position of women to men.[92] Mary might have been equal, but her role was hidden "behind the chair" of her husband. Still, this is good evidence that black activism mitigated gender roles, especially where important religious and emancipation work was concerned.[93]

* * *

Black codes were designed to permanently circumscribe the rights and privileges of undesirable immigrants, but steadfast activism resulted in circumstances that were constantly in flux. The dynamic of the push and pull between white and black groups was nearly Newtonian: for each action there was an equal and opposite reaction. Each time that whites proposed some new law or punishment, African Americans held a meeting to discuss how to mount legal opposition. For every school that denied entrance to black children, congregants began a campaign to build their own school or fight the segregation statute. If African Americans were sure that the Midwest was a good place to call home, then white midwesterners were equally sure that they wanted to be left alone. Self-professed "friends of the black race" occasionally supported some of the codes that were less draconian, so activists spent hours articulating the ways in which biracial efforts by whites and blacks to share the same land would benefit everyone.[94] Activists suffered gains and losses as they struggled to secure freedoms. Runaway slaves needed a place to go, families wanted to be reunited, and emancipated slaves leaving the slave states wanted to settle in free states.

In Illinois, the law sanctioned brutal repercussions for runaway slaves, stipulating that escapees could be subject to thirty-five lashes at the hands of a justice of the peace before being shipped back south. Laws governing the assembly of blacks in Illinois and Indiana were not dissimilar to those adopted by southerners. African Americans in Illinois who were caught assembling in groups of three or more could be jailed and flogged. One black man challenged Indiana's anti-immigration rule when a jury convicted him for bringing a black woman into the state to marry her. The state supreme court upheld the conviction, noting that the "policy of the state is clearly evolved. It is to exclude any further ingress of negroes, and to remove those among us as speedily as possible." Such was the long road activists had to tread before their new states offered any type of sanctuary whatsoever.[95]

Save for Quakers, the Midwest was not a place where African Americans could seek the friendship of whites.[96] In Indiana, Quakers considered themselves to be good neighbors to black settlers but were often divided over whether or not slavery would best be handled by colonization or gradual emancipation.[97] Even when proponents of emancipation, white people were often unable to envision an integrated society. Not surprisingly, the hostility that many black men and women confronted in the Midwest eventually forced them to move on. For example, in his autobiography, formerly enslaved Benjamin Drew explained the lack of legal protection for blacks in Indiana: "I was dissatisfied with the laws. I had a good deal of property [in Indiana]. It was not safe, for any loafing white might destroy or steal, and unless a white man were to see it, I could get no redress."[98] Indiana state law, which Drew described as "oppressive," angered him in part because it denied black men the opportunity to testify against white men. Under these circumstances, many African Americans like Drew decided to continue north to Canada.[99]

White hostility and violence were ever-present threats in the Midwest. For example, in 1844 in Jeffersonville, Indiana, a gang of white men attacked two African American men who were supposedly guilty of having sex with two white women. The beating took place in public as town residents looked on. In 1848, a group of proslavery whites assaulted Frederick Douglass after his speech in Pendleton, Indiana. Incidents like these were not uncommon, prompting one Quaker woman to observe that "Indiana was a hard state for a colored man to live in."[100] Later in the decade, an all-white jury in Indianapolis found a black man called Jordan Woodward guilty of "making a murderous assault upon a white man." Woodward's lawyer, John Ketcham, attempted to introduce testimony from an eyewitness claiming that Woodward had acted in self-defense against the deceased, who provoked the attack. The court disallowed the testimony because the witness was black. Legislators had designed black codes to keep African Americans legally mute.[101]

Midwestern freedpeople heard stories of other enormously successful blacks, and this motivated them to become heavily involved in church and community activities. This allowed black people to continue their battle for emancipation, despite the leaden pace. In these midwestern communities, "conflict was an integral and permanent aspect of a pluralistic community in which no single hierarchy of authority and values could instill consensus."[102] This was true of New Philadelphia, a town founded by a black man, "Free" Frank McWhorter of Pike County, Illinois, in 1836. At the age of forty-two, McWhorter negotiated with his master to determine the price of his and his wife's freedom. McWhorter immigrated to Illinois and purchased 160 acres of farmland, along with his son's freedom and that of thirteen other family members. Not only did McWhorter supervise a bustling farm, but he also transported his goods to market along the Mississippi River, amassing enough wealth to become a leader in the town and respected among his peers. New Philadelphia served as a stop on the Underground Railroad some twenty miles from the Mississippi. The town of Hannibal and the slave state of Missouri lay just across on the farther bank.[103] "Free" Frank's town was also strategically located near roads that ran to Quincy and other sites near the Illinois River, an important crossing point for fugitive slaves. McWhorter died before the Civil War and a chance at real citizenship.

* * *

Religion was a crucial component of emancipation activism, as African Americans relied on their church associations for spiritual, social, and economic guidance in their quest to be free. It is difficult to overstate the importance of religious life for emancipation activism, which would not have survived in the Midwest had it not been for a particular brand of urgent zeal. Activists denounced slavery as offensive to God. Members of the Bristol congregation extolled their Christian principles: "We testify against the whole system of human slavery as practiced in these United States. We consider the chattel principle or holding property . . . as a most heaven forbidding and God-provoking sin. [It is] the 'sum of all villainies.' We cannot voluntarily hold fellowship with voluntary slaveholders. . . . We cannot permit their preachers to occupy our pulpit, or . . . to sit at our communion."[104] Black midwestern settlers routinely equated God's will with the destruction of slavery.

In the early period of migration to the Midwest, African Americans had yet to organize their own churches, but a handful of antislavery whites had established an important precedent. Beginning in 1835, Congregationalists established churches in Plano, Little Rock, Newark, and Lisbon.[105] The Northern Baptist Association of Illinois, founded in 1838, gathered at the Community Baptist Church in Warrenville. The constituents voted on, and eventually passed, a resolution condemning slavery. By 1844, the Baptist churches in Illinois held a mass meeting to discuss the issue of slavery, and this time the delegates argued for the establishment of an abolitionist newspaper. The next year, black activists published the first edition of the *Western Christian*.[106] During this same period, groups of white Reformed Presbyterians also immigrated to Illinois, where they set up Underground Railroad stations that passed through Eden, Coulterville, and Oakdale. Fresh from the religious revival in Oneida, New York, Congregationalists settled towns in Illinois such as Galesburg and Lyndon and Bailey Grove. By 1848, the Baptist church convention reported that there was "a colored association of 14 churches, 9 preachers, 6 licentiates, and 243 members, scattered over the state from Shawneetown to Galena and Chicago."[107] In this way, friendly whites fashioned spaces for their new neighbors.

The majority of white residents in Illinois and Indiana believed, of course, that they had sufficient justification for laws that denied citizenship rights to their black neighbors. Attendees at white constitutional conventions continued to debate migration problems and devote their efforts to the maturation of their state's racial caste system. Many whites felt that, before the war, their towns had been too often visited and inhabited by free blacks and fugitive slaves; during and after the war, whites had to deal with the same problems, only this time in the form of emancipated persons and contrabands. White men in Illinois went so far in an 1847 constitutional convention as to demand "protection" from African Americans, lest they resort to violence in order to protect themselves from this perceived injury.[108] Many attendees at the convention, especially antislavery Democrats, urged a relaxation of the black codes, but the majority still insisted that Illinois refuse entry to blacks. One local newspaper summed up the mood of the convention this way: "No fears need be entertained that the Convention will outrage popular sentiment by authorizing a relaxation of those distinctions between the two races, which are found in human nature and are so essential to the safety and dignity of society."[109]

Three years later in 1850, when the Indiana state convention met again, whites were casting their votes for laws that forbade "negroes and mulattoes" from settling in the state at all. Another law stipulated that any contracts formed with blacks who entered the state would be declared null and void upon their relocation. This was an attempt to impair the white Quakers and Baptists from eastern and northern Indiana who were abolitionists and employed African Americans. When statewide voting occurred, Indianans overwhelmingly voted for the exclusion of blacks from their state.[110] White legislators continued to enact laws designed to deter black settlement. The most comprehensive of all came from Illinois in 1853, a law that completely prohibited any black migration into the state and subsequently enforced the portion of the 1848 Illinois State Constitution that had denied blacks entry.[111] African Americans again faced fines if they were caught crossing into the state. If they were unable to pay the fine, they were subject to sale until a sufficient time had passed or the fine had been "paid" through involuntary servitude.[112] This law was known as Logan's Black Law, named after John A. Logan, the leader of southern Illinois Democrats who had proposed the law. Though this law generated relatively few arrests and sales of enslaved people, the mere presence of it was enough to intimidate and frighten African Americans who wanted to pass through or settle in the state.[113]

Emancipation activists continued to battle the black codes by trying to frame their arguments in terms of constitutionality. Although they could not vote to overturn the legislation, activists used local people and local places to fight white encroachment. Instead of attempting to alter a system commanded by the power of white privilege, African American activists created political processes of their own. Black conventions provide the best evidence of these processes, within which activists also made use of committees and their publications as part of their civil disobedience.[114] For his part, activist John Jones joined the Illinois constitutional convention's debate on black immigration to Illinois. In September 1847, John wrote and published two articles strongly urging white Illinois residents to accept African Americans into the state. Both essays were published in the *Chicago Tribune* and were also reprinted in the *Western Citizen*. At the constitutional convention, John opined that blacks were indeed citizens of the United States since the eighteenth-century framers had not specifically used the word *white* in reference to freedom. John cleverly utilized a variety of sources, including black Revolutionary War military service and the ideals of republican government, to bolster his argument. Unfortunately for the Joneses and the community they represented at home, lawmakers amended the state constitution to include the new anti-immigration portion. The restrictions that limited the movement and conduct of African Americans were now part of state law.[115]

For Mary and John Jones, the codification of black codes represented a watershed event in their lives, as they would spend the next two decades fighting to repeal them. Activists like the Joneses decided almost immediately to begin speaking out against the new restrictions, for it was now abundantly clear to them that, although many white voters claimed to detest slavery, these same voters also wanted little to do with free blacks who had escaped from slavery.[116] The Joneses also understood their world in terms of their gender roles. Black women like Mary found themselves denied the opportunity to perform the obligations of white republican motherhood, so they instead assumed a collective stance as standard-bearers for their communities as they built homes, churches, and schools. Later, they would become war workers as they crossed into increasingly public activities. In all of these activities, a defined sense of black gendered maternalism informed women's roles.[117]

Black codes were critical to white power and so oppressive that they severely circumscribed free blacks' engagement with civil society, but activism flourished nevertheless. In the case of the Midwest, people linked their struggle for self-fashioned local places with the fight to eradicate slavery everywhere: "we claim to be citizens of Illinois to all intents and purposes, and are of right entitled to all the immunities of other citizens of the commonwealth. . . . [W]e intend to avail ourselves of that only constitutional guarantee now inviolate from the ruffianism of American servitude."[118] For emancipation activists who chose to carve out a homeland in Illinois or Indiana, conditions were regularly disheartening. Despite the fact that many midwesterners disapproved of slavery, black emigrants understood all too well that a white man's right to own slaves was well protected across the nation. Free blacks who searched for a new land, new home, and new environment had little choice but to continue functioning as committed activists against the black codes. But white racists were equally determined to stop African Americans from creating thriving free communities. Still, activism retained its force and fervor. Blacks had quite clearly stated their intention to wage their own battle for emancipation—on their turf and on their terms.

2. Legal, Educational, and Religious Foundations

Despite an incredibly complex set of political and social circumstances, community and religion were still the centralizing forces of African American life. The founding of Quinn Chapel in 1844 illustrates both the commitment to collective activism and an unwavering faith in God among Chicago's black community.[1] Free blacks used Quinn as their meeting place, school, and most importantly, a place of worship and prayer. Initially, a group of seven people met regularly to pray in the home of John Day. When the parishioners expanded their membership, Maria Parker, one of the organizers of the prayer group, acted as hostess in her home.[2] In 1846, the group chose an old schoolhouse for their prayer meeting, whereupon the participants decided to ask the AME Church to accept them as a congregation and send a minister to serve them. The elders approved their request, and on July 22, 1847, the group officially became a congregation of the AME Church. They chose the name Quinn in honor of Bishop William Paul Quinn, a missionary who had organized numerous churches in the Midwest.[3] Much later, Quinn Chapel functioned as a farewell and provisions post for Civil War soldiers and their families.

Black Chicagoans often used Quinn AME as their central meeting place. Quinn and Zoar Baptist were both responsible for turning out high-profile members of Chicago's activist community. In 1858, members of both churches met at Quinn to discuss emigration and colonization. Famed activist H. O. Wagoner summed up black Chicago's refusal to leave the Midwest: "[We] have already planted our trees in the American soil, and by the help of God we mean to repose under the shade thereof."[4] The church itself, and the religious fellowship it represented, was the most important locus for black organizational activity. In fact, white racists understood so well the power of the African American church as an institution that they often focused their loathing on the buildings themselves as a way to obstruct the trajectory of black activism. Such is what happened to a black church in Indiana. Led by white missionary Reverend Charles Satchel, blacks established the Second

Baptist Church of Indianapolis in 1846. At first the congregants met in a private home; then a small frame structure was built in 1850. One year later, the entire building went up in flames, the target of white arsonists' ire.[5] Undeterred, congregants rebuilt the church one year later.

Quinn's congregation was friendly and supportive to its women in their efforts to secure leadership roles. Women who hailed from Quinn became activists not only for antislavery and emancipation but also for women's rights. In 1893, when Susan B. Anthony traveled to Chicago for the World's Columbian Exposition and needed a venue for her speech, "None but a colored church called Quinn's Chapel would open its door to a woman speaker."[6] Churches like Quinn emerged as centers for abolitionist and Underground Railroad activities and thus were viewed as havens—and as models—for black communities.[7]

Activism in the 1850s proceeded from the assumption that, even though creating a solid community infrastructure might not resolve their claim to emancipation, access to educational and religious resources within their communities would at least allow African Americans to augment their communal foundations.[8] Moving forward, activists decided to center their organizational and protest activities on two specific goals: the continued establishment of churches and the creation of schools. Congregations often constructed a building that housed both the school and the church, although some towns managed to build two buildings. Church leaders led proper searches for doctrinal and academic staff for both institutions, yet African American Christianity often blurred the lines of secular instruction and spiritual devotion. Activists expected that they could depend on the church to pave the way: "Mr. John Jones, of Chicago, who represents the colored people of the great North-West . . . declared the A.M.E. Church to be the most powerful instrument of elevation which the colored people had."[9] Overall, midwestern blacks continued their quest to both destroy slavery and create sanctuaries through the dissolution of the black codes, but now they had other areas upon which to focus their efforts. It is not surprising, then, that activists held political gatherings and planning forums in these new schoolhouses and places of worship.

The final antebellum years are crucial to understanding how African Americans were able to structure their lives so as to adapt to myriad, and sometimes merciless, changes that sectional crisis and the war would bring. Throughout this conflict, activists located the struggle for their existence almost entirely within the domain of group organization and collective power.[10]

As it happened, this was a clever move on their part: by highlighting the importance of schools and churches founded and led by their own people, activists tied their claim to regional identity to their emancipation activism. Black America, however, was not monolithic, and historians have shown how regional differences—even within the same state or territory—played out in these communities.[11] In this sense, the creation of a unique black regional identity was key.

While black emancipation activists focused on building schools and churches in their new homeland,[12] they faced fresh challenges in the form of the FSL in 1850 and the 1857 *Dred Scott v. Sanford* decision, both of which slowed the pace of emancipation by erecting critical barriers. The enormous implications of these events would reverberate in the black community until and throughout the coming Civil War, and activists immediately recognized these edicts as a twofold threat. On the one hand, the FSL posed a peril to their safety and bodily integrity with the possibility of removal to the slaveholding South. On the other hand, *Dred Scott* declared the Missouri Compromise, and its prohibition of slavery, unconstitutional and denied that African Americans were even citizens. Naturally, midwestern blacks paid close attention to the case, as the situation of Dred and Harriet Scott (along with their children) mirrored that of many blacks living in the Midwest: they lived in free territories but did not have the citizenship rights they believed they deserved as Americans. Of course, Dred and Harriet Scott never got much of a chance to discuss the right to vote and run for office, or the right to own property and sue in court, or the right to seek federal employment and sit on a jury because Chief Justice Taney's decision turned on race and the supposed inferiority of enslaved African people and their descendants.[13] The national conversation sought by so many African Americans never really happened in a way they had envisioned. Taney insisted that blacks were inherently inferior, thereby justifying the belief that black people lacked the character and moral capacity to govern themselves. He articulated ideas that white racists were already thinking: slavery could be justified as a duty of white men to care for and guide an inferior race.[14] Midwestern blacks, like so many others across the country, were dealt a terrific blow with this language. All along, their activism had turned on the basic premise that they too were God's children—deserving of the rights due to full and equal citizens.[15]

Political groups sought effective leaders who were adept at creating and disseminating rhetoric about blacks as citizens, as Americans, as people who deserved emancipation.[16] Several black Indiana communities flourished in the decades before the Civil War. The Roberts and Beech settlements were close to hamlets of Quaker-supported black communities, especially in Wayne, Randolph, and Henry Counties.[17] Most of these black settlers had escaped slavery in North Carolina and Virginia, so they knew all too well the horrors of bondage.[18] The African American population was constantly changing because both the federal FSL of 1850 and the state's 1851 constitutional exclusion article frightened more and more settlers into fleeing to Canada or avoiding the state altogether. Underground Railroad conductor Levi Coffin noted a significant decline in the black population of southern Indiana counties following black emigration to Canada after 1850.[19]

For their part, African American women took a lively interest in local, state, and national politics, despite the fact that they were excluded from many of the traditional forums used for protest and activism. Black women may have been barred from the pulpit in most churches, yet they chose, and often created, other types of activist positions within their churches. Black women also enacted emancipation and political change as Underground Railroad conductors and hosts. Moreover, the women worried about the moral state of their community members, so they formed temperance societies to keep a watchful eye on vice. In 1850, twenty-five black women in Greenville, Indiana, created just such a society. The organization lasted for twenty-four years, until the group became an auxiliary of the national Christian Temperance Union.[20]

* * *

The long fight against the black codes likely prepared the activist community for the next big challenge, the FSL, which was simultaneously the most frightening and the most invigorating event to galvanize the black community. For the majority of blacks, the best option was to retreat to church and pray for God's direction of their activism. Although black people were afraid of bounty hunters, their attendance at church did not suffer. Not long after the law's passage, one newspaper reported on attendance at Wells AME: "Our readers may not be aware that the colored population of this city has a very neat edifice on Wells Street, and that it is crowded every Sabbath to its fullest capacity. [We] have rarely seen a better appearing congregation whether in point of apparel or decorum."[21] The African American community remained committed to worship as the driving force in their lives, and church construction continued as planned. In 1850, black Chicagoans erected another AME church, this time at the corner of Jackson and Buffalo Streets. This sanctuary is particularly notable because it was accompanied by a schoolhouse for the children. Congregants raised three thousand dollars for the combined cost of the church and school.[22] The Women's Sewing Society held a fair to "materially aid their brethren in the good cause."[23] With their handiwork for sale, the women raised more than two hundred dollars, which they proudly presented to pastors A. T. Hall and J. M. Warren.[24]

The FSL allowed for the deputization of private citizens to aid in recapture, and bounty hunters could simply swear before a judge that their captives were fugitives, while the captives were prohibited from presenting testimony on their own behalf.[25] In one case, bounty hunters seized a black barber from Petersburg, Indiana, and removed him to Tennessee. Robert La Plant, a white man, signed a statement swearing that the barber once worked for the La Plant family and was now indeed free. Police freed the barber, but only because La Plant was willing to testify.[26] In other cases, bounty hunters took runaways or free blacks to be sold in slaveholding states. Indiana law made no provision for the protection of runaways; in fact, it allowed masters or agents from other states to enter the state and remove so-called runaways.[27]

In Chicago, black activists concentrated their efforts on the legal repeal of the FSL. Although African Americans often spoke of their appreciation for the church as a haven, they were still concerned for escaped people who might be on the run in the Chicago area.[28] In the fall of 1850, activists held several meetings to discuss the legal underpinnings of the FSL and debate the most efficacious ways to secure its repeal. At the end of the first meeting, John Jones and seven other men composed a "committee on resolutions." John reported the existence of a "strong, deep resolve to resist every attempt to bring back to bondage any black," as well as the "[the determination] to defend ourselves at all hazards, even if it should be to the shedding of human blood." Two days later, the group offered its proposals to a standing-room-only gathering at the Wells AME Church. John Jones began his speech by stressing the community's commitment to the emancipation of *every* black person threatened by slavery. He also noted that the black community's interpretation of the FSL's objective was simple: "to enslave every colored man in the United States."[29] John went on to outline the committee's stance on the regional ramifications of the law. Activists claimed that the FSL was a brazen example of the North's subordination to the South, since slaveowners were using the North as nothing more than a hunting ground for fugitive bondspeople.

Although the FSL represented tremendous additional challenges to their plans for immediate emancipation, activists became more determined than ever. On September 28, 1850, three hundred Chicagoans—out of the population of five hundred—gathered at the Wells AME Church for their second meeting regarding the FSL.[30] Prior to the meeting that evening, John met with leading activists H. O. Wagoner and William Johnson to write resolutions concerning the FSL.[31] Jones drew upon early republican rhetoric for his inspiration, evoking both Patrick Henry and George Washington in his call to "stand by our liberty at the expense of our lives" and refuse to be "taken into slavery or permit our brethren to be taken.[32] John's speech that evening also contained references to the fact that although Chicago blacks were free from chattel slavery, activists remained committed to aiding enslaved people who were still in bondage or who were runaways.[33] At the end of the evening, the group decided to create a number of committees, including a correspondence committee and a resolutions committee.[34]

Church records indicate that committees were key to the overall organization and planning of activism as it related specifically to the FSL. Along the way, however, community leaders reset the goals of the committees as they saw fit. One such group, a correspondence committee called the Chicago Liberty Association, set out initially to disseminate literature on the "general principles of human freedom,"[35] but the committee morphed into a different group during the first few weeks of meetings. The committee of forty-two men decided that safety was a more urgent need. This new group, the Vigilance Committee, intended to "examine any attempts on the part of individuals to presume upon the liberties of [our] brethren in any way."[36] The Vigilance Committee functioned like a police force arranged into seven divisions. Composed of six men each and assigned to specific neighborhoods, the seven divisions then "patrolled the city each night [to] keep an eye out for interlopers" who might be slave catchers.[37] Vigilance committees gave black activists an opportunity to feel safer and more secure in their neighborhoods, while also pointing at the necessity of self-defense.

Vigilance committees were not new to African American communities. As early as the 1830s, committees on surveillance indicated a deep commitment to the aid and welfare of runaways. Although documentary sources about the Chicago Vigilance Committee are scant, one can draw inferences from other similar groups in the Midwest and Northeast.[38] David Ruggles established the New York Committee of Vigilance in 1835. Abolitionists (white and black) also formed a vigilance committee in Boston in the 1840s. Vigilance groups also emerged in Philadelphia, Detroit, and other northern cities. These groups fended off slave catchers, swelled the ranks of activists, and staffed the Underground Railroad. Black women and day laborers served as lookouts as they went about their jobs, and women in particular raised money and ran activist groups in their churches. The Colored Vigilant Committee of Detroit prepared a lengthy annual report in 1843 spelling out the concerns of emancipation activists who worked with committee members to "watch over [their] interests."[39] Urban centers like Boston, Detroit, and Chicago were indeed alluring to those who wanted to put great distance between themselves and slaveholding states. Activists in these cities sought to countermand the FSL with elaborate plans and schedules to ensure that fellow blacks watched out for one another.

In their struggle against the FSL, activists split themselves into groups, each with a different theme or set of tasks. The Resolutions Committee in Chicago drafted position statements on a variety of issues pertaining to the FSL and its interpretation. Black Chicagoans wrote eloquently about their "strong, deep feeling to resist" the FSL because its "tendency was to enslave every colored man in the United States" and because it carried no provisions "to guard against false claims." Sadly, activists admitted that they had "abandoned hope" that their government would protect them, leaving them with only "self-protection" on which to rely and a fierce "determination to defend each other at the risk of imprisonment, fine, limb, or life itself."[40] Activists also formed education committees, signaling their belief that self-help and uplift were crucial stepping-stones to emancipation. Michigan's activists expressed their yearning for black male suffrage, their plan to draft petitions to legislators, and their hatred of slavery. Their goals could be achieved, they stated, with "education as their shield" in the "moral and political" war they were fighting. The Colored Vigilant Committee of Detroit commended its members for establishing a day school (taught by an African American man) and providing financial support. The committee recommended to the community that anyone who wanted to "make strides in moral and intellectual improvement" could join a temperance society, the Young Man's Society, the Debating Club, or attend the "Reading Room with a Library of Historical Works." Detroit's Colored Ladies Benevolent Society, of the Methodist Church, had been active since 1843, but activists announced "with much joy" two new female societies whose missions included education, temperance, economy, and the "universal reformation of the present, as well as the rising generations."[41]

For black families, the definition of emancipation certainly included suffrage for men, but they were almost entirely at the mercy of state constitutional conventions, legislatures, and courts. In the early years of statehood,

Indiana (admitted in 1816) and Illinois (admitted in 1818) had deliberately added constitutional provisions to disallow suffrage for black men.[42] For this reason, suffrage would play a critical role in emancipation activism through the late antebellum period. White citizens, save for some Quakers and Free-Soilers, were overwhelmingly and adamantly opposed to black suffrage. In Indiana this opposition was especially strong in the southern counties, where residents became so vocal that representatives for the 1850 Constitutional Convention refused to allow the *question* of black suffrage to be put to a vote.[43] The situation was much the same in Illinois, and it would take an act of the federal government and the passage of the Fifteenth Amendment to provide for black suffrage.[44] For many black settlers, though, reason for hope nevertheless persisted, as they ramped up their efforts and attempted to locate pockets in the Midwest where the proslavery, anti-suffrage argument did not exist as the prevailing sentiment.[45]

Once FSL activists moved past the committee-formation stage, they continued to be hypervigilant of their own comings and goings—after all, many of them had either been freed on dubious terms or had escaped from slavery. In October, the *Western Citizen* reported that two southern bounty hunters were in Chicago searching for escaped slaves. The Resolutions Committee in Chicago conducted an investigation and eventually established the falsity of the report.[46] But the following week, a bounty hunter did appear in the city. People saw Uriah Hinch circulating photographs of the alleged escapees, and he had even brought his own slave with him to assist him in his apprehension effort. The slave later escaped to England on a steamer. After advertising his intention to tar and feather people who had aided and abetted the enslaved man, Hinch applied to attorney Justice Lowe for help and was told that "nothing could be done." Hinch left Chicago, "never to return." The town newspaper proudly reported that an antislavery lawyer had advised Hinch to leave immediately: "It is proper to add that our colored population are ready for any emergency. While they do not propose to use violence, they will not suffer the new law to be executed upon their persons."[47]

Chicago's activists had one monumental stumbling block in their resistance to the FSL. They needed to gain the support of the Chicago Common Council, which was the city's main governing body, headed by the mayor and staffed by aldermen, all of whom were white. The Common Council had the power to direct the police force to ignore the demands of bounty hunters and slaveowners who wanted to detain enslaved fugitives. Activists gained that support in October when the Chicago Common Council interpreted the law in the same way the Resolutions Committee had: "the Fugitive Slave Law lately passed by Congress is a cruel and unjust law and ought not to be respected by an intelligent community." The Common Council voted not to "require the police to render any assistance for the arrest of fugitive slaves."[48] Council members added that they believed that the law was not only unconstitutional but was also "contrary to the practice and propagation of Christian principles."[49] Additionally, like other whites, the aldermen resented the law's implications for themselves: white citizens could be deputized against their will to apprehend slaves, while local courts were bypassed altogether. With Chicago's city government publicly opposed to the FSL, there were rumors that southerners referred to Chicago as a "ni—r loving town."[50]

Slavery's supporters in Illinois, as well as Free-Soilers, vehemently disagreed with the Common Council's interpretation of the law. Midwestern whites had good reason to welcome the FSL if it fit into their vision. One newspaper wrote, "We of the south do not regard Chicago as belonging to Illinois. It is as perfect a SINK HOLE OF ABOLITION as Boston or Cincinnati."[51] In Indiana, Robert Dale Owen, a Democrat and editor of *New Harmony* newspaper, asked in 1859 if any decent person desired "the continuance among us of a race to whom we are not willing to accord the most common protection against outrage and death." His rhetoric was hardly an exaggeration: during the constitutional debate in the state that year, one speaker frankly acknowledged, "It would be better to kill [black people] off at once, if there is no other way to get rid of them. . . . [W]e know how the Puritans did with the Indians, who were infinitely more magnanimous and less impudent than the colored race."[52] Whites would continue these malevolent kinds of attacks on black settlers throughout the entire antebellum period.

Meanwhile, African Americans used a carefully planned model of attack to cope with the onslaught of discrimination, segregation, and outright violence. Activists were never content to gauge their plans according to an old-line protectionist model. Instead, they cleverly attached their meaning of freedom to the lands they already occupied and owned. They truly believed that they had a legitimate domiciliary right to peace on their own land. In this "ownership is nine-tenths of the law" scheme, they again used principles of local political culture to both legitimize emancipation activism and recruit new members. No one group in America owned antislavery, abolition, or emancipation activism, but the emerging controversy over popular sovereignty absolutely equaled allegiance to state, region, or territory for people on all sides of the slavery debate. Black activists in Illinois and Indiana were not content to allow Frederick Douglass and other notable leaders to speak for them, because they believed that their brand of activism was specific to their communities. Midwestern activists claimed their rights in relationship to their land, especially since they had to battle opposing state and local politicians. Community leaders believed that the protection of local blacks should fall to them. There were myriad challenges to the community's position that the FSL was unconstitutional. For instance, Democratic politicians sought either to assure their present constituencies of the law's efficacy or to gain new voters by defending its desirability. Stephen A. Douglas, the famed Democratic congressman from Illinois, vehemently defended the FSL's necessity, earning him the ire of many black and white Illinoisans alike.[53]

Throughout the 1850s, black activists continued to rally against the FSL, but whites reacted by tightening the black codes. The harder and longer African Americans fought—and the more visible they became—the more determined white racists became to rid Illinois and Indiana of black settlers altogether. If whites had hoped to deter black emancipation in the Midwest with the black codes, then they must have been disappointed to discover that African Americans renewed their commitment to emancipation following the passage of the FSL, despite the intensity of the conflict. Activists, however, often directed their protest activities to other pursuits related to community building and equality. Although public schools were supported by taxes paid by blacks and whites alike, no provisions were made for the education of black children. In 1850, the Indiana State Supreme Court ruled that African American children could not attend public school, even if they were willing to pay tuition and find a school district that would welcome them. Finally, in what was perhaps the most alarming evidence of statewide racial prejudice, Article XIII also contained appropriations for a colonization fund and the salary of a state agent whose job it was to encourage Indiana blacks to return to Africa.[54] The black codes effectively constituted a structured and legal repudiation of civil rights. For black settlers, the codes meant (among other things) no serving on juries, testifying in court, or attending public schools.[55]

The contest reached a fever pitch when, in 1853, the Illinois legislature approved the passage of additional black codes. Much like the federal FSL, this new state legislation specifically targeted runaway slaves, as well as anyone who dared to help them. These codes were quite specific, and Indiana and Illinois now boasted the harshest codes of all states and territories in the Midwest.[56] In Indiana, for instance, no black man could testify in any case involving the crime of a white man.[57] The law in Illinois required that any white person bringing an African American, free or otherwise, into the state would be fined from one hundred to five hundred dollars and be jailed for a year. Blacks who came into the state on their own (and stayed longer than ten days) could be sold to the highest bidder if they could not pay a bond. Joseph Barquet's letter to the *Western Citizen* provides some sense of how many African Americans responded to the legislation: "What means Illinois when she lately spoke those words of inhibition? . . . The house added insult to injury. . . . [T]he friends of justice and right have been tramped under foot."[58]

* * *

Meanwhile, as activists mounted their attack on the FSL, the black national convention movement prepared to battle the continuing ferocity of race discrimination in the Midwest.[59] At the same time, the national abolitionist movement had undergone some changes whereby blacks in the Midwest held more leadership positions.[60] This was good news for activists, many of whom did not possess the middle-class status of elite blacks in the Northeast. In fact, convention activists used the type of skills they honed as community builders. For these local people, taking part in a national convention did not mean that they left behind their local places. In fact, the desire to sustain those free communities is one of the things that motivated regional black activists to align themselves with larger groups and make long trips away from their families.

Black conventioneers who attended mass meetings in large cities drafted all-encompassing manifestos outlining their demands for freedoms in American society. These documents were strikingly similar to the demands articulated by midwestern black activists in their own small towns and neighborhoods. In 1853, following Frederick Douglass's call for a new convention, 140 delegates representing nine states assembled in Rochester, New York. Delegates there drew up the "Address of the Colored Convention to the People of the United States," which laid out the basic rights of black communities. Those included education, suffrage, inclusion in the legal system (such as sitting on juries), and all other opportunities to "assert their rights on their own native soil" as American citizens.[61] Activists also created the National Council of the Colored People, which was composed of two members from each of the ten northern states. John Jones served as one of five vice presidents of the convention, and delegates chose him as president at the first black Illinois state convention. Jones also became chair of the colonization committee, to which he submitted a report representing his Illinois constituency. In an 1853 newspaper editorial, Jones denounced all proposals encouraging blacks to emigrate to Africa.[62] At the same time, he also criticized Martin Delany's call for a national emigration convention. This statement, articulated by one of the black community's vociferous defenders, sent a clear message that many blacks in the region were uninterested in leaving their homes for Africa.[63] Moreover, black citizens articulated their resentment toward any plan that encouraged them to do so.

Across the Midwest, as black communities continued to hold meetings to discuss and debate the most efficacious approach to opposing the FSL, women continued to carry out their ecclesiastical and activist duties. Once again, religious and political roles overlapped for both men and women. Church membership was often fluid, so John and Mary Jones attended several different churches while they lived in Chicago. In fact, they helped found Olivet Baptist Church. People often attended the church that was within walking distance or went with relatives to their church when other transportation became available. Women rarely traveled to attend political conventions, but participants observed political cooperation strategies between men and women. Some women may have accompanied their husbands on these trips, but it is more likely that they would have remained home to perform reproductive and paid labor. Since they were denied a ballot at black conventions and other meetings where their husbands, brothers, and fathers voted, black women exercised their agency as activists within all manner of religious, educational, and self-help organizations. Black women adopted a profound sense of maternalism in this period; as black freedom was widely and openly enervated in the Midwest, women clung tightly to the idea that their efforts would make a better world for their children and grandchildren.[64] Mary Jones would have made her views clear to her husband, and despite the fact that she could not take the floor herself, her familial and communal values were reflected in John Jones, who represented their kin and community.[65]

Newspapers were full of stories about enslaved people being caught and returned to the South, so whispers in the pews might have threatened to disturb sermons were it not for the religious devotion these congregants possessed. Local newspapers were vitally important for the activist community, which relied on literate brethren to read and disseminate information about slavery. Among community members, news was then passed by word of mouth, an important oral tradition for a people who had been denied the opportunity to become literate. For instance, one news story reported was about a former slave named Mitchum, who had lived in Jennings County, Indiana, with his wife and child for several years. A group of bounty hunters seized Mitchum, alleging that the black man had run away some nineteen years before.[66] Mitchum did receive a trial, but he was awarded to the claimant slaveholder and transferred to Kentucky, leaving his wife and child alone. The local newspaper commented, "We think our Kentucky neighbors leave our town satisfied that how[ever] great our abhorrence to the institution of slavery may be, we are still a law abiding people."[67] Also in 1851, slave catchers abducted a woman named Martha Rouse, who had been living peacefully in Washington County, Indiana, with her husband, Charley.[68] A group of black neighbors followed the band of Kentuckians who carried Martha away and offered the men six hundred dollars for her freedom. The slave catchers agreed, insisting that the contract should be legalized in Louisville, but the bounty hunters refused to sell her when they arrived. Martha was never heard from again.[69]

Midwestern activists knew that stories like these, repeated in their local newspapers, meant that the FSL was no mere scare tactic. The ordeal was undoubtedly horrifying for the person captured and transported to the South. First, there was the initial discovery by abusive, and often violent, bounty hunters. Then, the captured person was forced to travel, mostly likely with hands bound, with men who considered a slave no more than a piece of property. Finally, the enslaved person would have been placed with auctioneers or returned to a slaveowner—alone. No matter how poor they were in the Midwest, no black person wanted to return to the hell that was slavery. For women in particular, this forcible removal to the South was equated with rape and other violence, forced pregnancy, and the rupture of the mother-child bond at an early, or any, age.

As speeches and newspaper accounts show, African Americans in Illinois and Indiana combined the most pressing national political questions of the midcentury with local black antislavery and emancipation activism. But this was a tall order for a community that needed to convince its settlers that they would be safe if they remained in the region. Many Chicago blacks were so frightened by the implications of the FSL that they fled to Canada in the first forty-eight hours after its passage, but activists were determined to protect their remaining community members.[70] So many black members of local churches had already fled to Canada in fear of bounty hunters that activists tried to ease the fears of the community. The Midwest could not be considered a haven if the black population ran away as a result of the law.[71] State and local activists cleverly took a federal law and outlined its regional implications for both a local and national audience: "We have the same work before us that we marked out in 1848. Slavery is to be excluded from the Territories by law, it is to be abolished in the District of Columbia, the fugitive law is to be repealed, and the influence of the slave party as such is to be abolished."[72]

It is clear from source material that blacks did consider all of the options available to them—settlement farther west, emigration to Canada, and emigration to Africa—although they were all clearly cut from different theoretical cloths. Leaders of the African emigration movement succeeded in convincing only a small number of blacks to move to the African continent.[73] Nevertheless, emigration rhetoric permeated black political and intellectual life from the early colonial period into the early twentieth century, and it was especially relevant as activists tried to weigh their choices for equality. Residents of the slaveholding states, border states, and free states who contemplated emigration saw it as an opportunity to break free from white control and confinement.[74] In 1858, Henry Highland Garnet founded the African Civilization Society, but the enterprise required a great deal of money, white patrons, and a huge leap of faith. In fact, colonization is a historical phenomenon that must be understood as occurring in a particular—and perhaps peculiar—historical context. Activists formulated ideas about African emigration as part of their response to white America's refusal to extend citizenship rights. Yet many blacks living in the Midwest had so much invested—literally and figuratively—in their free communities that they rejected colonization almost instantly. Colonization was anathema to the goals for their homegrown schools and churches; it was, in the words of John Jones, "fatal to our hopes and aspirations."[75]

Up until 1850, black activists who had participated in many years of sustained protest continued to organize themselves around issues that were of greatest concern to their particular black community.[76] Free communities boasted a range of fraternal, social welfare, and educational societies. Although the membership rolls of these groups often contained the names of the same active individuals, each society's goals and activities tended to differ—some groups spent more time building schools; some spent more time with Underground Railroad activity; others concentrated on church endeavors.[77] The FSL meant that diversified black organizations would have to become more adept at exploring the linkages among seemingly disparate issues and communities.[78]

Migration patterns—however difficult to measure—show that the first two years following the passage of the FSL were difficult ones for Indiana and

Illinois blacks. The law forced settlers to assess their personal situations (as well as the relative threat to their safety). Northern counties in Indiana, for instance, reported an increase in the black population since some African Americans had fled from proslavery southern counties but decided to remain within Indiana state lines.[79] Southern counties were more likely to require blacks to register according to the state's black codes. In Franklin County, for instance, there were 150 blacks registered in 1850. By July of 1853, only 14 persons were registered. These numbers give a glimpse of the reality of demographic change for African Americans.[80] Henry Bibb, writing in the Canadian newspaper *Voice of the Fugitive*, indicated that Indiana blacks were leaving for a good reason: "22 from Indiana passed through to Amherstburg, with four fine covered waggons and eight horses. A few weeks ago six or eight such teams came from the same state into Canada. The Fugitive Slave Law is driving out brains and money." Black families who fled the Midwest often needed money and supplies to make the journey. Some had a fair amount of wealth. Later that month, on July 29, the same newspaper reported, "We know of several families of free people of color who have moved here from the northern states this summer who have brought with them property to the amount of £30,000."[81] Levi and Catherine Coffin reportedly helped some two thousand slaves escape from slavery during their twenty-year stay in Newport, Indiana. Mary Bibb reported that she had harbored twenty-three fugitives in her own home in one ten-day period.[82]

As in Illinois, African Americans in Indiana formed a state convention movement. Conferences to discuss resolutions were generally held just before meetings of the state legislature so that members might craft their appeals to lawmakers. The AME churches in Indianapolis were common sites for gathering to plan for state conventions. AME churches boasted cross membership with black Masonic lodges, which had first been organized in the state in 1848.[83] Masonic orders provided leaders for emancipation activism, but meetings, society memberships, and other organizational activities were inspired by (and nearly always filtered through) the church.[84]

* * *

The church was the centralizing force for African American activists in the 1850s. Parishioners and conventioneers identified with regional and national denominational leadership, but they did so in order to shore up local resources and local people by building churches and congregations. National and larger regional conferences were important because they provided networking opportunities. They also allowed regional activists to make their own arguments to activist leaders who tended to train the spotlight on abolitionism in the East and slavery in the South. In Indiana, attendees at the national AME conference established their state conference in 1840. The first meeting was then held at Blue River, Indiana, on October 2, 1840. Upon his arrival in Indiana, Bishop Paul Quinn found that there was a great desire among African Americans to establish independent congregations.[85] By 1844, Quinn exulted that Indiana and Illinois had "47 churches with 2,000 members, 20 traveling preachers, 27 local preachers, 50 Sunday schools with 200 teachers and 2,000 students, 17 camp meetings, and 40 temperance societies."[86]

Religious work in the activist community also focused on literacy, education, and relief for the poor. The South Cavalry Baptist Church, located in Indianapolis, was one such parish. Founded in 1851, the church's congregants had fled from slavery in Kentucky. Prior to raising the funds to buy property for the church building, members lived together in an old farmhouse and, later, held Sunday services in an old blacksmith's shop. Most of the original members had taken part in a weeklong revival meeting led by Reverend Moses Broyles, who possessed an evangelical fervor for emancipation from sin and slavery.[87] Among South Cavalry's groups were a Masonic brotherhood, a women's missionary society, and a women's deaconess society. A few years after South Cavalry's inception, a subset of congregants split from the membership and founded another church called Mount Zion Baptist Church, also in Indianapolis.[88]

Raising funds for various ecclesiastical needs was crucial to activists' goals and fell within women's purview. Congregants who used private homes for worship wanted a church building for Sunday school, fund-raising suppers, and other meetings. Gender mores dictated that women assume leadership roles such as these, especially where the founding of churches (both literally and figuratively) was concerned. African American men were more likely to spend their time in the political arena, especially in terms of speaking engagements; all women in the nineteenth century were discouraged, or even banned, from public speaking.[89] In Chicago, black congregants founded the Zenia Baptist Church in April 1850. Sallie Jackson hosted the first meeting in her home, along with her friends John Larson and Samuel McCoy.[90] Three years later, under the leadership of a woman named Annie Simpson, church members organized another church, Zoar Baptist. Eventually the Zoar congregation changed its name to Olivet Baptist, most likely to avoid confusion with Zenia. In their first year as a congregation, members collected seven dollars and fifty cents to send to the Wood River Baptist Association, an assemblage of black churches providing aid to their poor congregants.[91] In return, itinerant pastors from the association visited Zoar regularly for about two years because the church lacked a permanent pastor.

* * *

Black emigrants had always put a heavy emphasis on education, and African Americans sought solutions to the hardships of midwestern settlement through institution building.[92] It is little wonder, then, that church and school were somewhat interchangeable in this regionally determined milieu.[93] Schools had existed with some success in Indiana and Illinois in the early abolitionist period.[94] Since the 1840s, both the AME Church and the Quaker Friends had provided some sporadic schooling for black children. Because they understood that the maintenance of white supremacy depended on segregated schooling, activists insisted that they needed excellent day schools, permanent Sunday schools, and a state seminary.[95] Formerly enslaved people especially wanted better educational opportunities for their children. John Randle, from Greensfork, Indiana, reported in 1833, "I went to school a little in South Carolina to make up for lost time of white children. My mistress taught me some, and the rest I have picked up as I could. I tried to send my children to school at Spartansburg, but they were treated so unkindly that I took them out. Afterward there was a school in the colored settlement east of me, and I sent [them there]. [Our teachers] taught them."[96] Elisha Weaver, pastor of the Bethel AME Church in Indianapolis, set up a boarding school for African American children, whom he promised instruction in "spelling, reading, writing, arithmetic, grammar, geography, history, anatomy, physiology, [and] hygiene on fair terms."[97] Many church fund-raising campaigns were designed to sustain schools.[98]

Emancipation activists sought educational rights on a national scale, but local strategists were in charge of the actual nuts and bolts of making sure the schoolhouse doors were not locked to black children. In fact, John Jones mentioned the desire for education at a political convention: "We want education and we want money. With these two potent instruments we have the 'Aachimedian [sic] lever' with which we may turn the wicked institution of this country upside down, and pour Slavery into the pit below, its only congenial abiding place. Let us profit from the teachings of history until each one of us shall fully realize the truth of which Lord Bacon taught, that 'Knowledge is power.'"[99] In this, John reveals a great deal to us about his background and beliefs about uplift. He lacked a formal education, so most of his skills were largely self-taught. Whatever else he knew was likely garnered from literary and debating societies within the Chicago churches he attended in the span of his adult life. John, like so many other activists, believed that one key to emancipation lay in the availability of quality education for African Americans. John knew from his own experience that education had allowed him to grow a successful business and hire his own employees so that he could devote his time to emancipation activism. In the speech quoted from above, he linked money and education because he believed that a good educational system in Indiana and Illinois cities and towns required money, but he also knew that money meant power. In the case of so many of his brethren, having money meant that they could buy property, which could equal access to citizenship rights—like voting—or it could mean buying family members who were enslaved. Finally, John probably understood that his classical education allowed him to speak on the same level as figures like Frederick Douglass and Abraham Lincoln. He was proud, in part because his literacy allowed him to stand tall, and he clearly wanted that for his people.

Rudimentary schools were almost always located within churches and other religious meetinghouses, so children matriculated in places where people commonly met. For instance, the African American Presbyterian church in Shawneetown, Illinois, had its own small school by 1850, with classes taught by Francis Smith, who was listed as a black teacher in the 1870 census.[100] In nearby Lakeview, black resident Zachariah "Byrd" Taborn donated an acre of land so that an already-existing log building could be used as a church, school, and cemetery.[101] The school was open only a few weeks a year, but it existed nevertheless.[102]

Midwestern black activists were keenly aware that while they were working to establish schools, white opponents were spreading the word that blacks should be denied education on the basis of their perceived lack of intelligence.[103] Activists also recognized the need to craft a regional response to inter- and intrastate hostility, especially from whites who were sympathetic to slaveowners or were worried about black encroachment on their locale. Activists understood that much of this segregationist rhetoric was coming out of the South. As a result, the antislavery politics of blacks was local and statewide. The women of the Henry County Female Anti-Slavery Society wrote a letter to the editor of the Greensboro, North Carolina, *Patriot* in which they specifically addressed slaveholders. In the letter, the women maintained that there was no evidence that blacks were inferior in intellect; if this claim were true, they noted, then African Americans should be allowed and *encouraged* to seek education.[104] In this way, black women activists stepped away from the local politics of their towns to comment on the destruction of slavery, which had always been a crucial piece of emancipation.

Of course, African Americans were denied entry to public schools in the Midwest. In Spartanburg, Indiana, a group of high-school-aged black students from the Union Literary Institute formed a protest society. Local community members joined the students, who decided to publish their own newspaper. This particular group must have felt that they had little recourse in the legal arena, so they used the printed word to remonstrate against "an abominable and most shortsighted provision in the laws of Indiana." The group gathered information to make their argument, which centered on the fact that some twelve thousand Indiana blacks (according to their reading of the census) were being denied educational opportunities. Contributors stated that they hoped to "cultivate and develop the latent talents, and elevate the intellectual, religious and moral character of the colored people." Before that could be accomplished, however, students had a host of complaints. In 1863, they wrote, "Look at the barbarous code of Black Laws. . . . We are denied the benefit of the schools funds and at the same time compelled to pay taxes for the support of the government. The worst and most deplorable feature of those proscriptive laws is, that they shut us out from the public schools, and leave us (so far as the state is concerned) entirely without the means of education."[105] Much of what was written in the *Repository* was deliberately provocative (and typed in boldface and capital letters), but *Harper's Weekly* gave its stamp of approval nevertheless: "If we as a race ever become educated, elevated, and respected, we have got to do the work ourselves. No one else can do it for us. We must prove to the white man that we are as susceptible of improvement as he is."[106]

Churches and schools were interconnected as a form of institution building. Churches were more than a local place for religious worship, and black activists continued to wage battles for the education for their children. That education was never equal to what white youths received, but that fact alone was an excellent motivator for activism. Back in 1836, when one black family in Indianapolis, Indiana, tried to send its children to Sunday school in an integrated church, white congregants refused to allow interracial learning. Superintendent A. C. Washburn, who was sympathetic to emancipation, decided to put the African American children in a separate room during Sunday school. When he could get away from his duties with the white children, he spent some time instructing the black children.[107] The 1850 city directory listed white women who taught at the "colored" Sunday school, but they received about half of what teachers at the white school earned.[108] In 1856, the School Fund Association of Illinois had collected eight hundred dollars over a period of three years, but progress was slow, and the group decided to disband until the situation improved.[109] Legislators established the public school system in 1857, but it did not serve black children. By 1860, black parents were pressing the school board on a weekly basis, and the school board finally relented and established a separate school for their children.

Women combined their gendered and raced responsibilities with their demand for the education for their children.[110] Women wanted their children to receive religious education for all of the obvious reasons, but they also wanted to send a message about their organizations' activist principles. Activists viewed education within a religious paradigm. In Ripley Township, Indiana, for instance, there were several schools for black children (with both black and white teachers), mostly located within black churches. Church members understood the need for self-improvement, and they commonly wrote about their longing for it, especially where their parenting skills were concerned. In 1859, one African American woman who was trying to organize a "Mother's Association" spoke of the need for a group whose sole interest would be child-rearing with an intellectual and moral focus. She wrote, "If one half the time which has been spent in blaming and denouncing our oppressors had been employed in working out the results of such an institution, much, very much would have been accomplished to demonstrate [our position to] the respect and consideration of mankind."[111] This indicates that some black women believed that there were other community pursuits equally as important as emancipation activism.

Black communities believed that racial uplift, as it related to education, fell within the purview of women especially. For Indiana and Illinois blacks, uplift was primarily rooted in the local relations of power and could offer a clear path to full civic inclusion. African Americans resolutely sought education because they equated literary, scientific, and mathematical skills with the chance to own their own homes, property, and businesses. Racial uplift was a bulwark against race-based denial of citizenship rights, and it provided for black political success as well. The black community stressed imbuing children with academic skills early on.[112] At Quinn AME, women activists known as the "Big Four" provided shelter, clothing, and food to escaped slaves on the Underground Railroad, but their important work also included instructing children in day schools and Sunday schools in the church. One of the women, Emma J. Atkinson, arrived in Chicago around 1847 with her husband, Isaac, but appears to have left no other records.[113]

Schools in Indiana and Illinois that encouraged interracial schooling were training grounds for young men and women who would eventually become community and congregation activists. Leaders were laying down roots, and they wanted their children to learn to read, write, and do math. Although some proslavery whites lived in southern Indiana, there were also groups of Quakers and paternalistic whites who tried to help blacks as they built their communities. In Jefferson County, Indiana, Thomas Craven (a white man) established Eleutherian Institute (known as the "abolition school"), which he encouraged blacks to attend. Church leaders and pastors who led the fight for emancipation in the late antebellum years often attended these schools. Moses Broyles, who became a legendary pastor of Indiana's Second Baptist Church, was one of Eleutherian's most prominent students. Black women established a women's society at the institute and advertised their desire to see more black students come to the school from around the state.[114]

Black women believed education was "the key to the future of their community."[115] One can well imagine the kind of planning this took for free black women who had only recently escaped slavery and immigrated to the Midwest. Luckily, white benefactors provided help along the way. In 1845, Benjamin Thomas, a white resident of Randolph County, Indiana, donated 150 acres of land for the creation of the Union Literary Institute. The institute was surrounded by three thriving rural black communities in Greenville, Cabin Creek, and Snow Hill. The school was one of the few educational institutions to encourage the enrollment of both black and white students, and it also included African Americans among its board members. Supported by the antislavery Society of Friends, the school began accepting students in 1846. A fugitive slave, Louis Talbert, was one of the first to attend the institute.[116] The state legislature granted the school its first charter in 1848, although the charter lacked explicit wording about black educational rights that would have most assuredly raised the ire of slavery's supporters. The school's constitution, which was drawn up at a Friends meetinghouse, noted that the institute was meant for the "benefit of that class of the population whom the laws of Indiana at present preclude from all participation in the benefits of our public school system."[117] Whites, however, were not excluded.

The building and administration of black schools was met in many areas with staunch white resistance. In one case, a white man from Mississippi had married and freed an enslaved woman, mother to several of his children. The family moved to Lancaster County, Indiana, so that the children could enroll at Eleutherian Institute. A former slave from Alabama who had traveled north with his family also enrolled. In 1850, white racists burned both families' homes, along with another African American home. Another group of whites attempted to prosecute three administrators associated with the school. White antagonists argued that the black teachers had violated Article XIII of the state's constitution by "encouraging Negroes to come into the state." The three African Americans were indicted, but the case was eventually dropped when antislavery lawyer and judge Stephen C. Stevens represented the defendant before the court.[118]

African American activists, along with some like-minded whites, developed sophisticated protest dialogues against discriminatory educational laws that prohibited black enrollment in public schools. In the 1850s, the state legislature in Indiana introduced two measures to eliminate the whites-only educational provision, but antislavery legislators were as divided on the issue as Democrats were united. During these legislative battles, African Americans found themselves divided along two lines: those who pushed for admittance to white schools and those who pushed for a share of taxes for black schools.[119] In 1852, fifty-two property owners (white and black) petitioned the Indiana state legislature to "set aside the portion of School Tax arising from the property of Colored Citizens for the education of colored persons in the State."[120] Three years later, in 1855, the Illinois legislature finally provided for this tax plan by instructing individual townships to allot portions of school taxes to black schools. As a result of black poverty and the limited size of the black population, the amount of tax funds that blacks received was but a pittance. They needed private donations to establish schools and keep them running. In Gallatin County, Illinois, African Americans did use some of those tax funds to create small schools.[121] According to the census, twenty-nine black children attended school in that county in 1860.[122]

These legislative "victories" were a mixed bag for black activists. The uneven consequences of these battles crystallized black dissatisfaction with the excruciatingly slow pace of emancipation. In fact, for every small victory, there were many more defeats. Records suggest that these men and women rejected any other sort of plan (such as moving elsewhere or group dissolution) because slavery affected all parts of the country. This they knew all too well. Furthermore, these setbacks might have threatened the precarious nature of confidence in emancipation activism, but activists continued to associate the meaning of emancipation with the politics of both building a home and destroying slavery. Emancipation in Indiana and Illinois could mean freedom elsewhere, and vice versa.

Despite these challenges, African Americans in Indiana and Illinois continued to make education for their children their top priority, along with religious instruction and training. By 1860, 1,122 black students were enrolled in some sort of school in Indiana.[123] Although this number represented only about a quarter of school-aged black children, it was certainly a step in the right direction. Samuel Smothers, a black educator and 1856 graduate of the Union Literary Institute, wrote in 1860 that the most damning feature of all the black codes was the barring of African Americans from school. Smothers held Republicans particularly responsible: "Republicans, how long! Oh! how long will this be the case? When you support, by your votes and by your influence, the other proscriptive laws of this State, you indeed commit a crime against God and humanity of great magnitude; but when you deprive us of the means of education, you commit an outrage upon the SOUL; *a war upon the immortal part!*"[124]

Beyond this, much of the language used by black activists centered on the destruction of slavery, a goal that was funneled almost entirely through their insistence that they would not leave the Midwest. Place, and the dedication to it, was the pivot on which black midwestern organizing and activism turned. Convention members who had insisted on a western tour of black speakers could now celebrate an improved motherland: "But times have changed very much of late. The Abolition lecturer speaks to a different audience, moves in a different atmosphere, and treads a less rugged pathway. We therefore bring no discouraging news from the West. The cause of freedom is onward and upward in [all the states.] The work is not done; there is much more to be done, till the last yoke is broken and the last captive set free. But it is soul cheering to observe how much has been accomplished."[125] Activists also highlighted the importance of individual cooperation and group teamwork. Put simply, there was safety in numbers. But as the above passage shows, there was also safety in hope. Blacks shared a bond borne by fear and injustice, and they used their networks to act collectively. Furthermore, they understood the allure of Canada and worked to make their grassroots campaigns more attractive: "Twenty years ago the number of colored men in Canada West was 3,400; now there are more than 49,000. In four months after the F.S.L., 10,000 poured into the country."[126]

Whether they were building schools or erecting churches, activists stubbornly reiterated their intention to remain in the Midwest, in the communities they had worked to build. Their homegrown groups had their own set of leaders and followers, and activists never became dependent on eastern abolitionist leaders for their impetus or ideas. African Americans who had already settled in the Midwest had enough familiarity with (and fear of) the FSL to have spent considerable time aiding fugitives on their journey. The *Western Citizen* hosted meetings of Chicago activists when it came time to raise money and food for travelers, and it was proud to report this type of philanthropy in its pages.[127] Emancipation, then, was sometimes a tangible objective—one that could be garnered with horses, wagons, food, and conductors to light the night sky.

3. Antebellum and Wartime Emancipation Activism

Black emancipation activism took crucial turns in the late antebellum period, because much of what was happening on the federal scene was mirrored in small midwestern settlements. Activists linked the "slave's restoration of freedom" directly to their own precarious citizenship status, reasoning that "the elevation of the free man is inseparable from, and lies at the very threshold" of the destruction of slavery. Emerging sectional crises, convention delegates argued, also fell within their purview because the "elevation of the free man" was directly related to outcomes for states' rights, free soil, and free labor.[1] Of course, these same black men recognized that white men (save for a handful of radical abolitionists like John Brown) cared little how black communities would fare as the sectional crisis and later the war shook the nation. Throughout the late 1850s, activist strategies included growing local and state networks, chipping away at the FSL and black codes, and church and school construction. All the while, combative whites continued to make the Midwest a place antagonistic to black settlers.

Free blacks in the Midwest theoretically had the power to act independently and make their own choices—they were not slaves, after all—but their choices were often limited by their white neighbors' disaffection. Emancipation for black state activists signaled freedom from local systems dominated by white racists.[2] While African Americans imagined creating new lives in these places, it was the very place that held them back—a place where slavery had been so entrenched that white society felt compelled to enact black codes. For most whites, African Americans were mere pawns in the game. White loyalties could and did shift suddenly in the last few years before the war. Republicans, especially, underwent transformation as the sectional crisis drew them closer to the question of extending slavery, an issue that most of them would have rather avoided altogether.[3] Republicans were cautious at best when it came to black activism or apathetic and hostile at worst.[4]

This constantly changing terrain characterized midwestern politics in the 1850s. Migration to, from, and through Illinois and Indiana must have occurred at a dizzying rate, given the presence of runaway slaves. In fact, activists recognized that there was some degree of safety—and saliency—in numbers. Following the passage of the FSL, a group of prominent Chicago activists (including John Jones, William Styles, H. O. Wagoner, William Johnson, and the Reverend Abraham T. Hall) met to make plans for repudiating the law.[5] They decided that success would depend largely on attracting large numbers of local African Americans to sign a petition, so the committee and its workers canvassed the Fourth Congressional District (which included Chicago) for the names of all blacks living there.[6] In doing so, they would make sure that no one became an activist by accident—African Americans would join the ranks because they had been sought out by community leaders and because everyone understood that total emancipation might be at stake. The 1860 population of Chicago was 109,260, including 7,628 free blacks.[7] The more black voices that could articulate the message of emancipation activism, the better.

Political treatises written by activists at the conventions of the 1850s often focused on education and religion, or a combination of both. The concerns of the 1840s had not lessened. Black activists repeatedly mentioned in their political documents their offense at paying school taxes when there were no educational provisions for their children: "We pay school taxes without the privileges of sending our children to public schools. . . . [I]t is a subject that should commend itself to every colored man and woman in the State, and their duty in regard to it is plain."[8] Convention proceedings mentioned black women's "auxiliary associations," the goals of which were to "pray and provide relief from the repressive laws" under which the community suffered.[9]

As their next step toward emancipation, African Americans in Illinois participated in the second State Convention of Colored Citizens in 1856. Attendees were appointed by community members who met at church meetings to nominate delegates.[10] Black churches were customary venues for civic meetings—religion was enthusiastically combined with political goals.[11] Evelyn Brooks Higginbotham's conclusions on the late nineteenth- and early twentieth-century church hold true for the antebellum and wartime church as well: "In time the black church—open to both secular and religious groups in the community—came to signify public space. . . . The church also functioned as a discursive, critical arena—a public sphere in which values and issues were aired, debated, and disseminated throughout the larger black community."[12] The convention delegates, who were chosen at the Colored Baptist and AME Churches of Chicago just before the convention, included Joseph H. Barquet, H. Ford Douglas, John Jones, and H. O. Wagoner. They, along with their wives, are important to the story of state and local emancipation, not only because they were relatively wealthy and educated but also because they were chosen to represent thousands of other African Americans who lacked the socioeconomic status and education to plead their own case. This is an important fact that cannot be overlooked: these men were only representatives, and countless public meetings were held to decide what the men would orate in public speeches, assert in pamphlets and newspapers, and opine to government leaders.

The 1856 State Convention of Colored Citizens signals an important turning point in the time line of emancipation activism. The convention reveals three of the most important features of black antebellum activism. First, the event itself highlights the importance of all-black state and local meetings. Abolitionists had been holding conventions throughout the antebellum period, but regional black activists wanted to have conventions of their own.[13] Black activists were now hosting their own regional meetings rather than attending national ones, which was a new and important departure. Second, African Americans now chose to embed the language of "home" in their political propaganda: "We the colored citizens of Illinois, in Convention assembled, feel ourselves *deeply aggrieved* by reasons of the cruel prejudice we are compelled to suffer in this our *'native land,'* [italics in the original] as dear to us as it is to white men—as the blood-bought inheritance of our ancestors."[14] This they proclaimed publicly to all who resented their encroachment in the Midwest, and they would continue to do so throughout the Civil War. Free blacks considered themselves to be Indianan and Illinoisan—they were staying and refusing to leave.

Activists had already opened up their houses to runaways and freedpeople, and now they intended to make their state and local communities attractive to any other emancipated person. Enslaved people regularly crossed the Ohio River and took refuge in the homes of other blacks already in Indiana and Illinois. This deliberate act of unlawful defiance infuriated whites in the region. With scare tactics that foreshadowed Jim Crow, whites used the newspaper to warn blacks of severe recriminations if activists continued to violate the law that forbade aiding fugitives. One newspaper threatened, "The [black] keeper of the house should be taught a lesson which would make him more careful in the future how he violates laws."[15]

Black activists fashioned their colored national conventions platforms to promote a range of positions, especially those concerning the relationship between slavery and black codes. Attendees agreed that slavery was an insidious evil because its effects were so sweeping. Additionally, they argued, all race hatred bore the same fruit: "while slavery is sectional, it is in itself destructive and fatal to American liberty."[16] In these records, African Americans reveal themselves to be courageous and unwilling to back down in the face of white intimidation. Their plans included what they called "an enlarged democracy" in which black men would gain the same citizenship rights as white men. "Freedom should prevail everywhere and slavery nowhere," they insisted, sending the message to white supremacists all over the country.[17]

As the third important feature of their antebellum activism, African Americans cemented their commitment to midwestern politics by taking on the responsibility of emancipation advocacy for themselves. Blacks had accepted assistance from Quakers, for instance, but they did not rely on them. Throughout this period, Americans bore witness to the maturation of self-help ideology within the black community. Individual cooperation had been a major cornerstone of black activism in the previous two decades, but moral suasion and white philanthropy had both lacked the momentum needed to effect emancipation. African Americans could not use the democratic process to end slavery. They could, however, push for the type of enlarged democracy that they envisioned. Black self-reliance and agency were more important than ever, and by 1856, state activists found themselves at a crossroads.[18]

The black codes had been deliberately designed to marginalize blacks as second-class citizens, and activists knew it. By the mid-1850s, the black codes still had not been repealed. John Jones was especially maddened, and he reminded his audiences that whites in the region were tenacious in their malevolence.[19] Jones added that the codes were deliberately designed to act symbolically, too, so that African Americans would understand that their rights were restricted even in "free" states.[20] Black people were cognizant that they would remain vulnerable in America unless emancipation for all occurred, and even abolition would not necessarily guarantee their rights.[21] And as the regional and federal crises of the 1850s unfolded, black activists appreciated the real crux of the matter: everyone was talking about them and what they did or did not deserve, but no one was delivering.

Perhaps even more crucial to identifying themselves as activists and citizens of the Midwest was the insistence on the part of African Americans that

Alfred Jackson Tyler, *John Jones Fights for the Repeal of the Black Code*, oil on canvas, 35⅛ × 44¼ inches. Illinois Legacy Collection, Illinois State Museum, transfer from the State Historical Library; photographer, Dannyl Dolder.

they would stand together in their quest to destroy slavery and its statutory cousin, the black codes. Attendees of the 1856 Alton convention declared that "the thorough organization and united effort of the colored people is absolutely essential to the successful termination of the great struggle in which we are now engaged for the attainment of our rights." Activists committed to hiring itinerant agents to travel throughout the state to hold meetings with black settlers. In addition, those agents would "establish auxiliary associations, lecture, circulate petitions and memorials among the white people of the State, and pray for relief from the oppressive law under which we suffer."[22] Proceedings also included a great deal of antislavery rhetoric. In addition to naming their group the Illinois State Repeal Association,[23] black activists added a constitution and bylaws.[24] These documents instituted a host of rules and regulations to be followed by any member of the community who participated in the association. The rules included, but were not limited to, an executive committee with a president, vice president, treasurer, and secretary; regular attendance and timely arrival at meetings; and dues paid to the local associations.

The Repeal Association devised its list of goals with an eye toward fastidious organization and all-inclusive membership. The associates' motives for inclusivity may have had some type of altruistic intent, but it is more likely that they understood their true statistical minority status—at any one time in the antebellum period, they constituted less than 1 percent of the total population in Illinois and just over 1 percent in Indiana.[25] The men included a call for "Female Repeal Associations" in towns and cities, most likely because they knew they needed a good portion of the black population to fill the ranks. Men knew that women were critical to activism and institution building, but separate groups for men and women were still expected. And if they had any sense of the type of activism women practiced in their communities, then they had an appreciation for how women could help achieve their goals.

The combination of the black codes, the FSL, and the lack of schooling for black children meant that African American settlers had to recruit every man, woman, and child for emancipation activism. H. O. Wagoner was unable to attend the convention but sent a letter to be read aloud.[26] Wagoner was a busy black activist and president of Chicago's (African American) Literary and Debating Society.[27] Part of his letter included his opinions on how to achieve the Repeal Association's goals: "Of course we all agree that *union of sentiment* and *concert of action* are first necessary. But how shall those be brought about? ... [We must] institute a thorough and efficient system of *organization*, as the first step in this great work. By well-organized associations, we assign to each and every man a place to work; and surely every individual can do something, however small, in this great movement."[28] Conventioneers did not elaborate on what type of small tasks they were thinking about, but their words reflect the ethos of emancipation activism in the late antebellum period. As Wagoner noted, unity among activists was an exigent matter.

The Repeal Association also represented hope—an expectation that blacks could create a voice loud enough for whites to listen.[29] After all, white people possessed virtually all of the power. With this in mind, conventioneers elected Wagoner (despite his absence) one of the Repeal Association's secretaries, along with Joseph H. Barquet, from Wagoner's close-knit circle of activists.[30] Barquet was a Chicago mason who made his living by "brick laying, plaster hanging, and paper hanging" with his business partner, Andrew Jackson Pertect.[31] Barquet had been active in northern Illinois and Chicago abolition-ist groups for some time. In 1853, Barquet had argued that the exclusionary laws in the state would lead black men (already living there) to marry white women: "The recent law of inhibition against the negro, passed by our leg-islature . . . bears hard, very hard against Sambo. . . . Well, sir, [if] I wish to annex myself to a wife, but the commodity in colors is scarce in our market! What shall we do? If we go from home to import one, the dear creature will be sold to some heartless Logan."[32] Barquet finished with a warning: "the laws of Illinois do not recognize the marriage tie between a white and negro, and if Mr. Logan shuts out the black girls, why we must take the white ones."[33] In this statement, Barquet shrewdly manipulated one of the foremost fears of whites, miscegenation, by insinuating that black women should be allowed to settle in free states so that black men would not try to claim white women as wives. Of course, interracial marriage was illegal in Michigan, Ohio, In-diana, and Illinois.[34]

Whites continued to fear that immigration into the Midwest would result in the "mixing of races." Indeed, whites strenuously enforced the endogamous color line in the North, even more so than in the South.[35] Even George W. Julian, a radical Republican from Indiana who supported emancipation, be-came squeamish at the thought of miscegenation. Julian insisted that in the Midwest, whites and blacks did associate with one another, but there were "no such *intimate* relations" as in the South, where "slave mothers and slave masters . . . are brought on to the level of social equality in its most loathsome forms."[36] White racists sometimes vacillated between two competing ideas— on the one hand, they abhorred "mixing" races, but on the other hand, they wondered whether miscegenation could eventually rid the United States of black faces.[37] Local Republicans defended their policies toward blacks: "[We want] to let the African race alone; neither marry nor cohabit with them; to give them their freedom . . . separate the whites from adulterous communication with them; and preserve the purity of the Caucasian blood from African admixture."[38] Therein laid another reason for whites from Indiana and Illinois to support the black codes: race mixing was simply too detestable to allow.[39]

Homesteads, churches, and schools were crucial to both black political culture and psychological and physical survival. Black people located their daily lives in these places, where work, kin, and children thrived. Pride in numbers was a crucial component of these places. In Charleston, Indiana, there were thirty-six black families, with just over two hundred "industrious enterprising" people altogether. Among those, thirty men owned the land with "handsome farms." In winter, Charleston's black children went to school, but as soon as spring came, they returned to the land with "ax, plow, hoe, spade, [and] rake, thus training to education and industry both."[40] These were the images that African American men and women carried with them when they attended meetings and met with leaders in their communities. Later, pride in these places would play a meaningful role as African Americans enlisted in the United States Colored Troops.

At the State Convention of Colored Citizens, place was part of a significant, and often contested, discussion about black settlement. Participants knew it was important that they choose an advocate of emigration rather than an opponent of it, because they wanted to represent several topics for debate.[41] Conventioneers chose a luminary in the movement, H. Ford Douglas, to supervise a committee on "addresses."[42] (Douglas's spouse, Sattie Douglas, was also well known in the activist community and would later spend a significant amount of time helping to recruit black men for military service.) The committee's stated mission was to organize and fund lectures on citizenship rights and emancipation across the Midwest. Delegates likely thought that Douglas would be a good candidate for this job since he was already a traveling and lecturing agent for the *Provincial Freedman*, the main organ for the Canadian emigrationist movement.[43] Although there was disagreement among activists as to whether settlement in free states was an appropriate choice for them, blacks could at least agree that slavery was still the insidious evil. Attendees' debates were energized with knowledge of the Midwest's essential role in emancipation activism.

Whether or not African Americans welcomed the idea of emigration is essential to the story of black activism.[44] Not only were abolitionist luminaries spending time talking to black farmers on dusty stages in Indiana and Illinois—meaning that they considered them a worthy audience—but ordinary men and women were taking part in a national conversation among black activists from the East and the North. Activists refused to allow the very idea of emigration to overshadow their desire to settle the Midwest and assemble their communities. African emigration was a common topic at church meetings, where it was openly debated, and differences of opinion could inspire congregations to challenge ministers.[45] This highlights an important power dynamic in the black community, especially since churches were the center of political activity. For instance, after one African American minister in Covington, Indiana, called for free blacks to join him in colonizing Liberia, congregants in Fort Wayne called for a caucus.[46] The result of this was the formulation of a strong message against the colonization movement, which was published in the *Anti-Slavery Bugle* newspaper.[47] The congregation's statement read,

> Because we are at present denied some of these rights in this State, we should not abandon the hope of attaining justice for ourselves and our posterity, when already the leaven of justice is beginning to show . . . [and], though not yet arrived to a state of maturity, is so far improved as to assure us that patience and perseverance are only needed on our part; and if we should at such time flee our country, forsake the graves of our fathers, desert the places of our birth and the scenes of our childhood, we should show ourselves unworthy of the enjoyment of those things now withheld from us.[48]

In this statement, black settlers reveal their commitment to their homesteads, farms, and towns.

Although they viewed black emancipation from two different ideological positions, H. Ford Douglas and Frederick Douglass toured the lower and upper Midwest together in 1859.[49] H. Ford's philosophy was characterized by his pessimistic view that slavery would never be crushed, but he continued to labor for abolition through the war, eventually joining an infantry regiment from Illinois.[50] Their recollections of their journey were printed in Douglass's newspaper. The men made nearly fifty speeches in twenty-two midwestern cities, acting as agents for the *Provincial Freedman*. They reported that "[n]o matter what might be the subject of our discourses, whether before lyceums or elsewhere, slavery was really the uppermost in the minds of our hearers. Every town we visit, every audience we address, seem to regard us as the medium of an acquaintance with our enslaved people."[51]

Chicago black activists approached H. Ford Douglas' emigrationist stance with a combination of mistrust and apprehension.[52] In the late 1850s, emigrationists separated themselves into two camps. James T. Holly led one group, which championed Haiti as their destination. Martin Delany guided the other group, which endorsed a move to Africa. Douglas never truly allied himself with one group or another, although he seemed to be leaning toward Central America as a better option. Following an 1856 emigration convention, in which these factions revealed themselves, Douglas increasingly spoke about America and slavery rather than emigration. Later, after Chicago blacks were compelled to form vigilance committees to deal with the threat of the FSL, they had agreed as a group "not to fly to Canada but to remain and defend themselves."[53]

Activists did at least consider emigration, if only for a brief historical moment. Meetings to discuss international emigration do appear in the historical record, but the record overwhelmingly suggests that activists had discussed the issue and decided to remain in their present homes. On October 2, 1851, *Frederick Douglass' Paper* reported that a group called the Convention of Colored Freeman met at the Methodist church in Pendleton, Indiana. They discussed emigrating to Jamaica, Canada, or Liberia but adopted a declaration stating "their intention to remain in their native land." Primary sources may privilege those who stayed, rather than those who had already left for other countries. When, in February of 1859, Frederick Douglass spoke at Chicago's AME church on Jackson Street, the audience implored H. Ford to lecture on emigration and the *Dred Scott* decision (even though he had not planned to give a speech that night).[54] H. Ford gave what was presumably a provocative lecture, because Frederick later commented that his Chicago friends were "in a ferment" over emigration to Haiti.[55]

There is no evidence that African Americans in Chicago ever seriously considered the idea of emigration, even though they were the ones who had asked for H. Ford's lecture on the topic.[56] When H. Ford went east to deliver some speeches on Frederick Douglass's turf in late 1859 and early 1860, he was mostly unknown to his audience there. The newspaper reported that H. Ford was well known and popular enough, however, to be called to speak by audiences in Illinois. Later, the Convention of Colored Citizens passed a resolution opposed to emigration: "Resolved, that we are opposed to the call of a National Emigration Convention, as put forth by M. R. Delany and others, and discover in it a spirit of disunion which, if encouraged, will prove fatal to our hopes and aspirations as a people."[57] Although black activists in Chicago never warmed to the idea of emigration to either Africa or Haiti, H. Ford Douglas continued his friendly relationship with Chicago's activists.[58]

Local activist leaders and pastors, along with their congregations, repudiated emigration as an affront to their local and state settlements. John Jones abhorred the idea of emigration and wrote that "he was one Chicago black man who was not going to Haiti."[59] The Progressive Library Association in Chicago claimed that "all forms of expatriation whether emigration, colonization, civilization, or whatever were unacceptable to its members."[60] In 1860, the association took great pains to "utterly condemn" the plan, which sought "notoriety at the expense of the colored man." The association's president H. O. Wagoner characterized black Chicagoans' covenant with the Midwest in a letter: "America is our home, and we abide in the belief that though justice be tardy, we will yet enjoy the rights of man in this land. . . . We will labor and want. We favor our people going any and everywhere their good sense and inclination may dictate, as individuals, but we oppose a relinquishment of their homes."[61]

Black codes, the *Dred Scott* decision, and the FSL were the other commonly addressed topics at local meetings and state conventions in the late antebellum period. By 1858, however, some African Americans began to question the efficacy of these conventions. At a colored convention in Ohio, activists debated the creation of a statewide antislavery society in Illinois. Peter H. Clark, noted Ohio abolitionist and educator, voiced his concerns: he "desired the Convention to pause before they added another to the long list of failed Anti-Slavery Societies, State Organizations, etc. . . . The thing to be done was to get the colored people themselves, interested in their own welfare, and then would be the time for the organization of societies, to operate upon Slavery in the South, or caste in our own state."[62] Many of Clark's colleagues vehemently disagreed with him, arguing that patience (and trust in God) would be rewarded eventually. Clark warned, however, that only urgency and political maneuvering would offer any real chance at equality.[63] Clark's frustration signaled the preponderant problem in small black midwestern communities—poverty was grave enough to give pause to African Americans who knew that speeches and pulpits could not feed a starving family. The dream of emancipation would be woefully incomplete without also having the basic necessities for family and community life.

* * *

The next stage of emancipation activism is best understood as an endeavor that functioned within—and despite—a context of racialized violence. Black activism remained steady in the last few years of the 1850s, as the business of states' rights and western settlement was now incorporated with activist efforts. Grassroots leaders provided the enthusiasm with which they embraced their activist duties by defending their homes with ardor. The local newspaper in Bloomington, Illinois, carried stories of blacks who continued the physical and legal fight for their freedom and that of others.[64] J. H. Lancey, an African American, gave a speech one evening in 1858 in College Hall, asking for donations to a local elderly woman who was trying to buy her daughter's freedom.[65] Black settlement in central Illinois was on the rise, and blacks continued their activist work, reaching out to new immigrants. White racists were undoubtedly paying attention, because in 1859, when the townspeople held an African festival, "a party of [drunk] white revelers invaded the room, turned off the gas, played smash generally, and in short, broke up the frolic."[66] Charlotte Wells, a black woman from town, dared to gather lumber from the yard of Sidney Haley, a white man. Upon discovering her, Haley began throwing bricks and clubs at Wells. The police arrested Haley, and he was fined.[67] The story was much the same in other towns like Bloomington—talk of emancipation generated enthusiasm among blacks and drove racist whites to continue their regular attacks.

John Brown's raid on Harper's Ferry played an integral role in shaping black politics on the eve of secession. As in other towns, blacks in Bloomington listened with awe to reports of John Brown's raid and subsequent public hanging. Mary Jones's prognostication that "somebody would have to give up his life before [John Brown] was done" came true on October 16, 1859, following the raid on the federal arsenal at Harper's Ferry. Despite its antislavery stance, central Illinois's *Daily Pantagraph* called the raid "absurd." Editors contemplated what would happen next: "The inevitable and irrepressible conflict between light and darkness, between freedom and slavery grows fiercer and the irresistible current of events is sweeping our country on, whether to a precipice or to a peaceful lake, we know not."[68]

The next series of events would have everlasting effects on black midwestern emancipation activism. The Republican Party placed Chicago in the spotlight when it chose to hold its national convention there in May of 1860. The Republican platform was decidedly unsettled: it denounced the *Dred*

Scott decision as judicial activism while at the same time condemning John Brown and his partners for choosing racialized violence. Republicans also opposed the expansion of slavery into the West but said virtually nothing about slavery as it existed in the South. When the dust had settled, Abraham Lincoln was the Republican presidential candidate.

African American demographics and civil liberties were the subject of intense regional debate as the presidential election drew near. The Republican Party, though in its infancy in Indiana, needed to carry that state to win the presidency. Indiana Republicans had deliberately chosen Abraham Lincoln as their candidate because he was cautious on the topic of abolitionism. Meanwhile, Stephen A. Douglas warned from his campaign pulpit that Republicans would support large-scale emigration of blacks from the South, especially once slavery was destroyed. Douglas, despite being from Illinois, derided its boastful big city by sneering, "Abolitionist Chicago!" One Indianapolis newspaper summarized Republican goals to white racist Democrats: they intended to give suffrage to black men, to allow black men free access to compete in the labor market (thereby harming the white laborer), and to allow miscegenation.[69] Many activists understood Lincoln to be a supporter of "Negro" rights. Few whites in the Midwest (or in the country, for that matter) supported any type of racial egalitarianism. Lincoln and his fellow Republicans responded with their stock answer: they had no wish to interfere with slavery where it already existed. Free blacks were certainly not and would never be equal to white men, at least in the opinion of the party of Lincoln.[70] Republicans and Democrats alike viewed blacks as both political pawns and subjects of legal scrutiny—but only as they benefited or impinged on the lives of whites.

Popular history treats Lincoln as the "Great Emancipator," but the decision to craft the Emancipation Proclamation was a militarily expedient one. He himself characterized the proclamation as a "war measure." For African Americans, on the other hand, the document was a symbol of liberation. In 1854, in a speech in Peoria, Illinois, Lincoln pondered southerners, slavery, and equality for blacks: "What next? Free them, and make them politically and socially our equals?" he asked, as though he found the idea preposterous. Save for radical abolitionists and Quakers, very few whites in late-1850s America advocated for black emancipation.[71]

The Republicans carried Indiana and Illinois in the 1860 election, but the real political battles had only just begun. Once the southern states began to secede in December, accusations of blame and responsibility for the war began in earnest by April of 1861. Midwestern Republicans were united with Lincoln and the Union under Indiana's Governor Morton, but Democrats clamored for some type of compromise, blaming the Republicans for not responding to the Crittenden Compromise in the first place. Crittenden would have effectively reinstated the Missouri Compromise, which had been destroyed by the Kansas-Nebraska Act and the *Dred Scott* decision. Southern slaveowners welcomed the compromise's promise to extend slavery westward, but Republicans did not agree. Generally, Indiana voters opposed turning the war into one that would eradicate slavery. As one Indianapolis newspaper opined, "The best blood of the North will never be shed in so disgraceful a cause as that of negro emancipation."[72] Another of the state's newspapers hailed Lincoln while warning of the power of abolitionists: "The present administration is trying to do right, but is so hampered by the Abolitionists that it can hardly move."[73]

Indeed, throughout most of 1861, it seemed to people in Indiana that the president was primarily concerned with preserving the Union, but when Lincoln suggested to Congress a plan to give federal aid to states providing for gradual emancipation, Indiana Democrats reacted with intense hostility. The *Daily Sentinel* of Indianapolis printed portions of the Democratic State Committee meeting, in which one speaker noted that Lincoln's plan would result in "transcendent injustice and oppression to the white race."[74] In 1861, one black man expressed to *Douglass' Monthly* how difficult it was to live in the Midwest, where racism was rampant: "It is my ill luck at present to live in the darkest corner of Egypt. As I am about the only abolitionist in the place, your journal is a standing offense to those lovers of mental and moral darkness."[75] In short, whites from Indiana and Illinois not only doubted whether blacks could handle emancipation (gradual or not) but were also irrationally fearful of the fate that might befall white communities should it occur.

Eminent Indiana historian Emma Lou Thornbrough characterized the state's prevailing antebellum attitude as "neither proslavery nor antislavery but anti-Negro."[76] Democrats were afraid of what was going to happen if formerly enslaved people moved north into the midwestern states and so insisted that emancipation had meaning for their lives as well. Of course, black people were heavily invested in the idea of gradual emancipation—any plan for emancipation—but whites showed little comprehension of the African American community's power to understand their place in the great upheaval of war. At county and state conventions, on the floor of the state legislature, and in speeches to constituents, Indiana Democrats decried President Lincoln, who seemed to have gone back on his promise not to make laws restricting the power of slaveholders. Reacting to the First and Second

Confiscation Acts, as well as the establishment of diplomatic relations with Haiti and Liberia, Democrats in Indiana lashed out at Lincoln and his party: "The legislation of this Republican Congress is devoted to the Negro. It is negro first, negro last, and negro all the time."[77]

With all eyes upon Lincoln, the president-elect from Illinois, the FSL was being strictly enforced in late 1860 and early 1861. The *Dred Scott* decision, proslavery and sympathetic to slaveowners, had been delivered by the highest court in the land. It also served to aggrandize its antecedent, the FSL. State activists understood *Dred Scott* to be cruelly inhibiting to their plans because Chief Justice Roger Taney had refused to recognize Dred Scott as a citizen and any part of America as "free territory." The FSL meant that *anyone* of African American descent could be mistaken for a fugitive and remanded to the South. The *Dred Scott* decision also meant that African Americans who had been removed from their homes (despite the fact that they lived in a free state or had been born free or manumitted) had no means of legal redress.[78] In 1848, a young black woman called Eliza Grayson had fled her master and made her way to Chicago, where she worked as a domestic servant in a bordello. Eliza confided her secret to two sex workers, who turned her in for a two-hundred-dollar reward. Luckily for Eliza, a group of African Americans rescued her from a city policeman and promptly sent her north via the Underground Railroad.[79]

Black activists, even during secession and war, continued to cope with the enforcement of the FSL. They were shrewd enough to realize that Lincoln was not necessarily their friend, but they were astounded nevertheless when he made an appeasement to the South following his inauguration. In April 1861, Lincoln called for federal marshals to make a sweep through Chicago's free black community, searching for escaped slaves. Local abolitionists were reportedly warned, and the Republican newspaper speculated that "perhaps in no other city [are] Negroes more apprehensive than in Chicago. The Negro community was panic stricken by a rumor that a group of Federal marshals was about to swope [sic] down on the Black population." The newspaper urged former slaves to run to Canada: "Don't delay a moment. Don't let the grass grow under your feet. You are not safe here and you cannot be safe until you stand on English soil, where you will be free men and women! It is folly for you to remain here an instant, for the slaveholders encouraged by their late success are ... making the most determined effort to reclaim fugitives from bondage. Strike for the North Star!"[80]

Instead of leaving the state, as they had been advised to do, blacks mobilized their resources in anticipation of federal marshals and bounty hunters.

A few African Americans were frightened enough to make the difficult decision to head to Canada. If the activists who remained in the United States were angry with other blacks for fleeing, their actions showed no sign of it. Activists met for an early worship service and meeting at Zoar Baptist Church, and then the "fugitives and their friends went from door-to-door" to bid farewell to each other. In some cases, entire families journeyed north, but in other cases "a wife left a husband, or a mother her children, amid tears," the newspaper reported. Church leaders ministered to the families and individuals, while other groups gathered provisions for the trip. Four freight cars had been commissioned to take the travelers to an embarkation point on Lake Michigan. The "fugitives" (as the newspaper referred to them) reminded each other that if they did not see one another again in Canada or the new country, they would surely meet again on "the other side of Jordan." Finally, before the cars pulled away, one minister reminded his male parishioners "to be [brave] men when they got to Canada."[81]

Blacks who had chosen to remain in the Midwest were disheartened to learn that emancipation was not one of Lincoln's war goals, but they kept their eyes on the prize nevertheless. Mary and John Jones, for instance, had spent ten years in a long quest to repeal the black codes in Illinois, and now they found themselves outraged by white assimilationists who reminded them that "at least slavery was illegal" in the North and West. For the Joneses, the war would culminate in a number of life-altering circumstances, not the least of which was John's fame as a vociferous protestor of black codes. Throughout the antebellum period, John had become a scholar of the Constitution, to the degree that his arguments against black codes rested on the Founding Fathers' intentions regarding universal freedoms.[82]

Later, as it became obvious that a war between the North and South might last longer than a few months, African Americans took another opportunity to articulate their place in the conflict. On the question of black citizenship, John Jones wrote, "if being natives, and born on the soil, of parents belonging to no other nation or tribe, does not constitute a citizen in this country, under the theory and genius of our government, I am at a loss to know in what manner citizenship is acquired by birth."[83] Here, John referenced what was most certainly on the minds of African Americans: Dred Scott had been denied citizenship rights because he was black, so too would they be until the law said otherwise. This was perhaps the tallest order for the activists: it was one thing to harbor fugitives, build schools, and praise God on their own terms, but it would be quite another to effect legal change.

Midwestern activists soon discovered that loyalty to the Union could not be assumed of other residents of free states. Many whites joined the Union forces as speedily as they could, but there were many midwesterners who sympathized with the Confederacy. Following General Benjamin Butler's decision to allow so-called contrabands to work and live in Union camps, some Indiana whites voiced their ire in the local Democratic paper: "Be that phrase forever nameless / Negro contraband, most shameless. / Get thee back into the rice fields / And the cotton-blooming shore. / See our country for thee bleeding— / Cease to prate of rights or freedom. / Dost-not know thou wert born a heathen. / Quit the bust above the door, / Niggers have no rights as humans, / So be gone from off the door. Quoth the darkey 'nevermore.'"[84] Abolitionists continued to plead with Lincoln to make slavery a war issue, but he refused. In the meantime, racist whites—in southern Indiana especially—continued to insist that the war had nothing to do with involuntary servitude: "About this war being to free the Negroes . . . it is all a fudge."[85]

While Republicans were trying to calm some of the tide by offering alternative plans for blacks (such as colonization), Democrats continued their attack on African Americans. Thomas A. Hendricks, a Democrat who was elected to the United States Senate from Indiana, epitomized the prevailing American attitude that blacks were unequivocally dissimilar to whites and therefore unequal. To the question of whether or not the "two races" could ever have a relationship of equality, Hendricks replied, "[In] terms of equality, it may be preached for; it may be legislated for; it may be prayed for; but there is that difference between the races that renders it impossible. If they are among us as a free people, they are among us as an inferior people." Later, Hendricks would add that God had deliberately designed the races with these differences; knowing this, he said, white men would refuse to fight alongside black men.[86]

Like the process of emancipation itself, it took a long time for Lincoln to finally agree that the Emancipation Proclamation was the best course of military action. As expected, Lincoln's September 1862 announcement of his intent to issue an emancipation decree provoked a furor among white state politicians.[87] Lincoln proposed a plan of gradual compensated emancipation in which all slaves would be free by 1900. He also offered to "buy" the freedom of the enslaved people in the border states, but the governors refused. Lincoln was quite clear on his position: the Emancipation Proclamation was a matter of political and military expediency, not a sympathetic move for African Americans. Fearful of how they would fare in the upcoming October state elections, Governor Morton and his fellow Republicans tried to portray the proclamation as a mere maneuver in the game of war.

Midwestern Democrats responded to the proclamation as others in their party across the country already had—they urged voters to understand that their next vote would be, plain and simple, a vote for or against the destruction of slavery.[88] The elections brought victory for the Democrats, who gained control of the Indiana legislature and upset several Republican bastions throughout the state. Democratic newspapers such as the *Daily State Sentinel* celebrated the elections as a strike against abolitionism. The same newspaper went so far as to hypothesize that white men had voted Democratic because they wished neither to fight with African American men nor be forced to compete with those same men for jobs once the war ended.[89] Republicans attributed their losses in Indiana (and in Illinois, Ohio, and Pennsylvania) to the lack of votes cast by white soldiers who were away at war.[90]

The Emancipation Proclamation went into effect on January 1, 1863, bringing—finally—some thrilling news to black communities in Indiana and Illinois, especially for former slaves. The fact that the proclamation applied only to states in rebellion was key, but activists celebrated nevertheless. Democratic newspapers waged a full frontal attack on Lincoln, his party, and anyone who supported Lincoln's plan for the war and for African Americans. Lincoln himself certainly did not espouse equality for people of color; indeed, in his speech to Congress in 1862, he reiterated his support for African colonization. He was careful to point out that the North needed a large labor force (thereby reassuring whites that they would not lose their jobs to incoming blacks). He spent a considerable amount of time addressing the differences between free blacks and newly freed slaves. Finally, Lincoln added, "can not the North decide for itself whether to receive [African Americans]?"[91] This statement "appeared [as] almost an invitation to the northern states to pass exclusion laws."[92]

Emancipation activists experienced the war surrounded by hostile whites, who for one reason or another resented Lincoln, his goals, or the war altogether. In response to the emancipation "scheme," as they called it, many white Indiana voters continued to express anger toward Lincoln and hatred for their black neighbors. Newspapers purported to carry letters from soldiers in the field who wrote of their hostility toward racial equality. Stephen Miller, a white Indiana soldier who was recuperating in a Louisville hospital, wrote, "As soon as I get my money I am coming home I don't care if they call it deserting or not. . . . I did not volenteer to fight to free the niggers and I guess that['s] what old black Abolition Abe is at now. if he don't go at trying to free the niggers I will come back . . . but if he goes at that I shall never shoulder another gun to fight the rebels."[93] Another letter from a soldier in the Army of the Potomac read, "We want this war ended. . . . We don't want the North flooded with free niggers. We want Indiana exclusively for intelligent, free, white men."[94] Other white Indianans claimed to oppose the Emancipation Proclamation because it would not be beneficial for African Americans: "Let it alone. . . . [L]oyal masters will soon rid themselves of the curse, not curse to the negro but to the white man. . . . [If they get rid of slavery] in 50 or 100 years it will be soon enough for the welfare of the negro."[95]

Once the Indiana legislature reconvened in early 1863, the Democratic majority wasted no time condemning the new presidential policy. Republicans and Democrats disagreed on abolition, exclusion laws, and emancipation so often and so vociferously that they failed to pass any appropriations bill for two long years. One Democratic-led state senate committee issued the following statement in one of its reports: "We are uncompromisingly opposed to all schemes the tendency of which is calculated to overrun the State of Indiana with a worthless and degraded negro population."[96] Republicans even proposed a harsher black exclusion law than the one existing in the state at that time, although the bill was never passed.[97]

The promise of the Emancipation Proclamation caused tremendous social upheaval. More blacks relocated to the Midwest, bringing their kin and others whom they had met along the way.[98] Republicans in Indiana held meetings across the state, encouraging citizens to support the Emancipation Proclamation as a necessary part of the war effort. Voters in both Indiana and Illinois had shown little support for it during recent elections, and Republican politicians knew that they would need the backing of whites to keep the war moving. African American emancipation was the subject of these meetings only insofar as politicians promised that blacks could be used as laborers and as soldiers. Politicians who hosted and attended these meetings crafted their messages carefully; black freedom could be leveraged to win the war, not to fulfill promises made to free and enslaved blacks.

Whites in Indiana and Illinois were alarmed at the suggestion that African Americans might become uniformed and armed members of military forces.[99] At the end of 1862, when President Lincoln announced his intention to authorize colored troops, Democratic Senator Hendricks of Indiana called the move a "gross insult to every man in whose veins flows the blood of our race."[100] Democrats unremittingly insisted that African American men were naturally cowardly and therefore not fit for service. Republicans defended the colored troops with equal vehemence, averring how brave African American men really were. Democrats also insisted that, mirroring the Northern free labor market, black soldiers should be paid much less than their white counterparts. In speeches before the Thirty-Eighth Congress, Indiana Democrats argued that since African Americans were not citizens anyway, the question of equal pay was essentially moot.[101] Congressman John Usher went so far as to claim that black labor was less valuable in the army.[102] Usher was probably referring to the fact that African Americans were used for labor (such as digging ditches and graves) that was considered much less important than those tasks assigned to the combat soldier.

Miscegenation—once again—also weighed heavily on the minds of politicians in Indiana and Illinois, since they believed that an influx of blacks might bring with them the matter of assignations. Newspapers frequently reported on this issue, usually referring to it as "amalgamation." In Indianapolis, women at Democratic rallies reportedly carried banners begging white men to save them from black rapists: "Oh Fathers, Oh Brothers, Save us from the Negro, Equality and Despotism!"[103] Democratic papers used unsubstantiated stories to drive fear into the hearts of their racist readers. One story told of young white women running away with black men, while another reported that white women were performing "favors" for African American soldiers.[104] The *Indianapolis Daily State Sentinel* even insinuated that President Lincoln played a role in the supposed "amalgamation" scheme, opining that he had "openly and publicly avowed . . . [the] beastly doctrine of the intermarriage of black men with white women."[105] Republicans responded to these accusations, insisting that the party was still most concerned about working white men and that there was little danger of a great black influx in the Midwest, since African American labor would be needed in the war-torn South.[106] These politicians promised that if any one group were to benefit from emancipation, it would be white men, whose marketplace value was sure to rise if black men found themselves in the local labor market after all.[107] In any case, Republicans carefully avoided the topic of miscegenation, seeming to imply that the issue lacked enough merit to warrant a response.

The Midwest was undoubtedly a place where the cacophony of racist speech was matched in vehemence only by the accompanying noise of emancipation discourse from black activists. Some whites from Indiana and Illinois were sympathetic to emancipation activism. Andrew and Sarah Hampton, of Wayne County, Indiana, were so "pronounced in [their] anti-slavery views that [they] refused to allow the use in [their] household of any product of slave labor, such as sugar, cotton, rice, etc., and it often involved much expense to procure free labor products." They also received fugitive slaves into their home throughout the war, aiding them "kindly and zealously."[108] All of the national debate over the spread of slavery to the West was critical to emancipation activism—for blacks, the quality of life lay in the balance. Black activists had worked for many years to build the institutions that helped their communities grow, and now they needed to concentrate on sustaining them. As the war made its long approach and finally took hold, emancipation activism kept pace. Activist goals would remain largely unchanged until black enlistment rocked free black communities back on their heels.

4. Black Soldiering and Emancipation Activism

During the Civil War, black Americans who had built midwestern communities now found themselves facing a battle for the republic. The Emancipation Proclamation freed no one, yet it made soldiers of black men and gave hope to many struggling African Americans. For midwestern African Americans, however, the Emancipation Proclamation, and the enlistment it encouraged, was a critical activist issue. For them, war was still located in those local places: the news of secession, the mustering of troops, the initial refusal to allow black enlistment, and so on—all of these were funneled through local activist political culture. Enlistment meant, on the one hand, that blacks could serve the Union, thereby securing citizenship rights they believed they were due as soldiers. On the other hand, enlistment meant that black men would have to leave their midwestern homes for camps and battlefields, most of them in slaveholding states. During the war, activists refocused emancipation on soldiering, both in literal and symbolic terms. If the efforts of African American activism in the region were focused on achieving emancipation in an incremental way, then black enlistment was another crucial step toward freedom.[1]

Enlistment was not a magic bullet for the racism and poverty that beleaguered the black Midwest. When menfolk marched to war, leaving women, children, and the elderly to fend for themselves, the community as a whole suffered. Historians have documented how African American men suffered inequities in pay, weaponry, housing, clothing, task opportunity, and overall humane treatment within their regiments.[2] But traditional military historiography has frustrated the study of war as a gendered and raced experience. The history of warfare has traditionally been treated as an entirely masculine activity—a story *necessarily* told through the eyes of (white) male combatants only: "Warfare is . . . the one human activity with which women, with the most insignificant exceptions, have always and everywhere stood apart."[3] Throughout world history, women have worked as everything from combatants to camp followers, sex workers to doctors, but they are most always historically invisible.[4] Black men understood this paradigm of undervalued and underpaid labor, and they longed to be skilled soldiers, not unskilled laborers. Midwestern blacks wanted to see their men fight as part of the Union army so that freedom would be doubly won. Black soldiers, however, were often assigned to "lowly" tasks like hauling garbage, digging and cleaning latrines, cooking, and performing menial tasks for white soldiers and officers. This was the fundamental issue upon which black military service turned: Since black men and their families had endured so much inequitable treatment as citizens, what compelled them to support enlistment and remain soldiers?[5]

Black attitudes toward enlistment were pragmatic. African Americans accepted responsibility for what they considered their part in the war. Samuel Smothers of Indiana's Union Literary Institute cast military participation as the long-awaited opportunity to perform manly duties: "The time has come for intelligent, decisive, and energetic action on our part. For thirty years we have been lecturing, talking and praying for this liberation of our enslaved brethren. God has answered our prayers, and our brethren are being liberated by the thousands. The wonderful changes which are now taking place in our condition brings upon us new duties." Smothers noted that the first duty was to defend the United States government because "our liberties, our interests and our happiness . . . depends upon the fate of this government. To fight in defense of the government will confer lasting honor upon us and our posterity, and secure for us the respect and admiration of our white fellow-citizens."[6] Midwestern blacks assumed a role in the military because they wanted to see the South and slavery defeated but also because they wanted to augment what they had built in the Midwest.

Black men believed that they could effect emancipation with their own blood. If they survived the war, they hoped they would then be able to vote, testify, sign contracts, and own property as heads of their households. It is somewhat ironic that the midwestern black men who wanted to defend their free black communities ended up serving in the East. About three hundred black men from Indiana and Illinois joined the Fifty-Fourth and Fifty-Fifth Massachusetts Regiments.[7] Men and their families were under a constant barrage of newspaper advertisements entreating them to travel to Massachusetts to muster into the army. Recruiters traveled west and brought men back to eastern states. Midwestern men, many of them former southern slaves, now found themselves on the Atlantic Coast.

The African American men whose war stories took them to Massachusetts and Connecticut for mustering can only be imagined, for they left few documents. On March 4, 1863, the New Bedford company of the Massachusetts Fifty-Fourth Volunteer Infantry gathered to receive a group of well-wishers prior to their departure to their training facility, Camp Meigs.[8] After receiving a pair of mittens each, fifty-four African American soldiers boarded a railroad car bound for a Union encampment at Readville, Massachusetts. When they stared beyond the windows of the train car as the countryside came into view, what visions of the past and images of the future crossed their minds? For men who had been born free, the true test of their manhood would be their success or failure to secure freedom for their enslaved southern brethren. For men who had been slaves themselves and subsequently escaped to freedom in the North, they were risking their lives by returning to the former site of their legal enslavement. Given the likelihood of combat violence, as well as the possibility of a return to slavery, the sheer bravery it took to board a train headed south amounted to an emotional and spiritual investment that would have everlasting effects on a generation of men caught between freedom and captivity.[9]

Following the attack on Fort Sumter, black communities remained deeply divided over the issue of whether or not they should "join" the war. Free African Americans responded to Lincoln's call for 75,000 volunteers by flooding northern recruitment centers. By autumn of 1861, some 8,500 black men had formed their own military units in cities such as New York and Cleveland. The War Department, however, rejected black men's offer of service.[10] Lincoln never had any intention of allowing black enlistment, fearing that it would drive slaveholding border states to secession. Even if Lincoln had pressed for black enlistment during this early stage, white men had already stated their refusal to fight alongside African Americans.[11] By the summer of 1862, however, a shortage of white volunteers forced Lincoln to order a militia draft. The Militia Act, enacted on July 17, 1862, authorized Lincoln to use contraband labor "in such a manner as he may judge best" and to conscript blacks for "any military or naval service for which they may be found competent."[12] Lincoln initially used this authority to allow his officers to employ contrabands as laborers, which the Union army had been doing for nearly a year anyway.[13] The net result meant that enslaved people could work for the Union army and theoretically earn their freedom. Their families could also be freed, provided that their owners had been disloyal to the Union.

By August 1862, however, Lincoln began suggesting publicly that he might support the enlistment of black men. He specifically avoided the topic of black soldiering as a harbinger of citizenship or equality for black men. By March of 1863, the president's discussion of black enlistment took on a somewhat more enthusiastic tone: "The colored population is the great available and yet unavailed of, force for restoring the Union. The bare sight of 50,000 armed and drilled black soldiers upon the banks of the Mississippi would end the rebellion at once. And who doubts that we can present that sight, if we but take hold in earnest?"[14]

Historians have theorized that enlistment equaled an opportunity for full male citizenship, and that is undoubtedly true.[15] But the role of race also problematizes the study of black soldiers because masculinity is inextricably intertwined with categories of sexuality and gender.[16] Ideals about freedom ultimately came to be universalized as male, both in language usage and in claims to citizenship.[17] The type of gendered discourse used by recruiters to encourage black enlistment was actually appropriated by African Americans in myriad ways.[18] Furthermore, the right and the need to perform wartime service was identified in gendered terms—as affecting men and their wives in terms of their manhood and womanhood. Black soldiers are best studied as affiliated with their families, and military opportunity influenced midwestern African American families as they contemplated the pros and cons of military service for the Union. The majority of them decided that the long-term benefits would outweigh the drawbacks. One black student from Indiana declared boldly, "The war is now in part our war, and the free colored men of the North must help fight it."[19] The young man who encouraged his brethren to join him probably envisioned the war for emancipation as something that took place far beyond the battlefield. Black men found themselves in an ironic situation when they became soldiers. They were suddenly allowed entrance into a culturally masculine institution, despite society's earnest castigations of black manhood. Emancipation activists hoped that the black presence in the military would personify the conflict as being about black freedom and equality for both men *and* women. Enlistment in the Union army meant that already-complex gender roles would have to be constantly mediated as the war progressed; indeed, military service was a hotly contested space where both male and female gender roles would undergo transition.[20]

One day prior to the New Bedford company's farewell, one midwestern member of the Fifty-Fourth wrote in the *New Bedford Mercury*, "[D]oes it not behoove every colored man in this city to consider, rationally with himself, whether he cannot be one of the glorious 54th? Consider that on this continent, at least, their race and name will be totally obliterated unless they put forth some effort now to save themselves."[21] This particular soldier articulated ideals that the African American community had been searching for as they fortified their homes and communities in the Midwest. One editorial from the *Chicago Tribune* complained that although black men were leaving to join Massachusetts regiments, they were nonetheless "impatient to get up an *Illinois* regiment."[22] Sending a loved one to a mustering station meant that black families believed that they owed fealty to the Union, to their city or town, and to their race. Authors who wrote about black enlistment in newspapers, speeches, and pamphlets used language peppered with words like *respectability, rationality,* and *commitment.*[23] Black men who wore the Union blue wanted a chance to prove their manhood and to earn citizenship rights. But African Americans also had a great deal to lose by leaving their homes and families without one or more wage earners.

Rhetoric reflecting idealized black masculinity was nothing new to antislavery advocates, since abolitionists had often encouraged slaves to "prove their manhood" by stealing their freedom. David Walker, a free black North Carolinian, had raised the ire of southerners and northerners alike when, in 1829, he referred to the Haitian slave rebellion in his call to arms: "Are we MEN!! . . . How we could be so submissive to a gang of men, whom we cannot tell whether they are as good as ourselves or not, I never could conceive. . . . If ever we become men, we must assert ourselves to the full."[24] Following William Lloyd Garrison's rise to popularity in the 1830s and his insistence on pacifism, many members of the free black community had questioned violent methods of emancipation and protest. Writers had continued, nevertheless, to encourage African American men to assert their claims to manhood, regardless of the form of protest they chose.

Black civic masculinity was rooted in the rhetoric of emancipation. The wartime experience was even more strained for African American soldiers, as the privileges of American manhood were much more difficult to gain for men who were neither white nor endowed with property and privilege. Recruiters employed a broad rhetorical method containing gender-specific language to entice and excite black enlistees. Black men responded to an idealized form of masculinity proposed by abolitionists and Union army recruiters. Activists discussed military manhood as though it were something that could erase centuries of servitude in one fell swoop. One officer in the Fifty-Fourth Massachusetts, for instance, wrote that black military service would "erase that semblance of inferiority of our race, which cruel slavery has created." He later noted that "if there is one spark of manhood running in the blood of the Race that has resisted the . . . waves of oppression, the school of the soldier will fan it to a glowing flame."[25]

Enlistment motivations are somewhat elusive, but it is clear that midwestern activists did consider soldiering to be a viable part of emancipation activism. The pernicious black codes and the FSL had been imposed on African Americans in an age when due process and equal protection under the law did not yet exist. Although black activists had fought long and hard against white supremacy, they still had little voice outside their activist circles. From the outset, some abolitionists (and a handful of radical Republicans) argued that the war was not only a fight to preserve the Union but was also a struggle to abolish slavery and racial discrimination.[26] While some blacks remained unconvinced that signing on as soldiers would help eradicate racism (since some African Americans believed that abolitionists were interested only in the plight of the enslaved), others decided to take their chance by mustering into the army. For instance, Sergeant Morgan W. Carter, a black soldier from Madison, Indiana, wrote to a friend that he thought it was important to fight "for the benifit of my race."[27]

Soldiering, not unlike slavery, placed black bodies squarely in the fray of a great civil war—both literally and figuratively. First, however, there was much persuading to do. Organizations such as the AME Church and newspapers such as the *Liberator* and the *Weekly Anglo-African* initially encouraged blacks to renounce enlistment, arguing that a Union that would not seek the abolition of slavery as its fundamental war aim did not deserve the support of the free black community.[28] Appeals such as this signaled a debate among activists about the appropriate choice for their communities. Over time, the tenor of black support for the war effort slowly shifted toward agreement that communities might benefit from black soldiering.

Of course, becoming a combatant carried tremendous risk of injury or death, so defenders of the enlistment "experiment" wrote to newspapers to outline the rewards, rather than the dangers, of service. In a letter to the *Weekly Anglo-African*, Robert Vandyne, a correspondent and financial contributor, argued that black men should consider service in terms of access to republican prerogatives. Vandyne argued that black men needed to prove their love of America: "any omission on our part to exhibit that patriotism so noticeable in the whites, will, when history shall record the doings of this memorable country, leave our names without one deed of patriotism or expressed desire for the success of the cause of liberty." Once again, the prose referenced the desire to "prove our manhood and the love of liberty" through soldiering. "Have not the two centuries of cruel and unrequited servitude in this country," he asked, "alone entitled the children of this generation to the rights of men and citizens?"[29] With rhetoric like this, black men could potentially see into the future and envision the affirmation of manhood and privilege. Once soldiers had served valiantly, a celebration of black heroism could be on the lips of every African American midwesterner.

Emancipation activists created shrewdly constructed enlistment propaganda directed at black men. These recruiters knew that most whites opposed black enlistment on the basis of racial inferiority. Newspapers contained "conversations" among activists arguing the relative merits of enlistment. One abolitionist, Alfred M. Green, responded to Vandyne, condemning the federal government for its refusal to commit to emancipation. Although Green disagreed with Vandyne about how black war mobilization should be deployed, Green utilized the same type of gendered language to argue his case. In his provocative letter, Green referenced the Lockean right to resist, to which the Founding Fathers had alluded during the Revolutionary War. Green encouraged black men to meet the war "with manly spirit" so that they could "protect their manhood" and avenge their fathers, who had been "cheated and disenfranchised after nobly defending the country." Green repeatedly reminded black men that they had to "defend their right" to military service.[30]

Black people accepted the fact that most white Americans, whether opposed to slavery or not, were not waging a war for black equality; the impetus to destroy slavery was almost entirely their own. Blacks also recognized that there was nothing in northern or midwestern public sentiment to support the notion that the Union sought to destroy slavery. As previous chapters of this book have shown, activists kept careful tabs on the national slavery debates. Chicago activist Sattira Douglas, H. Ford's spouse, read northern and southern newspapers alike, often sharing her views with her brethren in the *Christian Recorder*. She characterized the Richmond, Virginia, editors as "swaggering," "supercilious," and "exceedingly dolorous" in their discussion of Confederate conscription. Sattira further accused southerners of being most alarmed by the draft because they feared that leaving enslaved persons at home gave ample opportunity for insurrection. She argued that the "very institution" of slavery, which had previously been considered one the Confederacy's strengths, would soon be "converted to an element of weakness" by the "inevitable mutations of war."[31]

Sattira Douglas, like other activist women, also believed that she should disseminate information about emancipation activism in her community and beyond. She referred to black soldiers as "dark hued, determined avengers" who, she believed, should "swell the ranks" of the colored troops. Sattira also warned that "if black men do not enroll themselves . . . to do battle for the true and right, it will only prove the correctness of the aspersion indulged in by our enemies, that we are unworthy of those rights which they have long withheld from us." On the topic of the long struggle for freedom, she wrote,

It is no less true of nations than of individuals, that that which is the most dearly bought is the most highly prized, and the liberty, which we sacrifice our all to obtain, will be proportionately appreciated. This revolution, like all the others, is to act as a national purifier. We are now undergoing a process of fermentation, and all those false and unwholesome theories which have and do possess the American mind in regard to the relation which the colored race is to sustain towards the other nations of the world, are to work to the surface and pass off. This war is also to act as an educator, not only national, but individual. It is to teach us, regardless of sex or complexion, hard lessons of sacrifice, of courage, and of fortitude. We are to stand forth in our own individual light, either as cringing, cowering creatures, shielding ourselves from the duties and responsibilities of the hour . . . or, uncovering our brows and breasts to the tempest, stand fearless and undaunted, firm in our convictions of right, knowing that the storm, though violent, will have an end, and the sun of peace will shine through the overshadowing cloud. Colored men have everything to gain in this conflict: liberty, honor, social and political positions are now placed within their grasp. They have these on the one and on the other slavery, prejudice of caste, and all other attendant evils.[32]

Women like Sattira Douglas and Mary Jones spent their adult lives performing the reproductive labor associated with assisting runaway slaves and establishing homesteads and communities in the Midwest. But they also took up the mantle of cultural critic and moral persuader, and they fully expected that their opinions would be heard and appreciated throughout their congregations and communities. Not surprisingly, however, black women's letters indicate a particular sense of pensiveness regarding emancipation in a global and even universal sense. Activists were guided by an absolute commitment to inalienable human rights, granted by, as Sattira described it, "an unseen Providence" that protected black soldiers and would "lead them to victory."[33]

Recruiters also recognized that white paradigms of masculinity were essentially ideologically charged constructions serving to bolster the self-image of whites, so black male self-esteem became an issue in their campaigns.[34]

They also knew that the men were likely to equate their manhood with the successful completion of their obligations, which included providing financial support and protection for their families and kin. In speeches before crowds of poor black men and women who were aching for better lives, Frederick Douglass expressed his renewed belief in the possibility of liberty and citizenship for slaves and free blacks. Both blacks and whites would have to participate, he urged: black men would enlist, and white men would eventually demonstrate a willingness to allow African American men to perform wartime service with dignity.[35]

Even as recruiters were employing warrior metaphors to encourage black men to turn out at mustering stations, a fierce debate among activists ensued as to whether or not black communities would ultimately benefit from sending black men to become soldiers.[36] Men possessed a distinct fear of personal dishonor (which would have been appropriate for any nineteenth-century male), but they also considered war to be a test of their courage. Organizations such as the AME Church and newspapers such as the *Liberator* and the *Weekly Anglo-African* at first opposed black enlistment because the war did not seek the abolition of slavery.[37] The AME's newspaper, the *Christian Recorder*, was full of gendered rhetoric, biblical imagery, and political ponderings reflecting the black community's concern over enlistment. Although the tenor of black support for the war would slowly shift, many African Americans remained frightened and reluctant to send soldiers to war.[38] For women, the story would prove to be altogether different.

Frederick Douglass had supported black enlistment since the early days of the war, but his most famous rallying cry, "Men of Color, to Arms!" in March of 1863, presaged enlistment campaigns in the North. Later, *Douglass' Monthly* issued his writings "Why Should a Colored Man Enlist?" and "Another Word to Colored Men," among others. Douglass gave speeches, wrote editorials in newspapers, and published pamphlets and broadsides as part of his propaganda campaign. He repeatedly encouraged African American men to consider their proud wartime manhood to be something that would provide relief for the whole black community: "Enlist . . . and win for yourselves, a name and place among men, but secure to yourself what is infinitely more precious, the fast dropping tears of gratitude of your kith and kin marked out for destruction, and who are but now ready to perish."[39] Douglass's speech before a crowd at the Cooper Institute signified a renewed belief in the possibility of liberty for slaves and free blacks. Many African Americans were still dubious as to whether black enlistment would ultimately be a financial and social success.

To quell the concerns of activists who were afraid that black soldiers would be used for grunt work only, Douglass placed the onus on the government, whites, and military leaders: "When a man leaves home, family, and security, to risk his limbs and life in the field of battle, for God's sake let him have all the honor which he may achieve." Thus, he noted, black men and their families would willingly perform wartime service if they were allowed to do so with dignity, and if they were given a "fair chance at winning distinction and glory."[40]

American manhood had historically been equated with the rights and obligations of citizenship, so the denial was not only twofold but also deliberately excused women. Douglass understood that black men were essentially being denied the right to perform those manly obligations.[41] African Americans saw this war, like other wars, as a chance to fulfill their obligations under a republican democracy and thereby claim attendant prerogatives. Furthermore, Douglass purposefully conflated soldiering with familial and community commitments. From the beginning, conversations about enlistment were enveloped in the language of manhood and its link to eventual civil rights. Douglass's rhetoric contained numerous references to gendered obligations of citizenship. His message, though seemingly directed at fresh recruits, was also meant to compel government and military leaders to consider equal treatment for blacks. Douglass prepared speeches in which he claimed to have been "authorized" to assure black recruits that they would receive treatment equal to whites. In March 1863, *Douglass' Monthly* carried his "Men of Color, to Arms!"—a rallying cry full of promises for African American men who were willing to leave their homes: "I am authorized to assure you that you will receive the same wages, the same rations, the same equipment, the same protection, the same treatment and the same bounty secured white soldiers. You will be led by able and skillful officers—men who will take especial pride in your efficiency and success. They will be quick to accord to you all the honor you shall merit by your valor—and see that your rights and feelings are respected."[42] Douglass made good on his earlier promise to enlist his own sons, Charles and Lewis, who were his first recruits. The War Department, however, had never empowered Douglass to make any guarantees of equal pay or rank, so he took an enormous risk with his credibility by making those promises.[43]

Full-scale recruitment was the next step in the black military endeavor. Douglass was only one among several dozen formal recruiters, although he was certainly the most famous. In Massachusetts, Governor John Andrew (having received permission from Secretary of War Stanton) embarked on the first authorized recruitment campaign to raise a black volunteer regiment with white commissioned officers. In February of 1863, Andrew placed an ad in a Boston newspaper that read, "To Colored Men. Wanted. Good men for the 54th Regiment of Massachusetts Volunteers of African descent, Col. Robert G. Shaw. $100 bounty at the expiration of term of service. Pay $13.00 a month and State Aid to families."[44] Ads such as these initially attracted only a handful of men because Massachusetts had fewer than two thousand free African American men of appropriate age. Governor Andrew thus sought volunteer recruiters from other northern states. One such recruiter was Garland H. White, a former escaped slave and minister who worked in Massachusetts for some time before traveling to the Midwest.

Garland White has the distinction of being the first black man accepted into federal service as an active-duty chaplain; more importantly, he considered black enlistment a self-motivated duty for African American men who sought citizenship rights. White believed that slavery had been ruinous to American blacks, and he wrote several strident letters to the *Christian Recorder* insisting that black Americans needed to act as masters of their own destiny. In White's view, black men would eventually be liberated by their military experiences, so long as they could withstand the racist perversions of the paternalistic Union military machine in the meantime.[45] White was also steadfast in his belief that enlistment was an honor for black men, especially uneducated ones. When African American soldiers complained about their salaries, White wrote, "Those [men] . . . who complain more than all the rest of the colored troops of the nation, they are doing themselves and their race a serious injury. I sincerely hope that they will stop such nonsense, and learn to take things as soldiers should."[46]

White had a long history of petitioning the government for various things, and this reflects the tone of black midwestern activism. He wrote eloquently about emancipation and his desire to help the cause in a direct way. Since he was an ordained minister, it made sense that he would serve alongside the troops as their spiritual counselor. White's letters reveal how communities of African American men viewed their enlistment. As early as 1862, White wrote to Secretary of War Stanton to assert his belief that the war would result in the death of slavery: "Our offer [to serve] is not for speculation or self interest but for our love for the north & the government at large, & at the same time we pray god that the triumph of the north & restoration of peace . . . will prove an eternal overthrow of the institution of slavery which is the cause of all our trouble."[47] Among all Americans who pondered the cause and course of the war in terms of states' rights, constitutional issues, tariffs, and the rise of the Republican Party, black Americans understood the war to be for their own emancipation.

White is particularly important to the story of midwestern enlistment because he was both a recruiter and a chaplain—he experienced the war as a black man during recruitment, enlistment, as well as on the battlefield. He arrived in Indiana in late 1863 at the behest of Governor Oliver Morton, who had promised White the chaplain position in the state's colored regiment if he could recruit enough men to fulfill the state's quota.[48] The majority of white Indianans opposed the idea of black enlistment, and they either ignored or ridiculed the desire for enlistment in African American communities. Some white officers had even resigned when they heard about the Emancipation Proclamation.[49] Other white soldiers simply doubted the efficacy of the experiment altogether since they did not believe that suffrage could possibly benefit blacks.[50] But hundreds of recruiters from other states had flooded Indiana, so the governor turned to White to help meet the quota. White would later claim to have "recruited half the men in the 28th U.S. Colored Infantry Regiment raised in Indiana."[51]

The majority of black soldiers were recruited in the South, but in the Midwest white leaders began to acquiesce when quotas for soldiers could not be met with whites only. In December 1863, the state of Indiana issued a declaration "To the Colored Men of Indiana," urging African Americans to consider the "rescue of your suffering [white] brethren." The announcement ended with a now-typical appeal to manhood: "You can now show your detractors and the world the falsehood [of racist assertions], and place yourself in such a position that you may ask . . . from a grateful people a full recognition of your worth and rights as men."[52] White Americans had a great propensity to avail themselves of black labor when it most suited them.

Throughout this period of recruitment and enlistment, blacks in the Midwest proved themselves to be fiercely loyal to their home states. John Jones cleared out his office space in downtown Chicago so that it could be used for recruitment for the Fifty-Fourth Massachusetts. Since they had spent the past several decades building homes, churches, and schools in their respective towns, midwestern blacks had good reason to fear a threat that might rupture the Union. Garland White wrote that when he held meetings to educate men and women about the issues associated with black enlistment, their chief complaint was that they did not want to represent other states. Instead, they told him that they wanted an Indiana regiment instead of being "sent to other states against their will."[53] Over decades, the Midwest had become home.

There were plenty of proslavery white midwesterners who were loyal to the Union but adamantly refused to accept any government action (such as black enlistment) that would "elevate the Negro." These whites were savvy enough to realize what blacks were fighting for: "the equality of all men before the law, which means negro suffrage, nothing less," complained a Democratic newspaper.[54] White people also often blamed African Americans for any type of financial or business-related catastrophe. Salmon Hall, a storeowner in Groveland, Indiana, wrote when his business burned, "Read this your damned abolitionist for you are on your last legs. Mr. abolitionist of Groveland you have been cutting a pretty big swell for the last 4 years, Now sir I will just inform you . . . you had better prepare to meete your God for som of you shal follow old Abe soon or I am a damned liar—You have concluded that you had the South Whiped but you have just begun to hav trouble, We intend to destroy evry thing you have got and kill the meanest of you."[55]

Meanwhile, Republicans were busy drumming up support for the war. These campaigns for public support and public opinion were enormously important and were therefore conducted in the West as well as in the East. In Illinois (home to Lincoln, Ulysses S. Grant, and other Civil War notables), residents typically supported the plans of "their politicians." Illinois was also led by Governor Richard Yates, another Republican.[56] On the other hand, some of the most pernicious language used against Lincoln, and emancipation especially, came from the *Chicago Times*, a mouthpiece of the Democratic Party. In Indiana, meanwhile, some citizens urged white Indianans to protect the state and have no regard for blacks: "If, as . . . the State moves along, the negroes get in the way let them be crushed. If they keep out of the way let them remain where they are. . . . Is not this Government . . . worth more than the institution of slavery?"[57]

* * *

The War Department disallowed black men from assuming "higher" duties so that lower pay scales could be justified, but the inequity of this policy was not lost on African American men. For instance, almost all black soldiers were categorically denied line officers' commissions.[58] In 1864, seventy-four members of a Massachusetts black regiment sent a signed letter to President Lincoln protesting this policy. It was not unusual for some black men to refuse their pay because they had not been assigned "*soldier* tasks according to [their] enlistment" (emphasis added). The *Christian Recorder* documented this phenomenon when one of the last companies in the Twenty-Eighth Indiana left for the front. Although townspeople turned out to bid goodbye, "A considerable dissatisfaction existed in this regiment, as in other colored regiments, in regard to pay. [Soldiers] were offered seventy dollars, but refused to receive it. Some of the boys became unruly, we learned . . . some trouble was feared, and they were sent off sooner."[59]

White soldiers also wrote about task inequities in their letters home. African American men claimed to be humiliated by "trenches [and] fatiegue" duty because they had expected to train as soldiers until they went to the battlefield. Instead, blacks often worked as servants for whites. James Vanderbilt wrote, "Every [regiment] has a Negro for a cook and every Negro has a mule or a horse to carry the blankets. . . . First comes the regiment and then comes the mules, horses, and Negroes in the rear of the regiment. [White soldiers] have nothing to do. Our Negro does the cooking and we stand the guard."[60] This particular soldier wrote that there were four hundred African American men employed in his camp in Tennessee. Some of those laborers were probably contrabands rather than soldiers. Vanderbilt, however, did not distinguish between the two groups, probably because he assumed black men were a homogenous group.

Time and time again, black soldiers who lamented their circumstances outlined the emancipation motivations that had moved them to enlist. When black soldiers were taught military tactics and discipline—how to use their weapons and equipment and how to drill and march—they resented being denied the opportunity to use those skills. One group of soldiers explained this to President Lincoln: "we came to fight For Liberty justice & Equality. These are gifts we Prise more Highly than Gold. For these We Left our Homes our Familyes Friends & Relatives most Dear . . . To Do Battle for God & Liberty."[61]

Black recruiters considered themselves—as fellow African Americans—to be best suited to searching the country for the most able-bodied, courageous men. The delegation of recruiters who traveled to the Midwest included well-known abolitionists Mary Ann Shadd Cary, Martin Delany, Henry Highland Garnet, and Charles Lenox Remond. Their recruiting tours were mostly aimed at sending black men to the Fifty-Fifth and Fifty-Fourth Massachusetts Regiments. These recruiters realized quickly that War Department officials, too, needed to be convinced that black men were capable of handling tasks required of a soldier. Delany, for instance, wrote a carefully worded letter to Secretary Stanton suggesting that he, as a recruiter, might appreciate the special skills of black men: "The agency of intelligent, competent black men adapted to the work must be the most efficient means of obtaining black troops; because knowing and being of that people as a race, they can command such influence as is required to accomplish the object."[62]

In trying to counter racist charges that African American men would make poor soldiers, black Union recruiters sought to shape their portrayal of black male soldiers according to white middle-class definitions of masculinity. In their discussions of black enlistment, they oriented their language toward what rights blacks might earn, rather than the rights they lacked. White middle-class men voted, they owned property, they had constitutional rights, they served on juries, they brought lawsuits, they owned businesses, and they served in the military. But middle-class standards applied to black men in ambiguous and arbitrary ways. Only a small number of black families reflected a nineteenth-century bourgeois concept of gender and family relations. Most black women worked either in or outside the home for wages, both as young unmarried women and when they were older. Many households sent their older children to earn money by working in field or factory; black men were often unemployed for sustained periods of time; and there was never enough wealth or social capital to match the socioeconomic patterns of whites.

In fact, the federal government's informal recruitment program was in its infancy while black activists were traveling about and giving speeches. African American communities had provided the real momentum for black enlistment long before 1863, but by spring of that year, the War Department finally authorized the adjutant general, Major General Lorenzo Thomas, to recruit in the Midwest. Thomas had authority to appoint recruiting agents and to organize black enlistees into groups ready for military service, but he did this while on his regular inspection tour.[63] Governor Morton of Indiana supported black enlistment, although his comments reflected his political pragmatism rather than an abolitionist bent: "I am in favor or using anything to put down the rebellion, even dogs and tomcats. . . . The use of negro troops is simply a question of expediency, and if they can not be made available they will not be used. The use of such troops will . . . do away with the necessity of drafting so many white men."[64]

By January 1863, Lincoln's Emancipation Proclamation foreshadowed large-scale black enlistment.[65] Although experimental black units had been organized in Kansas, Louisiana, and South Carolina, official, wide-scale recruitment of African Americans for the Union army accelerated with the proclamation.[66] The War Department finally created the Bureau of Colored Troops in May 1863, but Lincoln and his advisors merely provided the administrative seal of approval—recruitment was not a new phenomenon in either the North or the Midwest. By May of 1863, the Union had no choice but to authorize the creation of the Bureau of Colored Troops since there was a shortage of white volunteers and the war had already lasted much longer than anyone had expected. As time passed, Lincoln became more enthusiastic about black enlistment. Initially, he was concerned that arming African Americans would compel more states to secede. Although he avoided the topic of empowerment as a rationale for black enlistment, Lincoln eventually admitted the value of black troops for the Union cause and finally provided monies from the war chest and commanders for the USCT units.

Although most white servicemen viewed black enlistment through a lens of racism, there were some reasons to welcome it. Many white Unionists had grown increasingly dispirited as the war dragged on, and white men at least felt gratified when the War Department promised them that they would not have to serve with black soldiers. Plus, since black men were expressly prohibited from becoming officers, white soldiers jumped at the opportunity for commissions, which would go exclusively to them. White racists were also pleased to learn that black men would be used primarily to garrison forts, to protect supply dumps and wagon trains, and to perform rear-area duties. (This, of course, flew directly in the face of Frederick Douglass's recruitment promises.) Once Congress passed the Conscription Act in March 1863, some white northerners came to the conclusion that "a black could stop a bullet as well as any white man."[67] Many northerners who were opposed to the war or were lukewarm about its leadership argued, in fact, that wherever possible, blacks be drafted instead of white men.[68] Members of the congressional Committee on Military Affairs noted that "the enrollment of negroes would be a popular measure because every colored man brought into the service would save from the service a white man, whose labor was of more value to the country than that of the colored man."[69]

Lincoln's government denied African American soldiers many of the military benefits they were promised, including equal pay, equal rank opportunity, and the chance to serve as combatants in the same capacity as white men. Inequitable policies affected black families in two important ways. On the one hand, there was the concrete issue of pay. On the other hand, there was the abstract issue of what black men would *earn* through their service: Suffrage? Jury seating? Property rights? Black men waited for their paychecks with great anticipation, only to discover less money than they had been told to expect.

Therefore, as day-to-day survival without male kin commenced, women and children at home had less money to buy food, shelter, clothing, and medicine. By being forced to cook food, clean latrines, and dig ditches exclusively, black men believed that they were not performing the manly duties that might allow them some control over their own lives and eventual emancipation.

In June 1863, the official policy of the War Department was that white soldiers were to receive thirteen dollars per month (plus clothing), while blacks received ten dollars, from which three dollars were subtracted for clothing expenses. Naturally, the recruiters who had worked so hard to enlist black men were embarrassed and outraged by this injustice. The Union's decision to pay black soldiers less than white solders threatened the integrity of Douglass and other recruiters. African American servicemen knew they would have to leave their homes, families, communities, and (for some) jobs, so they fully expected to receive the wage they were promised.

To make matters worse, Frederick Douglass had, in his recruiting speeches, linked the terms of equal pay with (eventual) citizenship rights for black men in general, promising that enlistees would also benefit from increased self-worth and strengthened manhood: "There is something deep down in the soul of every man present which assents to the justice of the claim [of equality], and honors the manhood and self-respect which insist upon it. Citizenship [will be] no longer denied us under this new government."[70] Black servicemen and their families were incredibly disappointed to discover that being black in the army meant that the whole family would have to do with less than expected wages; it would be another disappointment entirely, however, to lose a chance at emancipation.

Black communities did, however, experience a sense of pride when their citizens became soldiers. In the end, the tally was impressive: 1,811 black men from Illinois served in the Union army, while Indiana contributed 1,597.[71] Men arrived at mustering stations from black communities all over each state, and their communities were thrilled to call the soldiers their own.[72] A reader from Indianapolis wrote to the *Christian Recorder* to share news of the Twenty-Eighth Indiana Volunteers, who had marched in a parade through the city. Not only did the regiment contain hundreds of local men, the author declared, but enlistment was on the rise throughout all the northern states. Blacks in Indianapolis were thrilled to see black regiments march through the same cities where "mob violence [had previously] hunted own our people like so many animals."[73]

Men in the nineteenth century, regardless of race and class, believed strongly in their role as breadwinner for their families. But slavery, death, chronic illness, backbreaking labor, marital and familial separation, maternal and childhood mortality, single motherhood, and poverty were all woven through the fabric of everyday black lives with enough force to make the ideal of the male bread-winner nearly impossible to realize. Black soldiers and their families did take the responsibilities of the male head of household seriously, but this was an ideal, and not always the reality. Slavery certainly robbed many black men and women of the chance to fulfill their gender roles, but they remained undeterred in their attempt to perform their duties as parents and spouses. In a letter to his daughter's master, Spotswood Rice (a former slave himself) cautioned,

> I received a leteter from Cariline telling me that you say I tried to steal to plunder my child away from you now I want you understand that mary is my Child and she is a God given rite of my own and you may hold on to hear as long as you can but I want you to remembor this one thing that the longor you keep my Child from me the longor you will have to burn in hell. . . . Just hold on now as long as you can and the worse it will be for you now you call my Children your pro[per]ty not so with me my Children is my own and I expect to get them and when I get ready to come after mary I will have bout a powrer and autherity to bring hear away and execute vengencens on them that holds my Child. . . . this whole Government given chear to me and you cannot but help yourself.[74]

Rice felt both authorial possession of his child and also some degree of assurance that the same government that issued the Emancipation Proclamation would support his claim to his daughter.

While recruiters were creating rhetoric to support their cause, soldiers who had already enlisted found themselves pondering the economic status of their families at home. Williams J. Brown wrote,

> [W]e know that we have never had our Just Rights. . . . [T]he white officers of the other Reg. here persuaded me to join when there were no Reg. of coloured here to Join so I consented. . . . They promiced to pay us the same wages as was paid the whites & Rations & clothing the same. . . . Many of these people have families to support and no other means of doing it than what they get in this way. . . . [M]ay we Expect in the final settlement to get our full Rights as was promised us at the first.[75]

Other soldiers conveyed a sense of disappointment over how the public might perceive black soldiers' insistence on getting equal pay. Governor Andrew of Massachusetts promised the men of the Fifty-Fourth that if the War Department would not agree to raise the soldiers' wages, then he would personally guarantee that the Massachusetts legislature would pick up the slack. For members of the Fifty-Fourth, Andrew had missed the point entirely. Their objection was not just to the unequal pay but to the betrayed principle of equality. One anonymous soldier wrote, "Imagine our surprise and disappointment . . . to find [Andrew] making a proposition to [the legislature] to pay this regiment the difference between what the United States government offers us and what they are legally bound to pay us, which, in effect, advertises us to the world as holding out for money and not from principle—that we sink our manhood in consideration of a few more dollars."[76]

As they were interlopers in a nineteenth-century culture that proscribed equal access to wage labor in a capitalistic marketplace and to full republican rights on the basis of skin color, it is not surprising that black men responded to the sound of war drums. For black men, being "manly" meant being free.[77] Midwestern African American soldiers seemed to have possessed two sets of complementary ideals that drove them to become soldiers. First, at the loftiest, most idealistic level were citizenship rights.[78] This included freedom, which was deliberately broadly defined by recruiters such as Frederick Douglass, who encouraged black enlistees to believe that once slaves were free, a world of opportunity would open up to all African Americans in the United States.

Second, at the most human level, soldiers had to consider wives, children, and kin networks—concerns focused on basic day-to-day survival in black communities. In a society that, simultaneously, encouraged African Americans to adopt gender roles similar to those of whites and yet devalued the safety, health, and well-being of all African Americans, enslaved and free black men and women endured tremendous personal, familial, and communal hardships. While social ideals (both in white and black societies) meant that men were viewed as ultimately responsible for the physical preservation of their families and kin (in terms of food, shelter, and the like), black women bore the onus of reproductive labor (which included threats to their health through pregnancy, childbirth, childcare).[79] This explains, in part, why black men fought so hard for equal pay, although there can be no doubt that they wanted access to the type of liberty of which Douglass had so eloquently spoken. Black soldiers demanded the pay that had been promised to them because they depended on it for the provision of food, clothing, and shelter for their families. Black soldiers believed that they were fighting for their families and communities, not just for the sake of wages but for the sake of duty and honor to one's community. Sergeant Morgan W. Carter, who had enlisted in Indiana in 1864, wrote that he fought for the "benifit of my race," and he reasoned that any black soldiers who "lost theare life for theare country and theare people" would at least die "a noble death."[80]

When the guns fell silent, African American men and women reckoned the relative success and failure of black enlistment according to their household and community situations. Poor and working-class blacks (to whom recruitment discourse had been directed) did identify the right and the need to perform wartime service as a gendered concept. Soldiers waged a campaign for better pay, however—not only because of the affront to their honor but because their social role demanded that they take care of their family. It is doubly ironic that black men were trying to fulfill these roles by enlisting and remaining in the Union army (despite the inequitable circumstances), because insufficient pay ultimately forced them to desert or ask for furloughs. It was, in fact, the federal government that had not followed through on its promises of equal pay and equal treatment. Slowly, the black men lost their faith in the system that had promised them so much. Families could not survive with one wage-earning parent. They simply needed two sets of laboring hands to make emancipation work.

The voices in this chapter reflect a wide range of emotions felt by black men who were faced with two important tasks: to vindicate their manhood and perform republican obligations through soldiering and also to care for their families and communities by earning wages as a soldier. The realities of day-to-day African American life meant, of course, that ideas about how women should "remain within the home" while men served as the breadwinners were malleable. The question posed by James Henry Gooding to President Lincoln looms large if historians are to understand better the construction of black wartime masculinity: "Are we soldiers or are we labourers?"[81] The answer to that query is that black men served as both.

Black communities who sent husbands, brothers, fathers, and sons to the war showed sacrifice. But African Americans also broadcast an important message that their willingness to suffer—if temporarily—was grounded in their determination to self-govern on their own land and in their own homes, schools, and churches. Many black soldiers who returned to Indiana after the war were still in violation of anti-black immigration laws, compelling

Governor Morton to remark angrily that "more than one-half of the men have no right to come back again."[82] There was still a great deal of work to do, but soldiers still saw themselves as citizens-in-the-making, as fighters for the enslaved, and as people who would return to their neighborhoods, however troubled. The tenuous nature of soldiering—constantly moving from place to place—was actually antithetical to the fixed nature of midwestern free black communities. These efficient institution builders were united in their embrace of the war because it was the circumstance that actually seemed to hold the most promise for acquiring freedoms.

5. Black Women's Wartime Political Culture

Black women's uncompromising commitment to wartime community activism would help transform the war into a fight for citizenship rights and—eventually—emancipation. True enough, soldiering had eased black men's sense of emasculation and given them new claims to freedom and citizenship. But women, for their part, made their own claims to empowered womanhood as community leaders, but they did so within the morass of racism *and* sexism.[1] Through warwork and concrete political activism, black women crafted a tradition of institution building. For decades, black women had founded and sustained organizations through which they worked to alleviate social ills and improve the living and working conditions of their communities. Although African Americans would not always find the economic and political freedoms that they had envisioned, women like Mary Jones help us understand the larger picture of emancipation activism. Midwestern black women's particular brand of activism served both to bolster their communities at home and to provide relief to soldiers and poor families.[2] In doing so, African American women played a crucial role in emancipation and in the development of the region and the nation.[3]

The war encouraged free black women to augment the autonomy-bearing foundations they had already laid. This was a highly politicized activity, and it required a great deal of midwestern black communities. In the antebellum period, women activists had built churches and schools and had assisted in the legal fight against the black codes and the FSL, all the while performing their usual backbreaking labor. Those African American women who were lucky enough to have the opportunity and the resources stepped up their duties to include fund-raising, nursing, letter-writing campaigns, recruiting, speech-writing, and morale boosting. Wartime compelled women activists to become heads of households and to grow kinship networks in order to provide their families and communities the resources they would need to endure the war. Middle-class black women turned inward—back to their own communities—to create spaces for war activism. Meanwhile, working-class women, especially those who were widowed by the war, were still barely managing to provide food and shelter for their families. When it was over, the war had demanded that both groups of women reinvent their lives collectively.

The war was terrifically contradictory for African Americans because it carried both the nightmare of armed conflict and the dream of emancipation. Black women were no strangers to local, state, and national activism,[4] but the nature of the war created new political, social, and economic contexts for that activism. With the war nipping at their proverbial heels, African American women responded in numerous ways: they formed or expanded philanthropic groups in their churches and communities, protested poor treatment of black soldiers by waging letter-writing and petition campaigns, worked as nurses and caregivers at hospitals and camps, housed and cared for runaways, participated in fund-raising fairs, used changing ideas about gender roles in unprecedented ways to wield new kinds of power, and succored their kinfolk and communities, all the while performing greater shares of physical labor as a result of men's absence.[5]

As wage earners, wives, mothers, and caregivers for the community, African American women participated in service to their country along with their male kinfolk. Their service both held forth promise and posed a threat: on one hand, service to the Union could result in an increase in citizenship rights; on the other hand, worst-case scenarios conjured visions of increased poverty, starvation, family separation, and death. Black male participation in the Union army was only one of the many ways African American freedpeople sought to make themselves visible in American society. The outcome was uncertain, and black women had a great deal to lose by agreeing to the absence of their husbands, brothers, sons, and fathers. Yet individual black men who served on the battlefield and in the camps and trenches risked a great deal more than their own lives when they took up soldiering. One soldier, perhaps one who enlisted with his brothers or his cousins, represented a whole family and an entire community. One soldier's death or disability meant less muscle for work and therefore less food and shelter.

Family was the focus of nineteenth-century black communities, and domestic responsibilities were the first order of business for survival and racial uplift. There could be no community growth and triumph over slavery if the basic family and kin structure was irreparably damaged. In sum, the black military experiment was a tremendous opportunity for poor black families, but it also exposed them to other hazards. The precarious wartime position of families cannot be overstressed—many of them had emigrated out of the South as enslaved persons or had kin who had done so; they were still searching for their loved ones, for jobs, for friendly faces. Slaveowners persisted in the search for runaway bondspeople and their children. Family responsibilities often included supporting extended kin in addition to wives and children. Black women were also searching for their families; they were struggling to keep their communities intact and their families fed; and they wanted to be free and equal citizens, all at the same time. Additionally, many freedpeople had not yet had the opportunity either to become legally married or to reunite their broken families. Though nineteenth-century mores defined a "normal" family as white, middle-class, and united in marriage, many black communities possessed very little of the glue necessary to hold this façade together.

Wartime black families were decidedly non-nuclear and would defy the parameters of most modern demographers because slavery had broken the bonds of so many marriages and families. African American communities consisted of groups of kin who had experienced various stages of migration in their quest to move away from the South and settle in the Midwest. Slavery, as well as the inevitable escape from it, had torn the fabric of the black family with cruel family separations and disavowal of slave marriage.[6] African Americans responded by ordering their lives according to familial kinship networks, and both men and women bore a great deal of responsibility within these networks. If service to the Union was difficult for men because it threatened their ability to fulfill their manly responsibilities, women were also at a great disadvantage because they were left to bear the burden of paid work and unpaid reproductive labor while the men were away.

Black families who engaged in Union service dealt with two competing views of black masculinity. The rhetoric of exalted manhood, used so effectively in the enlistment process, would eventually become peripheral to the soldiering experience. The longer the war lasted, and the longer black men were away from home, the more they became concerned with the suffering of their families. Indeed, the gendered language used by African American men to describe their familial roles did not include terms like *citizenship*, *rights*, and *democracy* because they wrote more often about physical needs like feeding and clothing their children. Black soldiers could not gain these rights, let alone enjoy them, without first gaining reasonable access to food, shelter, and clothing. Although the war eventually resulted in the destruction of slavery, many black women and men would ultimately view black enlistment with bitter resentment because it placed such a heavy burden on their families.

African American women were no exception to the unspoken rule that war left most women to endure alone, along with the oldest and youngest folk, in their villages, towns, and cities. Black men joined the Union army in earnest. By February of 1865, Secretary Stanton was so convinced that the recruitment campaign for black soldiers in the Mississippi Valley had found all able-bodied black men that he ordered the program shut down.[7] Recruiter Lorenzo Thomas estimated in his final report that 2,872 white officers and 77,720 black enlisted men had joined the United States Colored Troops from the Mississippi Valley.[8] With the numbers provided by the 1860 census, that meant that about 9,500 free black women remained at home in Indiana and Illinois.[9] While the colored troops marched proudly into the South, women tended to businesses, churches, schools, children, farms, animals, and the infirm and elderly.

For every occasion in which a black soldier found himself in a life-threatening situation, a black woman faced a harrowing situation of her own. H. G. Mosee, a black recruiter stationed in Indiana, had originally come into the state much like Sarah Ann Lucas had—having been born in Kentucky, he was required to find a white witness so that he could apply for his freedom papers.[10] Mosee wrote to the secretary of war to summarize the situation for "Colored Soldiers Wives." According to him, many black families were starving, many had been robbed, and still others had been kidnapped and carried back into slavery in Kentucky. Mosee also said that whites offered money to black male heads of household (many of whom were contrabands from the South) if they would act as substitutes and muster into the army. The promised money often never materialized, so a wage earner and protector at home would be lost. Mosee described the women as powerless in these situations: "[Men go] into [black women's houses], stealing what they have and because the Colored Women have not got a White Witness they cant do any thing they can stand and look at their own property but cant get it because they have no . . . Military Man to speak in their favor."[11] Working-class black women suffered enormous losses during the war, with the majority of them having never laid eyes on a battlefield or hospital.[12]

Letters from African American women reflect their conscious acceptance of a range of caretaking duties in their neighborhoods, as well as the ways in which members of communities rallied together when necessary. Poverty, slavery, and family separation all meant that the gold standard of gendered middle-class familial values and ideals simply could not be met by most blacks.[13] Black families relied instead on substantial kinship networks. Women's letters indicate a deep sense of commitment to teamwork within marriage, emotional attachment, and the desire to keep their families intact. Through all of this, black women continued to perform their domestic work, as well as paid labor either in or outside the home. Often they were pregnant or nursing, but they could not afford to give up any extra wages that they might earn, especially when the number of mouths to feed might include in-laws, grandparents, cousins, friends, and "unrelated" family members.

If military service transformed black manhood, black womanhood also underwent its own changes. In this uncertain moment, when black men and women made the decision to send the men off to war, women became undeniably invested in the reciprocal relationship between soldier and state. Despite the fact that they had no appreciable citizenship rights, black women perceived themselves in a relationship to the state, and they expected the state to respond to their comments and complaints. African American women, like their male counterparts, wrote letters to state and federal officials describing their experiences with and problems resulting from black enlistment. These letters communicate emotions ranging from polite protest to quiet desperation to unrelenting sorrow.

While many African American women had wage-paying jobs, black families in the nineteenth century typically depended on two or more incomes (contributed by all able-bodied adults in one or more households) to support children and kin. The loss of one income for lengthy periods of time spelled economic catastrophe. Desperate black women wrote letters to the secretary of war begging for furloughs for their husbands. Mrs. John Wilson of Detroit, for instance, described herself as "compleatly distitute" because she had no means of support other than what "I earn by my own labor from day to day."[14]

Black women wrote to all manner of officials and described their destitute conditions. Recipients included President Lincoln, Secretary of War Stanton, midwestern governors, and many other politicians and bureaucrats, as well as family members. In these letters, women explained how the death of their soldier husbands affected their future as wives and mothers. Willie Ann Grey, a single mother whose husband had been killed in battle, expressed concern to her suitor that he not reject her children by another marriage: "I have three little fatherless girls. . . . I have nothing much to sell as I have had [some of] my things all burnt so you know that what I would sell would not bring much. . . . [Y]ou must not think my family large for if you love me you will love my children and you will have to promise me that you will provide for them al as well as if they were your own."[15] Gender dictated earning power, and Grey knew that she would need a husband to help support her and her three children.

Black women asserted that unequal or nonexistent pay jeopardized the welfare of their families. Rosanna Henson, for example, whose husband was in the Twenty-Second New Jersey Regiment, wrote, "my husband . . . has not received any pay since last May. . . . I have four children to support and I find this a great strugle. A hard life this! I being a col'd woman do not get any State pay. Yet my husband is fighting for his country."[16] The high cost of the war, including rising inflation and stagnating wages, took its toll on poor black families. In her letter to Massachusetts governor John A. Andrew, Rachel Ann Wicker, whose husband had enlisted in the Fifty-Fifth Massachusetts, referred to her community's inability to cope with rising prices: "a great many others as well as ourselve are suffering for the want of money to live on[.] when provision and Clotheing wer Cheap we might have got a long But Every thing now is thribbl and over what it was some thre year Back."[17] Many families welcomed enlistment because the promised army salary was at least more reliable than task-based labor and often more dependable than a farmer's pay. But no income at all was dire.

Letters also described in detail the plight of a soldier's family back home. Women sometimes described themselves as helpless and unable to fend for themselves. Families at home bore the brunt of inequitable policy such as uniform fees because it meant less money arrived home with soldiers' letters. Jane Welcome, the mother of a black enlistee from Pennsylvania, implored the president to release her son, because "he is all the subport I have now . . . his father is Dead and his brother that wase all the help that I had . . . now I am old and my head is blossaming for the grave."[18] Women frequently reported their domestic crises to their partners who had gone to war, and those men, in turn, wrote to federal officials in hopes of effecting some change. John Turner stated in his letter to the president that his family "are sick and absolutely naked, having no clothes to wear. They are also threatened with being turned into the street."[19] Lack of clothing was mentioned often. Ann, a woman still enslaved, wrote to her husband, "They are treating me worse and worse every day. Our child cries for you. Send me some money as soon as you can for me and my child are almost naked. My cloth is yet in the loom and there is no telling when it will be out."[20]

Lack of state relief meant that black men and women felt conflicted about their duty to the Union and their duty to their own families and communities.

Some soldiers simply asked to be released from duty so that they could help support their families again. Michigan soldier George G. Freeman wrote,

> I have not received my Back pay From the government yet. I am a man of faimley a Wife and two small children. I was foold in the first place. . . . my famley Receives no Relief from my state as was Promesed me. . . . I want them to Give me my discharge and let me go and work and suport my Familey for they are nearly starved and hav not suitabal cloathing to hide their neckedness. my Familey depends upon my daily labor for their suporte. when I entered the service I felt it my Duty to go."[21]

Others found themselves forced to desert. Warren D. Hamelton explained, "althou I am not but seventeen years old I have my old mother to support and as such expected that the gov. or its agents in this department would comply with its agreement I could have something to support my relitives. . . . if a genl promas or assureance is paid no respect to how much less could there be expectted of a poor soldier (pri.)"[22] Soldiers regularly noted that they would continue to serve in the army, provided they received their back and regular pay.[23]

Black Americans also wrote about their desire for racial equity. Lucy Bailey from Michigan wrote, "I am colored it is true but I have feeling as well as white person and why is it that colored soldiers letters cant pass backward and forwards as well as the white ones[?] I wish [you] would please look in this matter and have things arranged so we can hear from our Husband if we cant see them[.] I have not heard from my Husband in three months."[24] For historians of the black experience, these letters do two important things: they allow us to assess, as least to some degree, the extent of poverty in the black family, and they allow us to understand how letter-writing campaigns were designed to be another step toward securing emancipation.[25]

African American women believed that their opinions about the war were significant, and they communicated this to men in positions of power. In this way, black women were witnesses to the horrific situations caused by slavery and war; hundreds of letters to President Lincoln suggest that women believed that the highest power in the land ought to hear their opinion on how the war should be conducted. Hannah Johnson explained to Lincoln that she had reluctantly allowed her son to join the colored troops only because she knew that the president would never allow black soldiers to be sold into slavery. She also implored Lincoln to punish slaveholders for their sins: "[Slaveholders] have lived in idleness all their lives on stolen labor and made savages of the colored people, but they are now so furious because [blacks] are proving themselves to be men. You must put the rebels to work in State prisons making shoes and things, if they sell our colored soldiers, till they let them go. And give their wounded the same treatment."[26] Clearly African American women had contemplated the cause of the war—slavery and its supporters—in their own minds and decided that "rebels" deserved punishment.

Women's letters point to the relative state of poverty in wartime black communities. War mythology suggests that women were weak and helpless without men, yet the letters demonstrate how women bore the incredible burdens of their own jobs outside the home, their children, and their communities while their spouses and boyfriends were at war. Black families often lived on the brink of starvation, having already lost their shelter, families, and means of support. Many families were too scattered to support each other, usually because they had fled from the South or from a refugee camp. Northward and westward migration to find lost kin meant that African American populations in the region were constantly changing. Lovicy Ann Eberhart, a white woman from Illinois, wrote from a Vicksburg contraband camp: "Whenever a new crowd of negroes were brought in, everything had to stop until the general search for former husbands and wives, parents and children—who had been sold and separated years before—was over." But when former slaves were reunited with their partner, they were eager for a legal marriage ceremony. Eberhart was put in charge of a "conglomerated mass of would-be married people," many of whom asked if they could take part in the ceremony even if their betrothed's whereabouts was unknown. This was particularly the case for soldiers' wives, who said their partners were "up de Yazoo in de army." Eberhart reported that African Americans were "trying to get word to their husbands or wives who were not in the city," but when the day arrived, people "arrived in groups, and squads, and battalions, at the Baptist Church" for the marriage ceremonies.[27] The process of emancipation was an opportunity to mend families and solidify marriages.

Women's letters also reveal how they felt cheated when their husbands were unable or unwilling to help support their families. Catherine Massey accused her husband of neglect, noting, "I have not received a cent of money from him. . . . he has left me in detrimental circumstances and I know not how to meet my present wants. . . . I have toiled and am still striving to earn my bread. . . . I think it no more than right than that he should be made to do what he has never yet done and that is to help me to support myself as I helped . . . support him before he came in the army."[28]

Black women took on most of the labor when their husbands marched off to war. Additionally, women negotiated the tensions of the traditional white middle-class model of gender relations, which was mostly unattainable; they preferred instead to handle their marital and familial situation as their specific situation demanded. When the wages did not come, women voiced their concerns with their partner, the president, the secretary of war, or someone else who they thought might be able to assist them. In these letters, African American women show themselves to be heavily invested in the process of black recruitment and enlistment. They also indicate how blacks perceived wartime participation as a dismal failure when families did not have money for food, clothing, and shelter.

Black women taught themselves to complain—and loudly. Many of the letter writers probably had to find or hire someone literate to do the writing for them. While they understood that emancipation was the most significant goal, they refused to participate silently in an experiment that worsened their present situation. African Americans, though often illiterate, uneducated, starving, and penniless, directed their outrage over their inequitable treatment by dashing off letter after letter to the powerful white men who ran the war, the state, and the country. In these sources black women show themselves to be masters of their own destinies in that they refused to allow the government to alter their familial, marital, and financial circumstances without hearing from them.

* * *

Women's warwork was not just a mere extension, as American history mythology would suggest, of "natural" female benevolence and domesticity. Civil War historiography still follows a patriarchal paradigm of top-down history of men and the military. Additionally, American memory has privileged a fairy-tale type of philanthropy—not warwork—in which white middle-class women's culture was once referred to as the "cult of domesticity." Women were expected to use their unique God-given talents in the domestic realm as a natural extension of republican motherhood. As two scholars of African American women have noted, "the extraordinary participation of black women in the war effort is seldom mentioned, even in African-American histories. Of course, women had been involved in war before, but their participation had usually been limited to rolling bandages, knitting socks, and keeping things going on the home front."[29] Moreover, because women were inherently pious, they were supposed to spend a great deal of their time raising Christian children, setting a virtuous example for the community, and providing a haven for their husbands.[30] Women were presumed to be well suited for altruistic work, which explains the vast number of local charitable women's societies operating in the country when the war began. There is evidence to suggest that black women were thinking about their world—just like white women—in ways that have rarely been noticed by historians. For instance, one 1864 edition of a black newspaper printed the following: "Mr. Editor:—We, the members of the Colored Ladies Freedmen's Aid Society of Chicago, desire to announce, through your columns, what efforts we have made, and are still making, toward promoting the subject for which the society was formed. We do this in order to give publicity to the fact, that the colored citizens of Chicago are not wholly indifferent to the demands of the needy freedmen of the South."[31] This passage reflects the ongoing nature of midwestern emancipation activism, with its attendant focus on the eradication of slavery. Wartime aid societies are just one example of the types of organizations formed by African Americans to shape emancipation in the Midwest and in America.

The same set of circumstances threatening black working-class families gave middle-class women an opportunity to perform philanthropic work and hone their skills as benefactors. Midwestern blacks still believed that their fate was inextricably tied to that of their disadvantaged, enslaved brethren who were much less fortunate.[32] Black women especially believed that their gendered role including caretaking and nurturing. Much of the activism in the Midwest continued to be characterized by middle-class leadership and its long-standing devotion to the cause of emancipation and eventual equality.[33] As has been the case throughout American history, access to both money and leisure time was usually required for women to spend time away from their own homes and families. Women like Mary Jones immigrated to the Midwest because they wanted and needed places where they could grow and prosper as African Americans, as wives and mothers, as activists, and as women. This meant the pursuit of opportunities in the wage-labor market as laundresses, seamstresses, domestic servants, and sometimes nannies. They also took in piecework and mending, which allowed them to piggyback unpaid domestic labor on something that would provide a small yet critical wage for the household. Women with appropriate living conditions could also take in orphans, itinerants, and boarders.

Though the growing midwestern economy could technically sustain the addition of skilled tradespeople like Mary Jones's father, or even unskilled female laborers who were needed to work in homes or factories, the American economy was still fundamentally racist. For free blacks, especially those who had been slaves, the Midwest offered an exquisitely ironic state—the struggle for economic stability and endeavor for social respect were simultaneously onerous. Since, as Jacqueline Jones has pointed out, "the division of labor was calculated to demean the entire African American community by the collective humiliation of its women," black women bore the greatest burden of black midwesterners' relocated status, including the constant threat of rape, forced prostitution, harassment, and other kinds of sexual violence.[34]

Traditions of philanthropy were passed from generation to generation as black self-help strategies matured throughout the century.[35] Midwestern activists sought to build strong foundations for black communities in the antebellum period and to succor those same groups during the war, when the urgent need for citizenship rights demanded malleable gender roles. Middle-class women like Mary empathized with women who were poor, indigent, or orphaned. Perceptive African American women felt a special responsibility—they understood all too well how the system worked against them, and their response was meditative and altruistic. Mary learned the importance of mutual benefit at her father's knee, and she and John advocated for schooling for black children and the suppression of racially motivated state legislation.[36] In 1839, black congregants cofounded the Wood River Colored Baptist Association, located in St. Clair County, Illinois.[37] This was the third assemblage (or association) of churches in Indiana and Illinois led by free black churchgoers who pledged a commitment to antislavery, moral improvement, and self-help. The first two groups, known as the Providence Baptist Association, were founded by former slaves in Ohio from 1834 to 1836.[38] The association grew to include twenty-seven churches altogether, representing Indiana, Illinois, and Ohio.[39] A free black man called Alfred Richardson provided the impetus for founding the Wood River Association (initially known as Friends to Humanity Colored Baptist Association) when he contacted John Livingston, reputed to be the only ordained black minister in Illinois, because he had faced white racism in other churches he attempted to attend. Together, these churches announced their commitment to ending slavery because it was a sin.[40] The Wood River Association initially offered relief to the poor but later became more involved in constitutional battles, which members identified as crucial to emancipation activism.[41]

Parity in most relationships between black and white, male and female, rich and poor did not exist in nineteenth-century America, but midwestern black activists discovered that degrees of cooperation in gendered relationships helped them make greater inroads toward their activist goals.[42] Black women already had good reasons to seek degrees of equity—without stepping out of their nineteenth-century shoes altogether—in their married, religious, and community lives.[43] Like so many other activist women, Mary made her way in a country that was not ready for her. Mary was, for instance, a full participant in her marriage. Despite the fact that gender norms dictated a host of Mary's domestic roles, she stepped outside these boundaries on many occasions. Printer Rufus Blanchard interviewed Mary following John's death in 1879. Mary recalled how the couple's work with the Underground Railroad had commenced when she and John arrived in Chicago in 1845. She had a good deal of experience aiding fugitive slaves, who frequently took shelter in the Joneses' home for extended periods.[44] Mary also met her share of "famed" activists, including the ill-fated John Brown, whose first stay caused some marital stress. Initially Brown came to the Joneses' home one afternoon with Frederick Douglass, and they stayed up all night, discussing plans past midnight. Mary recalled that her husband asked "if I could make some provision for [Brown] to stay all night, [because] he did not want to send him away. [Brown] remained all night. I told Mr. Jones that I thought [Brown] was a little 'off' on the slavery question—that I did not think he was right—and that I did not believe he would ever do what he wanted to do. Somebody would have to give up his life before it was done."[45] This passage indicates that Mary and John discussed their antislavery activism when it came time to harbor fugitives and others. Not only was Mary prophetic, but she was also a cautious and complex thinker. Mary had carefully considered the issue of slavery's destruction and did not agree with Brown's plan of action.

Women like Mary cast a judicious eye on emancipation activists, workers, and beneficiaries. Nineteenth-century authors wrote copious amounts on the rules of propriety for men and women, but Mary had concerns of her own regarding appropriate behavior. Her activist skills revealed that she possessed a concept of personal worth, and she did not hesitate to voice her objections when her intuition was sparked:

One morning someone rang the bell, and Mr. Jones went down and answered the bell. About daylight, I heard several men talking. I had been reading about how many men [Brown] had around him, and I said to my husband, "I do not want John Brown's fighters. I am willing to take care of him, but not his fighters. He will lay himself liable." But [her husband] said, "They are here and I am going to let them in." I don't know how many, but four or five of them were the roughest looking men I ever saw. They had boots up to their knees, and their pants down in their boots, and they looked like they were ready to fight. They behaved very nicely, and I came downstairs right away.[46]

Later, after Mary and Brown were left alone together in the house, she asked him if he wanted more coffee. Brown responded in the affirmative, adding that he had had very little to eat in the past few days. Mary noted that this "showed that [Brown] had a system in all things," of which she heartily approved; she seemed to intuit that Brown had taken care of the fugitives first, rather than worrying about his own hunger. Perhaps because of his self-sacrifice, Mary gradually warmed to Brown, and later she arranged for him to leave Chicago with a new disguise of clothes: "I guess John Brown was hung in those same clothes."[47]

Activists savvily understood that their own fate was bound to the maturation of black equality. Numerous women's groups began to focus their efforts on warwork not long after the war began. In Springfield, Illinois, for instance, black women held a fund-raising festival to raise money for the Union, complete with ice cream, cake, and watermelon. Elisha Weaver, editor of the *Christian Recorder*, reported that Springfield had been in a state of martial law since the war began: "I think I hear some of my readers say, Were you not afraid to be out so late at night[?] . . . Oh, no! For it is as much as the authorities can do to keep down the secessionists, without interfering with free colored people, who are trying to serve God, and encourage our people to industry and religious elevation."[48]

African American women linked emancipation activism and institution-building successes with their commitment to mutual aid within free black communities. The maintenance of community order was chief among their concerns. In October of 1863, Sattie Douglas wrote a lengthy letter to the *Christian Recorder*, applauding the formation of Chicago's Colored Ladies Freedmen's Aid Society.[49] Its members included Mrs. John Jones (president), Mrs. James Blanks (vice president), Sattie Douglas (secretary), Mrs. George Lee (assistant secretary), and Mrs. Henry Bradford (treasurer). The society also had a board of directresses, composed of seven women. Women developed the group, she explained, "to alleviate the condition of the destitute, whose piteous wail floats up to us upon every Southern breeze."[50] To raise money, the women hosted a number of fundraisers in the Chicago area. Mrs. Ella E. Hobart delivered a lecture at Quinn Chapel, along with Mrs. Mattie Griffin, whom Douglas identified as a "distinguished orator from the Garrisonian school."[51]

Black women activists understood their role as a Christian one—secular warwork was also sacred.[52] The same women who had helped to build schools, churches, and coalitions in their antebellum communities now found themselves enmeshed in a religiously motivated effort to alleviate the war's devastating effects. Hunger, lack of shelter, and illness were chief among the worries of community leaders. The Ladies Aid Society, and others like it, had considered the black recruitment effort important enough to warrant hiring their own recruiters. But once that phase was over, meeting the day-to-day needs of the less fortunate, especially soldiers' families, was the best way to serve God.

Members of Chicago's Colored Ladies Freedmen's Aid Society (CCLFAS) were especially concerned for the people whom they referred to as "working class." Activist women sent numerous letters to the *Christian Recorder*, not only to promote the work that they had done, but to remind African Americans that Chicago had "a working class for the cause that cannot be excelled."[53] In this way, "black women provided a crucial link between the practical needs of the community and the ideology of the movement."[54] Black women frequently noted in their letters that all people were "His in God's eyes." This allowed activists to find common ground across the chasm of class insomuch as they were all united for one cause.[55] This was no small feat, as blacks were becoming increasingly aware of class distinctions in their own communities.

Activists were gravely concerned for other African Americans, especially formerly enslaved children who found themselves in a "naked" condition. Refugees from slavery had traveled hundreds of miles to find family members, reach Union camps, and settle in "free" states, with only the clothes on their backs. Women's aid groups formed circles in their communities to sew new clothes and mend old ones. Additionally, they made clothes in all different sizes for women, men, and children, since they were unsure as to whom the clothing might be allocated. The CCLFAS, for instance, held several sewing circles in the fall and winter of 1863. The activists were proud to note that the box they had shipped to Vicksburg, Mississippi, "contained several hundred pieces."[56] The same group of women was simultaneously busy circulating a petition for the "entire abolition of slavery," which they then sent to various federal officials in Washington, DC.[57] In this way, emancipation was both an act and a goal.

The CCLFAS tried to meet the needs of formerly enslaved people in two significant ways: by sending money to places where freedpeople lived and by sending goods directly to camps, towns, and cities where refugees lived.

For instance, one box sent south contained cooking utensils. This signaled an understanding of the most immediate and practical needs of refugees. Society members sent several boxes of fresh vegetables when the call went out for more food. Perhaps what is most significant is that members of the society employed "traveling agents" who were responsible for keeping tabs on refugee facilities. These agents went far beyond packing and sending bundles of food, bandages, and clothing: they were representatives sent to gather firsthand accounts of the freedpeople's conditions. In March of 1864, CCLFAS sent Mary Ann Shadd Cary to such a location because she was an "active and assiduous worker." In her letter to the newspaper, Sattie Douglas did not mention Cary's latest destination, but the tone of her writing gives the impression that Cary traveled often. On one trip, Cary transported the sum of $89.55, which was generously collected from a black church in Louisville, Kentucky. Upon hearing that refugees at Forts Scott and Leavenworth were starving, Douglas wrote that CCFLAS contributed to the "Kansas Relief Fund as generously as was consistent with our then limited treasury."[58]

Black activists showed their midwestern loyalty by arranging for goods to be sent directly to men from specific states. In 1863, a group of women from Indianapolis formed a committee to send parcels of gifts and sundries to Indiana's African American men serving in the Fifty-Fourth and Fifty-Fifth Massachusetts Regiments. The women collected about seventy dollars' worth of goods, which they proudly described as "things as will make the hearts of the boys glad to know that they are thought of at home."[59]

Black women on both ends of the class spectrum used the power of words to disseminate their thoughts about how the war had left many orphaned, widowed, homeless, or hungry. For middle-class women, this meant soliciting donations in journals and in newspapers. Once those donations had been made, black women followed up by posting public acknowledgments, which were designed to attract even more attention to their activism. Women composed descriptions of the needy in an effusive and maudlin manner, hoping that they could tug at some consciences. Perhaps poor and working-class women also considered the conscience of their readers, but they could not afford to use the same kind of sentimentality in their letters because they lacked a similar kind of power within their communities.

Black women adapted the tenor of their wartime activism according to the most urgent needs. In the antebellum period, women's activism had offered a more diversified roster: women chose among antislavery, Sunday school, Masonic, burial, literary, maternal, vigilance, and mutual aid societies. The destruction of slavery never failed to earn top priority but not to the exclusion of additional religious pursuits. In fact, racial uplift activities constituted the cohesive quality of black activism. The war, however, created a sense of immediacy as yet unmatched in the history of black activism. The jubilee was on the horizon but so was unmitigated horror and loss.

* * *

Middle-class women were motivated to leave their reproductive labor duties when the United States Sanitary Commission offered civilian women the opportunity to perform warwork. Women sanitary agents and their aides in camp sought to fight the rampant spread of disease and illness. In June of 1861, white northeastern philanthropists and politicians created the United States Sanitary Commission to deal with horrendous battlefield, hospital, and camp conditions.[60] The Sanitary, as it was colloquially known, was actually the brainchild of Doctors Elizabeth and Emily Blackwell, founders of the New York Infirmary for Women and Children. (White men who managed the Sanitary Commission from New York City took the credit, however.) Shortly after secession, the women doctors called a meeting to organize the efforts of women who had expressed an interest in relief work but had no formal governmental organization to guide them.[61] The document that grew out of that assembly—"An Appeal to the Women of New York"—is perhaps one of the most important missives in the history of women's collectives.[62] Women finally gave a voice and name to work that they had been doing in their communities for centuries—only this time, this was warwork that placed them squarely in a great civil battle.[63]

After much political debate, followed by a campaign to persuade Lincoln, the Sanitary Commission became a civilian branch of the Union army. It was a private war-relief agency dedicated to organizing home-front support efforts (including raising funds for the beleaguered army). As its name suggests, the Sanitary also offered proto-public-health advice to the government and became responsible for a wide range of duties in camps, hospitals, and battlefields. Sanitary agents taught soldiers proper camp drainage and use of water, placement of latrines, cooking skills, and personal hygiene.[64] The Sanitary also extended as far westward as California, under the aegis of the Western Sanitary Commission. This branch played a critical role in alleviating the suffering in the Mississippi Valley theater.[65]

Sanitary Commission activities shed light on black women's lives in two important ways.[66] First, given the climate of white racial hostility in the Midwest, as expressed in the law and practice of segregation, African Americans had every reason to believe that relief societies operating under the Sanitary Commission (conspicuously run by whites) would ignore black individuals and families. Second, sources indicate that when white relief societies turned black women away from their membership meetings, African American women formed their own groups. It is difficult to discern how often agents of the Sanitary refused to offer services to blacks. Since agents spent most of their time in camps, they would have had greater opportunity to assist African American servicemen. It is possible to surmise that black women were distrustful of white paternalistic groups, with the exception of the Quakers. Quakers themselves underwent attacks from other white midwesterners because they sought abolition—thereby "starting" the war—but did not wish to fight in it. An Indianapolis correspondent wrote that the Friends visited a black school so that they could provide advice about refugee relief and education: "[Quakers] urged our people to educate their children by all means, and those who had no children should assist those who were not able. They expressed a desire to assist in that direction. They set forth the condition of our people in their camps, where they had been visiting, their wants for clothing, and their desire to have missionary preachers and teachers among them; and the vast field opening for our young men and women teaching among those of our race just freed from the house of bondage."[67] The Quakers might have claimed conscientious objection to the war, but they did provide war relief nonetheless.

African American women planned for black communities to be responsible for their own soldiers' and families' relief.[68] Emily Elizabeth Parsons, a white nurse, wrote from St. Louis's Benton Barracks Hospital in 1864:

[T]hese colored women have got up a colored Union society among themselves. . . . There has existed in St. Louis, a Society for the colored among the white ladies since the beginning of the war. These [white] ladies visit the hospital constantly, taking comforts to the sick. The colored ladies wished the right of visiting *their* soldiers in this hospital, and they have at last obtained the privilege of riding in the cars on *one* day in the week, viz. Saturday. Some of them coming out a week ago were deliberately insulted by a white lady who was coming out to visit our soldiers. This is the state of things here.

Parsons also wrote about racist policies that forbade African American women from taking a seat on streetcars. Instead, she noted, they had to "*stand* on the platform among men who would and often do treat them rudely." Community meeting places such as Chicago's Quinn Chapel, so crucial to community activism throughout the antebellum period, now served as recruiting stations and farewell posts for servicemen.[69] So although the Sanitary Commission purportedly handled issues dealing with food, clothing, hygiene and shelter, black activist women had no intention of relinquishing their regular philanthropic duties, nor did the feel that they could.

Sanitary Commission activities also illustrate wartime conditions in the black community, especially where religion was concerned. African Americans continued to attend church throughout the war, as their faith in God was tied to philanthropic duty.[70] Black women's church groups, for instance, included the Sanitary Commission in their regular tithing pleas. The AME church in Indianapolis was composed "chiefly of women and refugees from bondage," since the men had gone to war. Worshipers were heartbroken when "an incendiary, of those who teach that negroes are fit only for slavery," burned their church to the ground. On the day that the congregation met to discuss renewal of their insurance policy, they decided instead to devote their time "to taking a contribution for the relief of the freedmen."[71] Five months later, the same congregation raised twenty-five dollars during regular Sunday service for the Sanitary Commission.[72] Newspaper editors noted that "small contributions from colored people" for freedpeople were common, but they were nevertheless proud to announce that this amount was one of the largest ever raised by the poor congregants.[73]

Midwestern black activism continued to thrive for the duration of the war. Black activists expanded their sphere of influence by using itinerant ministers to cross-pollinate their congregations, all of whom had motive to see emancipation succeed. For instance, the Indianapolis AME, like many other black churches, relied on these traveling preachers to spread their emancipation messages. Congregations frequently dispatched one of their junior ministers to other urban areas to preach to their sister congregations and raise money for their special needs. Black churches relied on these networks of congregations for information and camaraderie, both of which helped to create a cultural consciousness among black communities. Congregants from the ruined Indianapolis church sent W. J. Davis to St. Louis to solicit donations. Davis reported that the local auction block, identified to him as "Lynch's slave pen" by some soldiers, now held rebel prisoners of war. Davis heralded the change that had taken place in the former slaveholding city: "There is no more parting asunder the husband and wife, the brother and sister, the babe and the heart-broken mother. . . . There is no more closing up of the colored people's churches . . . no arresting colored people for coming into this State contrary to law. Colored people are not arrested here for being out after ten o'clock at night." Although he probably overestimated the relative safety of refugees, Davis nevertheless noted at the end of his letter that the "grand jubilee" was near.[74] Black communities shared despair and hopefulness alike.

Black women already had many of these relief groups in place before the war, in the form of church, antislavery, and literary leagues. It must not have been an easy task to envision a colored ladies' group that would garner firm support from local white officials or the larger political entity (the Union). There was nothing in northern federal policies or public sentiment to indicate that the impetus behind the war was the betterment of African Americans. Yet the formation of these local aid societies did not occur simply because black women felt left out. Black women were also genuinely fearful that relief societies like the Sanitary and Christian Commissions would not bestow their charity on *black* soldiers. Black women knew that the preservation of their families was intricately tied to the gendered roles of men. Thus, offering services to black soldiers offered protection for the whole community.

Proceeds from church collections were often divided among the Sanitary and Christian Commissions, local aid groups, individual needy families themselves, or other organizations. Proceeds varied from community to community.[75] W. R. Revels, a pastor from another Indianapolis church, noted that one service's tithes were "equally divided between the Christian Commission and our soldier's families."[76] When Bishop Daniel Payne took charge of Ohio's Wilberforce University's new incorporation plan in 1863, black activists across the Midwest earnestly resolved to send money. This they claimed to do because of the war, rather than in spite of it.[77] A bazaar notice from the colored ladies of Bethel AME Church in Philadelphia appealed to a sense of self-help and uplift: "Now is the time for elevation and education. Let us improve the moments while we have an opportunity."[78] In Chicago, residents pledged several hundred dollars for Wilberforce.[79] At Christmastime 1863, the Chicago Ladies Aid Society held a grand bazaar to celebrate and fund the black university.[80] An itinerant minister proudly claimed that "the heart of the great West is vibrating in unison" as students from St. Louis, Chicago, Danville, and Indianapolis "had moved to Ohio to enroll."[81]

* * *

Like their white counterparts, black women quickly recognized the amount of money and goods raised for relief activities could be augmented through fairs and bazaars. Perhaps some of them heeded the missive of the *Christian Recorder*, which encouraged all AME ministers to hold bazaars in their sanctuaries. Although the editors intended to persuade pastors, they also reminded Christians that "the people of every community should be especially interested in building up churches, school house[s] . . . for the good of their own community."[82] Fairs and bazaars always had goods for sale, in addition to the price of admission. Women utilized their understanding of material culture to convince their fellow citizens not only to attend the fair but also to contribute to the community war-relief effort by buying goods that were donated, auctioned, and manufactured specifically for the event. In doing so, women raised awareness of their own local auxiliary and activist groups, as well as the Sanitary Commission.

Black women made claims on the state when it came to their families and communities, but the same women also gave back as much as they expected, if not more. Members of the black Chicago Ladies Aid Society were engrossed in their work during the last two years of the war, and they divided their philanthropic prowess between larger groups like the Sanitary Commission and their own smaller, locally based associations.[83] White women organized their own warwork similarly, but they disallowed African American women's participation. The Ladies Aid Society took part in both of the Northwestern Sanitary Fairs held in Chicago during the war.[84] After the first fair in November 1863, the *Christian Recorder* noted that Chicago's "colored ladies" had "entered bravely into the work" of emancipation.[85] Following the second fair in June of 1865, the *Chicago Tribune* reported that "for the small charge of ten cents, there is a small booth presided over by a colored citizen polishing the boots of ladies and gentleman, 'for soldiers [aid].'"[86]

African American women used the skills they sharpened through warwork to improve their local fight back at home. Activists seemed to have believed that these accomplishments would ultimately have the effect of making their lives better at home, because when blacks experienced true uplift, communities thrived. Sources show how people wrote to the local newspaper to provide updates. For example, churchgoers were so insistent on community self-help that some congregations were angry when they thought they were being ignored: "all our well-to-do colored people who come north or come west, skip over [Indiana] and invest their means in Northern Illinois, Michigan, or Wisconsin."[87] At the end of the war, Chicago's black community was proud to announce that John Jones had been chosen to accompany President Lincoln's cortege to Springfield. But John Jones, though famous by now in the black community, was not the only part of the story. A woman named

Ruth wrote, "Were you to visit the three colored churches in our midst . . . and see the vast assemblage, you would [see our people] actively engaged in different movements for our political and moral elevation."[88]

African American women, much like white hospital and field nurses, bore witness to returning soldiers (many of whom had barely escaped with their lives) as they struggled to survive, to recover, and to return home and find their families. Because of this, black women sharpened their activist message as the war wound down. Whereas before they had wanted men to send money or letters or to come home altogether, now the same women wanted to put the pieces of their communities back together. Despite the war's imminent end, for instance, Chicago's women activists insisted that fund-raising should continue; if nothing else, they argued, the hospitals would now be nearly overrun with returning soldiers. To meet these needs, black women participated in sanitary fairs.

Activist participation at two sanitary fairs appears to have been somewhat circumscribed, especially since the organizational duties were dominated by white Sanitary Commission women—but black women participated nevertheless.[89] A local newspaper told the story of a young black man rushing down the street, having heard news of the capture of the Confederate capitol. A Chicago minister stopped him, asking why he was so excited. The African American man replied, "Richmond's took, and Weitzel's ni—r's in it!" The pastor informed the young man that Richmond's local laws forbade the entry of free blacks without a pass, but the black man shouted happily, "I 'spect sir, they's not enforcen' such laws as much as they used to be."[90] Chicago, where the city's African American population had fought so hard against black codes and the FSL, now hosted dignitaries and military heroes. Generals William T. Sherman and Ulysses S. Grant attended the 1865 Chicago Fair, along with their wives, Ellen and Julia.[91] The celebratory mood of the fair, however, was tempered by Lincoln's assassination, still fresh in the minds of northerners. Ann Hosmer, a white activist who normally worked in the Chicago Soldiers' Home, wrote in her diary that while in Vicksburg, the news of the president's murder incited tremendous "negro grief all over Mississippi and Alabama, grief for their Uncle Sam."[92] It is clear to historians from this and other sources that, by this stage of the war, southern blacks placed a great deal of faith in the man who had arrived at an emancipation plan only reluctantly.

Fairs in black communities were planned and orchestrated by African Americans, although it is ironic that activists made a point to send money and goods to the Sanitary and Christian Commissions despite their overt racist policies. When, however, the Chicago Ladies Aid Society held its own "grand concert and festival" in late 1864, the war had become so monstrously grotesque that whites were not in a position to limit black participation. The black women, however, remained almost entirely focused on black advancement. The *Christian Recorder* noted that the fair had been held to "defray the expenses of delegates [who were traveling] to Springfield to present a petition to the State Legislature for the repeal of the Black Laws of Illinois."[93] Local African American women "recited some fine pieces" of poetry and literature and also provided "some fine music on the piano."[94]

In this capacity, whether formally attached to the commission or a church, women activists created their own culture of warwork. Although no mention was made of women in the document that legalized the commission, the Sanitary Commission retained thousands of women working as operatives on all levels in all manner of local aid societies. Their skill set ranged from nursing to administration to public relations to fund-raising.[95] The Sanitary's far-reaching activities, and the money needed to carry them out, owed their existence to a multitude of anonymous women who ran countless bazaars and fairs; inspected camps, kitchens, and laundries; brewed coffee, cooked food, and prescribed healthier diets; rolled bandages and stocked medical supplies; nursed dying and wounded soldiers; cleaned up after surgeries and amputations; repaired tents, ambulances, and clothing; washed and sewed uniforms; campaigned against scurvy and the spread of disease; staffed hospital ships and convalescent homes; comforted men with stories from the Bible and from literature; acted as advisors in filthy conditions; searched for clean water; sang army songs and Christian hymns; collected shoes from the dead; decorated camps and hospitals during a holiday; traveled in Sanitary wagons from the East Coast to the West; took dictation for letters home; sold homemade patriotic goods to raise money (everything from cockades made of roses to socks to potholders); brought jelly, fruit, clean clothing, and soap to the soldiers; acted as or assisted nurses; aided families searching for prisoners of war and those missing in action; helped soldiers find their way home; and, in general, eased the pain and suffering of refugees, their families, and the Union army.[96]

African American women activists developed local, systematized spheres of influence that allowed them to have greater control over black life during the Civil War.[97] Black women leaders forged key alliances with politicians, neighbors, white women abolitionists, black soldiers, church ministers, newspaper editors, and anyone else who attended a fair or bazaar. If poor black women failed to form similar relationships with the men to whom they addressed their complaints, at least the powerful had been put on notice. To be sure, these relationships were incredibly complicated, but they constituted a political base nevertheless.

In the final analysis, *philanthropy* generally seems to be an appropriate word to describe self-help and relief activities, but the essential fact is that this warwork must be understood in the context of emancipation activism. This case was articulated by the activists themselves. In 1863, "Miss Clarissa Hill and Miss Minerva Williams" formed a committee to "procure some gifts for our noble and gallant volunteers." They sent their goods with a keen awareness that the men were "far from home, battling for the rights of their brethren and the cause of freedom."[98]

Both middle-class and working-class women exhibited agency in the face of dire circumstances, emboldened by the possibility of emancipation, which figured so heavily in the black imagination. Women's activism served as a conduit of racial uplift among black communities, although uplift still tended to operate according to class. Women like Sattie Douglas and Mary Jones, although privileged, played a multifaceted role in midwestern emancipation activism. Black activists, regardless of class, insisted that control over their own people was the most important element of human progress. Black Americans believed that although the fabric of society had been irreparably rent by the war, the greatest sufferers were the ones who had been forced into slavery in the first place.

For some insight into how women were able to accomplish so much in such a strictly gendered society, we turn again to Mary and John Jones. If John Jones's life and career are difficult to trace, then Mary Jones's story is even more elusive. Jones, for instance, hosted the great orator and abolitionist Frederick Douglass in her home on many occasions when Douglass came to Chicago to speak on behalf of the cause. When, in 1841, John's merchant tailor business had grown to such a degree that he was able to buy more property for his business, he took out an ad in the *Tribune*: "JOHN JONES. Clothes, Dresses, and Repairer. Gentlemen, I take this method of informing you that I may be found at all business hours at my shop. [I am] ready and willing to do all work that you may think proper to favor me. Yours for work, J. Jones."[99] Indeed, John had built a prosperous business. But he did not do it alone, for the couple's role in the partnership prompted and maintained John's fame among Chicagoans. Mary also had achievements that were solely hers—following the war, she added suffrage and social welfare to her already-burgeoning list of activist causes. But before she would have a chance to hone those skills, slavery (and later, the war) had to be reckoned with.

Portrait of Mrs. John Jones, also known as Mary Richardson Jones, 1820–1910, by Aaron E. Darling. Chicago History Museum, ICHi-089277.

Portrait of Mary Richardson Jones, 1820–1910, taken sometime after 1883. Chicago History Museum, ICHi-022363, cropped; Baldwin & Drake, photographer.

Mary Jones, like so many of the women who filled the ranks of the Sanitary Commission, churches, and private relief agencies, exercised her skills every time the war presented a new challenge.[100] As an active member of the Underground Railroad, Mary risked enslavement, forcible removal from her home, and death.[101] On countless nights, Mary (as the woman of the house) fulfilled the common caregiver role: she offered some warm beverage or food to the slaves; administered salves and medicines for their wounds; led them furtively through the dark to the outhouse or provided a chamber pot; mended their clothes; provided sleeping arrangements by laying out mats and blankets; and stoked the fire for the bone-chilled and road-weary travelers. She also rocked, soothed, or fed the fugitives' babies, in addition to caring for her own children. If there were any pregnant women in the group, Mary would have also offered a warm hand to the heaving belly, if for nothing else but to judge the position and size of the fetus. It is likely that Mary regularly attended births in the small community in which she lived, and so she probably possessed a certain degree of midwifery skill. This is how women became teachers of sanitation, how they managed to find food for refugees when there seemed to be no bread, and how they waged a battle for citizenship rights.

In the grand scheme of the nineteenth century, emancipation began early and ended late. African Americans who had immigrated to the Midwest hoped for long lives with all of the trappings that accompanied them—marriage, children, homes, jobs, education, and churches. In this, blacks were no different from any other Americans who hoped for longevity. This is evidenced by Mary's discussion of the whereabouts of former slaves whom she had helped: "One of the girls . . . that came here from Missouri covered with straw, is now living in Chicago. One got married and died, and I do not know what became of the other. . . . [One woman's] husband had been in the war, and she came here to see if Mr. Jones could identify her to get a pension. She had four girls, [one of whom] lived with us for five years, went to school and was accepted as a teacher."[102] Jones, along with the other tenacious women activists who would later join her, constantly sought updates about people whom they had helped.

Black women served as ambassadors of the midwestern emancipation activism ideology, which insisted that African Americans had the right to make whole their destinies in the new states. They shaped emancipation not simply because they met the ongoing material needs of the community. As John Jones articulated in 1864, "The Constitution of our state declares that *all* men are born free and independent, and have an indefensible right to enjoy liberty and pursue their own happiness. But this section denies the colored man equal freedom to settle in this state."[103] Still, African American women have been heretofore unrecognized in their dedication to emancipation. Women shared the activist arena with men, usually their husbands.

Black activists had brought legitimacy, integrity, and managerial prowess to their communities by creating long-lasting organizations. Indiana and Illinois boasted hundreds of black churches and schools; the Underground Railroad had transported thousands of slaves to Canada and the West; the black codes had undergone penetrating scrutiny (and would soon be abolished altogether); and organizational activity was on the rise. John Jones encouraged his fellow African Americans to continue to rely on black groups, which he called "associations," for collective power: "My colored fellow-citizens . . . vigilance, eternal vigilance, is the price of liberty. Vigilance on the one hand begets vigilance on the other. Then you must organize, for organization is power. Association is one of the first laws of the human condition. Union is strength, and division weakness, concert is power, isolation is inefficiency."[104]

Women's activism simply took on a different form from men's, but the goal remained the same: to bring emancipation to all African Americans. Women of varying incomes chose their path according to their ability and their life circumstances. In the nineteenth century, conditions of servitude and economic ability were the two most important factors that determined the level to which black people were able to participate in American life. Most of these women possessed a comfortable educational and economic status, especially when compared with the women they were trying to help, so socioeconomic status was a determining factor in how many women throughout the nation could take part in warwork.

Denied access to the public sphere (which was assumed to be white, male, and middle class), African American women employed both internal and external tactics to gain entry to social and political arenas.[105] Internal tactics focused on the black family and community itself, while external ones including letter-writing campaigns directed toward high-powered officials who might provide relief to those communities. Black women had almost no political or socioeconomic power, so they instead used what they did have access to—their own self-designed political culture—in order to conduct emancipation activism.

Conclusion

Free blacks living in Illinois and Indiana both affected and were affected by the process and ideal of emancipation. In order to secure even the smallest of freedoms, black men and women faced the colossal undertaking of shoring up their families and communities as slavery, the sectional crisis, and the Civil War encroached on their already-laborious lives. Black midwestern emancipation activism reveals itself to be much more than a reflexive or defensive reaction to white racism, black codes, or even the institution of slavery. Perhaps some of the protests planned by these activists can be viewed as a type of reactive struggle, but only on the surface. Free black activists met these challenges in inventive and extraordinary ways. They utilized their own communal and kinship ties, dictates and principles of gender, and powerful black institutions (constitutional conventions, churches, newspapers) to forge a highly politicized interpretation of emancipation.

To argue that free blacks constructed their own brand of political activism does nothing to eradicate the persistent theme of oppression that runs throughout their history. And why should it? There is much in these pages to celebrate and to mourn, and agency and structuralism are both apparent. This book asks historians to reassess their assumptions about who participated in black antebellum and wartime activism—and, indeed, what emancipation actually meant to a specific group of people. A sophisticated analysis of emancipation must define the process that was conceived, managed, and directed by black individuals and groups. This not only reduces the overstatement of white abolitionism but also enriches the narrative of American political culture in inestimable ways.

African American history has unbelievable quality to it, since institutionalized racism, legally sanctioned racial terror, and segregation all grew at rates equal to those things that scholars proudly offer as proof of the American Dream, including capitalism, republican virtue, and equality. Most ironically, the historiography itself reflects the centuries-long struggle of scholars and activists alike to establish the history of black agency and emancipation as a legitimate area of investigation. This book also asks scholars to consider how total warfare compelled activists to adjust the nature of their political activism as the war escalated and fluctuated. Additionally, a better understanding of black male soldiering and black female warwork, along with an evaluation of gender roles, will aid historians as we generate a comprehensive nineteenth-century periodization aimed at the subaltern group, rather than the dominant one.

In their quest to resist victimization, black women revealed a great deal about what was expected of them as wives, mothers, sisters, and community leaders. We know that emancipation inaugurated a period in which relations between blacks and whites would be indelibly altered, and the same is true for men and women. Black women faced an enormously incongruous situation—on one level, they were supposed to "practice" womanhood within domestic confines, but they also led campaigns to resist white supremacy and its focus on strict gender dichotomies. Thus, African American women found themselves entangled in debates over the "proper" behavior of women. Moreover, mutual aid societies and other women's groups fashioned possibilities for racial aspiration and self-expression, but it was difficult for poorer black women to take full advantage of these options. Furthermore, as free and freed women sought to adopt a new level of self-reliance, they subverted, sometimes unconsciously, the dictates of the public and private. If the structure of public and private had traditionally prescribed the tone of marital and familial relationships, as well affording specific rights to men (the commercial world, for instance) and to women (such as child-rearing), these boundaries changed when African American women welcomed both antebellum and wartime activism.

Rethinking emancipation as a gradual, incremental process will offer fresh periodization models for "the war" (without strict start/end dates), African American history, and the nineteenth century. As it turns out, the black women who wrote letters to Lincoln, taught Sunday school, and designed mutual aid societies really were trailblazers. Social activism narratives are central to identifying black women's instrumentality and sense of provocation. As the saying goes, these women did all of this "backwards and in heels," but in this case, they did so without the most basic set of freedoms most Americans take for granted.

Furthermore, black nineteenth-century activism dramatically changes the way historians understand the meaning and impact of emancipation *and* slavery. Despite the fact that slavery was illegal in the Midwest, black immigrants understood all too well that slaveholders' rights were protected in a de facto fashion. Conditions of indentured servitude were akin to the conditions of slavery, and state constitutions and black codes carried devastating consequences. In 1820 and 1848, the state constitutions of Indiana and Illinois explicitly banned slavery *again*, this time using more precise, strict language. Thus, even when enslaved people did escape or were freed, the Midwest was not necessarily the land of promise that it ought to have been. African Americans knew that they would have to be the architects of the conditions of midwestern freedom.

The Civil War was a great ideological and moral battle in which some Americans sought to solidify their right to enslave other human beings and create slave states, while others fought to see slavery contained or destroyed. African Americans also wanted the power to make occupational choices, acquire wealth and property, and participate fully in the civic arena. This was an extremely far-reaching goal—blacks were asking for full access to the very capitalistic marketplace that their labor had engendered. When African Americans imagined their lives in a new society, the images they conjured were devoid of slave auction blocks, paternalistic planters, and brutal paddy rollers; they imagined themselves instead as full-fledged members of society.

Scholars must continue to analyze how black men and women, free and enslaved, broadened their sense of self-sufficiency, agency, and authority following the passage of the Thirteenth, Fourteenth, and Fifteenth Amendments. Emancipation was clearly at hand when, on February 1, 1865, Illinois became the first state to ratify the Thirteenth Amendment. Indiana followed suit by ratifying the amendment to abolish slavery a fortnight later. Midwestern blacks rejoiced at the "miraculous" amendment in their churches, but they also knew that the Thirteenth Amendment had no direct legal role in their lives, only a symbolic one, since slavery was already illegal in their states. Indirectly, however, African Americans celebrated the jubilee with dreams of family reunification, financial successes, and the return of soldiers.

Emancipation, modeled by the Joneses and so many others, was something that required constant maintenance and vigilance in the postbellum years. Just one week after the state's ratification of the amendment, the Illinois legislature repealed the black codes, after hundreds of petitions demanding the same flooded the statehouse. This was undoubtedly a more significant achievement for local communities, who had always linked slavery to black codes. Black Chicago's celebration rightly praised Mary and John Jones, who went on to lead the fight to desegregate the city's schools in 1874. John was also an honorary pallbearer at President Lincoln's funeral and was elected a Cook County commissioner and the first African American to serve on Chicago's school board.[1] In Indiana, the 1865 legislature partially repealed the law banning blacks from testifying in court. Legislators finally did this at the urging of Governor Oliver P. Morton, who called the black codes "a stigma upon the humanity and intelligence of the state." In 1866, the Indiana State Supreme Court declared, in *Smith v. Moody,* that Article XIII of the state constitution was null and void because blacks were citizens of the United States. Since the Fourteenth Amendment had not yet been ratified, the decision rested on the Civil Rights Act of 1866. This signaled a major victory for African Americans in the Midwest, especially since the court had deliberately invoked *Dred Scott,* remarking that the case was "now disregarded in every department of government."[2]

This book chronicles the lives of African Americans who, in the middle of a great civil upheaval, made their way to the Midwest and settled there. African American men, women, children, and babies made trips of hundreds of miles from places like North Carolina—mostly on foot, sometimes in horse-drawn wagons, but hardly ever as locomotive passengers. They waded across streams and rivers, endured extreme temperatures, and lacked rudimentary maps. Many traveled on the Underground Railroad, and their stories of migration have been whittled down and generalized for museum placards and school textbooks. One can well imagine that the trip was long and hard, and when African-Americans arrived in the Midwest, they entered a violent and confusing landscape now known to historians as the sectional crisis. White residents who sought to use states like Illinois and Indiana to carve out their own political agendas found themselves faced with a group of black Americans who had plans of their own.

By taking a hard look at how black women wrapped up their meanings of freedom in the politics of home and institution building, we can better understand both their battle to survive and their place in the emerging world of women's political activism. It is one thing to reconstruct a mid-nineteenth-century history of Indiana and Illinois for the male-dominated world of political economy. For a history of free black communities, however, the picture is blurry because sources are less bountiful. Nevertheless, activists like John Jones and H. Ford Douglas did leave records of the ways they refused to submit to the will of the white man. For black women, the "third class citizens," the truth is even more difficult to discern.[3] African American women were thinking about their world in ways that have heretofore gone unnoticed. Social activism as part of the abolitionist struggle has often been portrayed as virtually exclusive to the white middle class.[4]

African American women sought to create—and sometimes redefine— their already-existing political networks, much of which had been developed during institution-building periods. The paucity of sources has generally meant that historians view the end of the nineteenth century as the height of black women's club work, so closely related to racial uplift. The black women's club movement now has its prequel. Historians can understand the ways in which these organizations had Civil War–era antecedents, although likely fewer in number and harder to document. By 1890, Chicago's African American community could boast a rich and thriving black women's club movement.[5] In 1896, black women created the NACW, or the National Association of Colored Women.[6] Indeed, Chicago has a rich tradition of women's organizational work, and by the end of the nineteenth century, the city boasted black women's groups with names like the Phyllis Wheatley Club, the Women's Civic League, and the Volunteer Workers Charity Club.[7] In 1905, the Indiana Association of Colored Women's Clubs (IACWC) held its first meeting in Marion, Indiana, representing more than thirty women's organizations. By 1933, the IACWC comprised fifty-six clubs representing forty-nine Indiana towns.[8]

The soul-crunching work of emancipation would continue as African Americans made their way out of war and into a new era altogether—one that was defined by more black codes, substantial racial uplift, and, inexorably, the maturation of Jim Crow. This activism occurred, in part, because African Americans extended the inroads they had made over several centuries: some escaped to freedom and got an education; many others were only functionally literate; still others took their dignity from the simple fact that they were parents or free laborers. As the war wound down, and refugees stumbled home or died from disease in camps, midwestern blacks continued to link slavery with their own freedoms, by utilizing a unique sense of agency in a world where their racialized subjugation was a matter of simple daily business for many Americans.

Emancipation is a term that scholars have increasingly used to direct our gaze to the totality of the black experience. The history of the Civil War needs to be rewritten to attend more to these social battles, because the eradication of slavery was a fundamental component of African Americans' understanding and construction of what it meant to be a free American in a democracy.

This study of free, self-conscious black activist communities shows how different groups throughout the wartime period defined home-front relief responses in varying ways. Black women's warwork also demonstrates how horror, violence, and sacrifice were not confined to the battlefield.

Furthermore, this book contributes to a significant historiographical shift that directs attention toward agency within a paradigm of organizational acumen and institution and community building. Excavating the emancipation activism of free blacks in the Midwest reveals people who tested the limits of so-called freedom by designing a local campaign to interpret, reinterpret, and, finally, live their emancipated lives in their new homes. This activism was creative, demanding, and assumed the right to resist. Throughout this process, black Illinois and Indiana residents became more self-reliant, which subsequently allowed them to capitalize on the prospect of legal emancipation. Identifying this activism, in turn, will help to mend some of the discontinuities in nineteenth-century women's and African American histories. Perhaps most importantly, the development of a more complex gender analysis of free women's emancipation activism will enlarge our understanding of black families and women's roles in them, women's access to public activism, and black women's perceptions of *themselves*.

Upon initial examination, free midwestern states may appear to be spaces where frantic, victimized runaway slaves and other refugees stumbled and landed, grateful for the promises of free soil. When they arrived, however, they found that slavery was indeed well protected by the white electorate, many of whom were antislavery but virulently racist. Yet the longer the immigrants remained, the more they cultivated a place to call home, anchored to a unique sense of regional citizenry. But painting a history of black Americans as one-dimensional sacrificial lambs subject to the slaughter of white racism can be nothing less than a total failure. In these chapters, African Americans aggressively and vociferously complain about the wrongs done to them, in spectacular venues ranging from newspapers to sermons to legal briefs to speeches and even letters to the president of the United States. Although American history has sometimes mythologized them as illiterate and unprepared for freedom, blacks appear in the historical record as a vigorous, aggressive, tenacious activist group. Over the course of a few decades, they did what any community-minded people would do: they busied themselves creating schools, churches, and political alliances. America, with its convenient historical amnesia, has long avoided the painful topic of a brutalized people who for hundreds of years were stateless, without property, and denied even the most rudimentary human right—freedom. If we now allow those same people to tell us what their activism meant to them, we can hear them characterizing emancipation as it really was: agonizingly slow and cruel but indisputably worthwhile. These are the self-determinate, resolute roars we hear above all other noises, because the American narrative remains incomplete without their voices.

Notes

Bibliography

Index

Notes

Introduction

1. Sarah Ann Lucas, "Proof of Freedom," 45. The county clerk described Sarah as a "light mulatto" in her first appearance but as "dark brown" in the second. Also quoted in Peters, *Underground Railroad in Floyd County*, 158.
2. "City Court Record," *Louisville Daily Courier*, January 9, 1854.
3. Finkelman, "Northwest Ordinance," 14–15.
4. Slavery became increasingly codified in the seventeenth century by usage of *partus sequitur ventrem* in colonial law, in which children assumed the status of their enslaved mother. For a discussion of how this affected slave mothers and their children, see Rothman, *Beyond Freedom's Reach*, 118–23.
5. See Foner, *Reconstruction*, xix–xxii.
6. Hahn, *Nation without Borders*.
7. See, for instance, Eicher, *Civil War in Books*. This work, numbering 407 pages, has only six pages under the headings of "Black Americans and the Civil War" and "Women and the War."
8. Guy-Sheftall, "Black Women's Studies," 38–39.
9. Yancy, *Black Bodies, White Gazes*.
10. Holt, "Reconstruction in United States History Textbooks," 1641.
11. Sinha, *Slave's Cause*, 147–48.
12. See, for instance, Martin, "Neighbor-to-Neighbor Capitalism."
13. Ginzberg, *Untidy Origins*; Jeffrey, *Great Silent Army of Abolitionism*; Yee, *Black Women Abolitionists*; Yellin and Van Horne, *Abolitionist Sisterhood*.
14. Lebsock, *Free Women of Petersburg*.
15. See, for instance, Myers, *Forging Freedom*, 2–7; Owens, *Medical Bondage*, 8–10.
16. Guy-Sheftall, "Black Women's Studies," 36–39.
17. Frankel, *Freedom's Women*.
18. Berkeley, "Colored Ladies Also Contributed," 184.
19. Bethel, *Promiseland*; Blocker, *A Little More Freedom*; Horton and Horton, *In Hope of Liberty*; Rael, *Black Identity and Black Protest*; Schwalm, *Emancipation's Diaspora*; Trotter, *River Jordan*.

20. Cayton and Grey, *American Midwest*.
21. Karamanski, *Rally 'Round the Flag*, 244.
22. Manning, *What This Cruel War Was Over*, 46–47.
23. Faust, *This Republic of Suffering*, xi–xii.
24. hooks, *Feminist Theory*, 39.
25. Curry, *Free Black in Urban America*; Holt, *Black over White*; Litwack, *North of Slavery*; Montgomery, *Beyond Equality*; Pierson, *Black Yankees*; Williamson, *After Slavery*.
26. Taylor, *Frontiers of Freedom*; Cox, *Stronger Kinship*.
27. Huston, *Calculating the Value of the Union*, 3–23.
28. Trotter, *River Jordan*, 37.
29. Griffin, "Brief Account of the Development and Work of African Methodism."
30. See, for instance, Masur, "Problem of Equality"; Bell, "Self-Emancipating Women."
31. Reed, *Platform for Change*.

1. Free Black Communities and Black Codes

1. On emancipation designed by African Africans, see Sinha, *Slave's Cause*, 65.
2. Griffler, *Front Line of Freedom*, 33.
3. Bordewich, *Bound for Canaan*, 4–5.
4. Phillips, *Rivers Ran Backward*, 224–28.
5. Salafia, *Slavery's Borderland*, 7–10.
6. Hammond, *Slavery, Freedom, and Expansion*, 17–19, 150–51; Schwalm, *Emancipation's Diaspora*, 11–42.
7. Brush, "Influence of Social Movements," 120–21.
8. Cord, "Black Rural Settlements in Indiana before 1860."
9. Kantrowitz, *More than Freedom*, 43.
10. Griffler, *Front Line of Freedom*, 15.
11. Rojas, "Social Movement Tactics," 2147–48. Social movement theory generally states that disruption, not violence, is one of the most effective strategies in achieving change.
12. Taylor, *Frontiers of Freedom*.
13. Harris, *History of Negro Servitude in Illinois*, 1–26; Cooper, *Black Settlers in Rural Wisconsin*.
14. Finkelman, "Northwest Ordinance."
15. Dunn, *Slavery Petitions and Papers*.
16. Finkelman, "Evading the Ordinance"; Cha-Jua, *America's First Black Town*.
17. Simeone, *Democracy and Slavery in Frontier Illinois*, 20–22.
18. Aldrich, "Slavery or Involuntary Servitude in Illinois," 121–23.
19. Morrison, *Slavery and the American West*, 46; Fehrenbacher, *Sectional Crisis and Southern Constitutionalism*, 13–15.

20. U.S. Bureau of the Census, 1840 U.S. Census, Illinois, Population Schedule, 341, 371, 396, 467.

21. 31 Annals of Cong., H.R., 15th Cong., 2nd sess., 305–10. See also Fehrenbacher, *Sectional Crisis and Southern Constitutionalism*, 13.

22. Thornbrough, *Negro in Indiana before 1900*, 25–32.

23. Onuf, *Statehood and Union*, 123–30.

24. Gertz, "Black Laws of Illinois."

25. Walker, *Free Frank*, 98.

26. Berwanger, *Frontier against Slavery*, 27–29.

27. Harris, *History of Negro Servitude*, 72–74.

28. Eastman, *Black Code of Illinois*, 20.

29. Litwack, *North of Slavery*, 72.

30. McDonald, "Negro Migration into Indiana," 33–34.

31. *Indiana House Journal, 1829–1830*, 35–36.

32. *Indiana Journal*, March 3, 1830.

33. McDonald, "Negro Migration into Indiana," 33–34.

34. Harris, *In the Shadow of Slavery*; Ripley, *Black Abolitionist Papers*, vol. 3.

35. Berwanger, *Frontier against Slavery*, 27–29.

36. Woodson, *Century of Negro Migration*, 4.

37. Voegeli, *Free but Not Equal*, 1–3.

38. Frederickson, *Black Image in the White Mind*.

39. Etcheson, *Emerging Midwest*, 162–63.

40. Dykstra, *Bright Radical Star*, 23–27.

41. Long, foreword, vii.

42. This compared to 1,338,710 whites.

43. U.S. Bureau of the Census, 1850 U.S. Census, Population Schedule, 817, 702, 755, 934; U.S. Bureau of the Census, 1860 U.S. Census, Population Schedule, 135, 137, 594, 595.

44. Siebert, *Underground Railroad from Slavery to Freedom*; Turner, *Underground Railroad in Illinois*.

45. Vincent, *Southern Seed, Northern Soil*, 26.

46. Thornbrough, *Negro in Indiana before 1900*, 31–33.

47. Thornbrough, *Since Emancipation*, 2–3.

48. Cord, "Black Rural Settlements in Indiana before 1860."

49. *Western Citizen*, February 23, 1843.

50. *Western Citizen*, June 20, 1844.

51. Muelder, *Fighters for Freedom*, 182.

52 *Western Citizen*, August 24, 1847.

53. The Zebina Eastman Collection is stored at the Chicago History Museum.

54. *Western Citizen*, December 14, 1847.

55. *Western Citizen*, February 27, 1849.

56. Bigham, *We Ask Only a Fair Trial*, 3–18.
57. Lusk, *Eighty Years of Illinois Politics*, 350.
58. On the "negative and feminist space" in black women's historiography, see Fought, *Women in the World of Frederick Douglass*, 4.
59. Bond, "Every Duty Incumbent upon Them," 210.
60. Jones, "Interview with Mary Jones," 298.
61. Walker, *Free Frank*.
62. Alton, Illinois, is located on the Mississippi River at the confluence of the Missouri and Mississippi Rivers.
63. *Harpel's Scrapbook*, "Obituaries, up to 1884: John Jones," vol. 8, Chicago History Museum. The *New York Times*, on March 3, 1875, reported that Chicagoans held a celebration of the thirtieth anniversary of John Jones's arrival in the city.
64. Berkeley, "Like a Plague of Locusts."
65. Blockson, *Underground Railroad*, 163–202.
66. The John Jones Collection is stored at the Chicago History Museum.
67. "Obituary: Death of Ex-County Commissioner John Jones," *Chicago Tribune*, May 22, 1879.
68. Conroy and Bontemps, *They Seek a City*, 44–45.
69. Payne, "Unearth Tale of 'Forgotten Man.'"
70. Conroy and Bontemps, *They Seek a City*, 45–46.
71. "Obituary: Death of Ex-County Commissioner John Jones," *Chicago Tribune*, May 22, 1879.
72. "Certificates of Freedom," John Jones and Mary Richardson Jones, John Jones Collection.
73. *Harpel's Scrapbook*, "Obituaries, up to 1884: John Jones."
74. "Lincoln and the Negro," box 5, "Negro in Illinois Papers."
75. Payne, "Unearth Tale of 'Forgotten Man.'"
76. Turner, *Underground Railroad in Illinois*, 25.
77. Jones, "Interview with Mary Jones."
78. "John Brown's Friend [John Jones]," box 1, "Negro in Illinois Papers."
79. Bontemps and Conroy, *They Seek a City*, 46.
80. "Carter Harris, Born Slave, Has Been Janitor for 27 Years," *Pantagraph*, June 30, 1924.
81. "John Brown's Friend [John Jones]," box 1, "Negro in Illinois Papers."
82. "Interview with Joanna C. Hudlin Snowden, February 3, 1938," "Old Settlers," box 10, "Negro in Illinois Papers."
83. Jones, *All Bound Up Together*, 27–28.
84. Heller, "History of Terre Haute, Indiana," 2.
85. *Provincial Freeman*, January 28, 1855.

86. *Report of the Debates and Proceedings of the Convention for the Revision of the Constitution of the State of Indiana*, 1792.

87. *Laws of Indiana Territory, 1853*, 478.

88. Dickson, *Manual of the International Order*, 358.

89. Dickson, *Manual of the International Order*, 356. The first "landmark" of the order is "Belief in God and the Christian Religion."

90. Dickson, *Manual of the International Order*, 27.

91. Dickson, *Manual of the International Order*, 28–29.

92. Adams and Peck, *Love of Freedom*, 103–15.

93. Scott, "Most Invisible of All," 5.

94. Farnam, *Chapters in the History of Social Legislation*, 219–20.

95. LaRoche, *Free Black Communities and the Underground Railroad*, 15.

96. Hamm, "Moral Choices."

97. Vincent, *Southern Seed, Northern Soil*, 26, 54.

98. Quoted in Sterling, *Speak Out in Thunder Tones*, 117.

99. Pierce, "Negotiated Freedoms."

100. Quoted in Cashin, "Black Families in the Old Northwest," 452.

101. Woodward v. the State of Indiana (1855), Supreme Court Papers.

102. Doyle, *Social Order of the Frontier Community*, 61.

103. Walker, *Free Frank*, 98.

104. Yorkville newspaper citation, 1846.

105. Muelder, *Fighters for Freedom*, 25–44.

106. Zebina Eastman Collection.

107. *Minutes of Illinois Baptist State Convention* (1848), 16.

108. Cole, *Constitutional Debates of 1847*.

109. *Illinois State Register*, July 8, 1847.

110. Thornbrough, *Negro in Indiana*, 54–59.

111. Middleton, *Black Laws in the Old Northwest*, 299–304.

112. "An Act to Prevent the Immigration of Free Negroes into the State," *Statutes of Illinois*, 1853.

113. Gertz, "Black Laws of Illinois," 463–67.

114. Mahoney, "Black Abolitionists," 37.

115. The following year, John attended the National Colored Convention of 1848, held in Cleveland. The conference was organized by the National Negro Convention.

116. Generally, see Litwack, *North of Slavery*; Roediger, *Wages of Whiteness*.

117. Dunbar, *Fragile Freedom*, 51–52.

118. *Proceedings of the State Convention of Colored Citizens of the State of Illinois*, 7. Alton was deliberately chosen because it was the site of Elijah Lovejoy's murder nineteen years earlier. See Cromie, *Short History of Chicago*, 54.

2. Legal, Educational, and Religious Foundations

1. Quinn Chapel, *110th Anniversary*; Quinn Chapel, *120th Anniversary*.
2. Gregg, *History of the African Methodist Episcopal Church*, 43–48.
3. Smith, *History of the African Methodist Episcopal Church*, 13–16. Carolyn Dodd (Quinn historian), interview with the author, tape recording, Chicago, Illinois, March 13, 2003.
4. Fisher, "History of the Olivet Baptist Church of Chicago," 9.
5. Broyles, *History of the Second Baptist Church*; Goebes, *History of the Second Baptist Church*.
6. Sorenson, *Illinois Women*, 55.
7. Petersburg Women's Club, "History of Pike County," reel 1.
8. Horton and Horton, "Violence, Protest, and Identity."
9. *Christian Recorder*, February 24, 1866. See also Williams, *The Christian Recorder*, 103–6, 119–24.
10. Pryor, *Colored Travelers*, 44–75.
11. Schwalm, "Overrun with Free Negroes."
12. Lincoln and Mamiya, *Black Church*; Billingsley, *Mighty like a River*, 35–37.
13. Fehrenbacher, *Slavery, Law, and Politics*, 121–50.
14. Fehrenbacher, "The Opinion of the Court," chap. 7 in *Slavery, Law, and Politics*, 183–213.
15. Giddings, *When and Where I Enter*; White, *Ar'n't I a Woman?*; Romeo, *Gender and the Jubilee*.
16. Mahoney, "Black Abolitionists," 22–27.
17. Seigel, "Moral Champions and Public Pathfinders"; Cadbury, "Negro Membership in the Society of Friends."
18. Thornbrough, *Negro in Indiana*, 22.
19. Coffin, *Reminiscences of Levi Coffin*, 111–15; Yannessa, *Levi Coffin, Quaker*.
20. Heller, "Colored People, Settlements, Temperance, Churches, Biography," 135.
21. *Chicago Daily Journal*, July 29, 1850.
22. *Chicago Daily Journal*, April 14, 1853.
23. Drake, *Churches and Voluntary Organizations*, 39.
24. Drake, *Churches and Voluntary Organizations*, 41.
25. *United States Statutes at Large*, 9 Stat. 462 (1850), 302–5.
26. Regional History Pamphlet Collection, Vincennes University, Vincennes Indiana.
27. Thornbrough, *Negro in Indiana*, 50–54.
28. Middleton, *Black Laws in the Old Northwest*, 202.
29. *Western Citizen*, October 8, 1850.
30. *Western Citizen*, October 8, 1850.
31. *City Directory, Rockford, Illinois, 1858.*

32. Jones, "Interview with Mary Jones."

33. *Western Citizen*, October 8, 1850.

34. *Liberator*, June 18, 1841. See also Ripley, *Black Abolitionist Papers*, vol. 3, 37–40.

35. *Chicago Daily Journal*, October 3, 1850.

36. *Weekly Chicago Democrat*, October 12, 1850.

37. *Chicago Daily Journal*, September 30, 1850; Pierce, *History of Chicago*, 382–84.

38. Blackett, "Freeman to the Rescue!," 135–40.

39. *Annual Report of the Colored Vigilant Committee of Detroit*, 8.

40. Mann, *Chicago Common Council and the Fugitive Slave Law*, 69.

41. *Annual Report of the Colored Vigilant Committee of Detroit*, 12. See also Scott, "Most Invisible of All," 7.

42. Constitution of the State of Indiana of 1816, art. XI, sec. 7; Constitution of the State of Illinois of 1818, art. VI, secs. 1, 2.

43. *Journal of the Convention of the People of the State of Indiana; Report of the Debates and Proceedings of the Convention for the Revision of the Constitution of the State of Indiana, 1850-1851* (1935).

44. Dickerson, "Illinois Constitutional Convention of 1862," 366–69.

45. Harris, *History of Negro Servitude*, 226–30.

46. *Chicago Journal*, October 14, 1850.

47. *Western Citizen*, October 22, 1850.

48. *Chicago Democrat*, October 22, 1850.

49. *Western Citizen*, October 8, 1850.

50. Longstreet, *Chicago: 1860-1919*, 37.

51. *Belleville Advocate*, July 17, 1851.

52. Claeys, *Citizens and Saints*, 47.

53. Johannsen, *Frontier, the Union, and Stephen A. Douglas*.

54. Kettleborough, *Constitution Making in Indiana*, vol. 1, xcii, 360–63.

55. Finkelman, "Slavery and the Northwest Ordinance," 346.

56. Sinha, *Slave's Cause*, 316–17.

57. *Report of the Debates and Proceedings of the Convention for the Revision of the Constitution of the State of Indiana* (1850), 1792.

58. *Western Citizen*, February 24, 1853.

59. Foner and Walker, *Proceedings of the Black State Conventions*, xiii.

60. Ripley, *Black Abolitionist Papers*, vol. 3, 27–28.

61. *Proceedings of the Colored National Convention Held in Rochester, July 1853*, 6–7.

62. Bell, *Minutes of the Proceedings of the National Negro Conventions*.

63. Delany's tract on emigration is *Condition, Elevation, and Emigration of the Colored People of the United States*, published in 1852.

64. Boris, "Power of Motherhood," 26–27.

65. Brown, "Negotiating and Transforming the Public Sphere," 111–50.
66. Money, "Fugitive Slave Law of 1850 of Indiana."
67. Quoted in Thornbrough, *Negro in Indiana*, 108.
68. *Indianapolis State Sentinel*, February 26, 1851.
69. Kotlowski, "Jordan Is a Hard Road to Travel," 6–8.
70. Landon, "Negro Migration to Canada," 22.
71. Mann, *Chicago Common Council and the Fugitive Slave Law*, 68.
72. *Western Citizen*, October 14, 1850.
73. Miller, *Search for Black Nationality*, 266–271.
74. LaRoche, *Free Black Communities and the Underground Railroad*, 106–10.
75. *Chicago Tribune*, October 11, 1853.
76. Robb, "Progress in Attaining Liberty and Justice," 6–12.
77. Watkins, "Some of Early Illinois' Free Negroes."
78. Bordewich, *Bound for Canaan*, 388–92.
79. Cord, "Black Rural Settlements in Indiana before 1860," 5.
80. Gliozzo, "John Jones and the Black Convention Movement," 234; McHenry, *Forgotten Readers*.
81. *Voice of the Fugitive*, July 1 and 29, 1852.
82. *Liberator*, November 12, 1852. For a discussion of the legal implications of the FSL, especially the *Prigg v. Pennsylvania* case, see Thornbrough, "Indiana and Fugitive Slave Legislation"; Crenshaw, "One Ran to Freedom," 4–6.
83. Grimshaw, *Official History of Freemasonry among the Colored People*, 214–15.
84. Fisher, "Negro Churches in Illinois."
85. Campbell, *Songs of Zion*, 52–56.
86. Payne, *History of the African Methodist Episcopal Church*, 170–71.
87. *South Cavalry Baptist Church Centennial Souvenir Booklet*, 2.
88. "Mount Zion Baptist Church Souvenir Program," 5.
89. Logan, *"We Are Coming,"* 1–22.
90. Souvenir Program, "Sixty-Fifth Anniversary of the Olivet Baptist Church," 4.
91. In 1839, African Americans in Illinois organized twelve churches into the Wood River Baptist Association. This group represented St. Clair and Madison Counties, Shawneetown, Vandalia, Jacksonville, Springfield, Galena, and Chicago. Washington, *Frustrated Fellowship*, 31–32, and quoted in Woodson, *History of the Negro Church*, 122.
92. Charles, "Economy-Cabin Creek Short Branch."
93. McCaul, *Black Struggle for Public Schooling*, 108–26.
94. Middleton, *Black Laws*, 251.
95. Hendrick and Hendrick, *Fleeing for Freedom*, 73–75.
96. Heller, "Colored People, Settlements, Temperance, Churches, Biography," 136–37.

97. Weaver, "Knowledge," 39.
98. Griffin, "Brief Account of the Development and Work of African Methodism," 6–20.
99. *Provincial Freeman*, December 27, 1856.
100. U.S. Bureau of the Census, 1870 U.S. Census, Population Schedule, 765.
101. *History of Gallatin, Saline, Hamilton, Franklin and Williamson Counties*, 172.
102. *Centennial History of Illinois*, 224–32. See also Saline County Historical Society, *Saline County, a Century of History*, 138.
103. Shepard, "History of the Negro Schools in Vigo County," 124.
104. Minutes of the Henry County Female Anti-Slavery Society.
105. *Repository of Religion and Literature and of Science and Art*, 12.
106. *Harper's Weekly*, October 31, 1863.
107. *Daily Pantagraph*, October 6, 1836.
108. Muirhead, *History of African Americans in McLean County, Illinois*, 9.
109. *Proceedings of the State Convention of the State of Illinois*, 3.
110. Taylor, *Frontiers of Freedom*, 127–28. On black women's autonomy in general, see Frankel, *Freedom's Women*.
111. *Repository of Religion and Literature and of Science and Art*, vol. 2 (1859), 30–32.
112. Stewart, "Emergence of Racial Identity." See also Gaines, *Uplifting the Race*; Jones, *All Bound Up Together*.
113. Quinn Chapel A.M.E. Church Archives, box 1, folder 3.
114. For example, the women activists sent "An Appeal to the Ladies of Indiana" to the *Indiana Free Democrat* on June 16, 1853.
115. Robertson, *Hearts Beating for Liberty*, 28. On other groups of white women abolitionists who also fought for schooling for black children, see Muelder, *Fighters for Freedom*, 181–83.
116. Tucker, *History of Randolph County, Indiana*, 196–97.
117. *Repository of Religion and Literature and of Science and Art*, 18.
118. Thompson, "Eleutherian Institute," 109.
119. Moore, *Southern Baptists in Illinois*, 62–65.
120. Petition of 52 Colored Citizens of Illinois.
121. Blackmore, "African Americans and Race Relations in Gallatin County, Illinois," 214–15.
122. U.S. Bureau of the Census, 1860 U.S. Census, Population Schedule.
123. U.S. Bureau of the Census, 1860 U.S. Census, Mortality and Miscellaneous Statistics, 507.
124. *Repository of Religion and Literature and of Science and Art*, 4–5.
125. *Douglass' Monthly*, April 1859.
126. *Douglass' Monthly*, November 1859.
127. *Western Citizen*, Summer, 1853.

3. Antebellum and Wartime Emancipation Activism

1. Foner and Walker, *Proceedings of the Black State Conventions*, 70.
2. Cox, *Stronger Kinship*; Schwalm, *Emancipation's Diaspora*.
3. Foner, "Republicans and Race," chap. 8 in *Free Soil, Free Labor, Free Men*, 261–300.
4. Morrison, *Slavery and the American West*.
5. Wright, *Centennial Encyclopaedia of the African Methodist Episcopal Church*, 103.
6. Gliozzo, "John Jones and the Black Convention Movement," 181.
7. Miller, *Black Civil War Soldiers of Illinois*, 12. The state population in 1860 was 1,711,961, so blacks composed a small percentage of the population.
8. Foner and Walker, *Proceedings of the Black State Conventions*, 70.
9. Foner and Walker, *Proceedings of the Black State Conventions*, 68–69.
10. Bell, "Some Reform Interests of the Negro," 18.
11. Raboteau, *Canaan Land*; Lincoln and Mamiya, *Black Church in the African American Experience*.
12. Higginbotham, *Righteous Discontent*, 7.
13. *Proceedings of the Illinois Anti-Slavery Convention*.
14. Foner and Walker, *Proceedings of the Black State Conventions*, 70.
15. *New Albany Daily Ledger*, May 31, 1862. Emigrants from Kentucky and Tennessee created most white settlements in Indiana.
16. Foner and Walker, *Proceedings of the Black State Conventions*, 72.
17. Scudder, *American Commonwealth: Indiana*, 47.
18. Adeleke, *UnAfrican Americans*, 4–12.
19. *Chicago Liberator*, November 11, 1853.
20. Thornbrough, *Since Emancipation*, 2–3.
21. Taylor, *America's First Black Socialist*. Clark wrote *Black Brigade of Cincinnati* about the honorable black men of the city's own black Civil War militia.
22. Foner and Walker, *Proceedings of the Black State Conventions*, 71.
23. McPherson, *Negro's Civil War*, 256–57.
24. *Proceedings of the State Convention of Colored Citizens of the State of Illinois* (1856), 14.
25. These percentages are based on the 1850 census. In Illinois, there were 845,034 whites and 5,436 blacks. In Indiana, there were 977,154 whites and 11,262 blacks. See U.S. Bureau of the Census, 1850 U.S. Census, Population Schedule.
26. Wagoner's obituary was printed in the *Rocky Mountain News*, January 28, 1901. See also Simmons, *Men of Mark*, 679–84.
27. Berwanger, *Frontier against Slavery*, 48.
28. *Proceedings of the State Convention of Colored Citizens of the State of Illinois* (1856), 10.

29. McManus, *Political Abolitionism in Wisconsin.*
30. *Galesburg Republican,* May 13, 1871.
31. Muelder, *Hero Home from the War,* 5.
32. Barquet was referring to southern Illinois Democrat John A. Logan, who led the General Assembly to adopt the Black Code of 1853, which disallowed all black migration into the state.
33. Quoted in Harris, *History of Negro Servitude,* xx.
34. Johnson, *Development of State Legislation concerning the Free Negro.*
35. Litwack, *North of Slavery,* 16–18.
36. Quoted in Voegeli, *Free but Not Equal* 181–82.
37. Julian, *Speeches on Political Questions,* 127.
38. *Chicago Tribune,* January 7, 1863.
39. Frazier, *Negro Family in Chicago.*
40. *Douglass' Monthly,* July 1859.
41. Harris, "H. Ford Douglas."
42. Clegg, *Price of Liberty,* 6–17. On the American Colonization Society, see Burin, *Slavery and the Peculiar Solution.*
43. In February 1856 an editorial in the newspaper announced that Isaac Shadd, Louis Patterson, and H. Ford Douglas were assuming ownership of the paper.
44. Rollin, chaps. 7 and 8 in *Life and Public Studies of Martin R. Delany,* 73–82.
45. Miller, *Search for a Black Nationality,* 140–41.
46. Mehlinger, "Attitude of Free Negroes," 300.
47. Bell, *Minutes of the Proceedings of the National Negro Conventions,* 112.
48. *Anti-Slavery Bugle,* August 11, 1849.
49. Hitchcock and Reynolds, "Ford Douglass' Fourth of July Oration, 1860."
50. Douglas also published articles in local newspapers. See *Weekly Pantagraph,* August 13, 1856.
51. *Douglass' Monthly,* April 1859.
52. Miller, *Search for a Black Nationality.*
53. Gosnell, *Negro Politicians,* 14.
54. Fitts, *History of Black Baptists.*
55. *Douglass' Monthly,* March 1859.
56. *Douglass' Monthly,* July 1859. Hitchcock and Reynolds, "Ford Douglass' Fourth of July Oration, 1860."
57. Foner and Walker, *Proceedings of the Black State Conventions,* 60.
58. Dixon, *African America and Haiti.*
59. *Douglass' Monthly,* April 1859.
60. *Douglass' Monthly,* April 1859.
61. *Douglass' Monthly,* August 1860.
62. Foner and Walker, *Proceedings of the Black State Conventions,* 62.
63. Taylor, *America's First Black Socialist,* 2.

64. *Daily Pantagraph*, August 17, 1858.

65. *Daily Pantagraph*, August 17, 1858.

66. *Daily Pantagraph*, December 28, 1859. The newspaper carried many reports of fights between the Irish and other white groups.

67. *Daily Pantagraph*, July 1, 1858.

68. *Daily Pantagraph*, December 3, 1859.

69. *Indianapolis Daily Journal*, March 8, May 19, September 15, October 1 and 16, 1860.

70. Stampp, *Indiana Politics during the Civil War*, 58–62.

71. Johnson, *Abraham Lincoln, Slavery, and the Civil War*, 46.

72. *Indianapolis Daily State Sentinel*, October 15, 1861.

73. *Marion County Clarion*, November 21, 1861.

74. *Indianapolis Daily State Sentinel*, August 11, 1862.

75. *Douglass' Monthly*, February 1861.

76. Thornbrough, *Indiana in the Civil War Era*, 13.

77. *Indianapolis Daily State Sentinel*, April 26, 1862.

78. Wilson, "Center City Origins of the South Side Black Community of Chicago," 20.

79. *Chicago Tribune*, November 13–16, 1860.

80. *Chicago Daily Journal*, April 8, 1861.

81. *Chicago Daily Journal*, April 8, 1861.

82. Gertz, "Black Laws of Illinois."

83. Quoted in Gertz, "Black Laws of Illinois," 457.

84. *Indianapolis Daily Journal*, December 19, 1861.

85. George Edwards to Sarah Edwards, January 13, 1862, George Edwards Papers.

86. Holcombe and Skinner, *Life and Public Services of Thomas A. Hendricks*, 94.

87. Zilversmit, *Lincoln on Black and White*.

88. Foner, *Free Soil, Free Labor, Free Men*; Holt, *Fate of Their Country*.

89. *Indianapolis Daily State Sentinel*, October 16, 1862.

90. *Indianapolis Daily Journal*, October 17, 1862.

91. Lincoln, "Second Annual Message to the Senate and House of Representatives" (address, Washington, DC, December 1, 1862).

92. Thornbrough, "Race Issue in Indiana Politics during the Civil War," 180. See also Voegeli, *Free but Not Equal*; Berwanger, *Frontier against the Slavery*.

93. Stephen Miller to Joseph and Nancy Brown, January 23, 1863, Stephen Miller Collection.

94. *Indianapolis Daily State Sentinel*, December 5, 1862.

95. John Hunt to Joseph A. Wright, March 17, 1862, Wright Collection, Indiana State Library. Quoted in Crenshaw, *Bury Me in a Free Land*, https://www.in.gov/history/3100.htm.

96. Stampp, *Indiana Politics during the Civil War*, 58–62.

97. *Journal of the Senate of the State of Indiana, 1863*, 696–700.

98. Johnson, "Out of Egypt."

99. Crenshaw, *"Bury Me in a Free Land."*

100. *Indianapolis Daily State Sentinel*, February 9, 1863.

101. *Indianapolis Daily State Sentinel*, July 26, 1864.

102. *Indianapolis Daily State Sentinel*, September 16, 1864.

103. *Indianapolis Daily State Sentinel*, September 19, 1864.

104. *Indianapolis Daily State Sentinel*, May 6, 1864.

105. *Indianapolis Daily State Sentinel*, March 30, 1864.

106. Thornbrough, "Race Issue in Indiana Politics during the Civil War," 187–88.

107. *Indianapolis Daily Journal*, September 16, 1864.

108. Votaw, "Andrew Hampton, Pioneer Nurseryman of Indiana."

4. Black Soldiering and Emancipation Activism

1. Westwood, *Black Troops, White Commanders, and Freedmen*; Glatthaar, *Forged in Battle*.

2. Hicken, "Record of Illinois Negro Soldiers in the Civil War."

3. Keegan, *History of Warfare*, 75.

4. Taylor, *Black Woman's Civil War Memoirs*; DePauw, *Battle Cries and Lullabies*.

5. Berlin, Reidy, and Rowland, *Freedom*, 1–34.

6. *Repository of Religion and Literature and of Science and Art* (1863–1864), microfilm, 81.

7. Drinkard, *Illinois Freedom Fighters*, 3.

8. Miller, *Black Civil War Soldiers of Illinois*.

9. Egerton, *Thunder at the Gates*, 63–96.

10. Ripley, *Black Abolitionist Papers*, vol. 5, 118.

11. Foner, *Blacks and the Military in American History*, 32–33.

12. Quoted in McPherson, *Ordeal by Fire*, 350.

13. Aptheker, "Negro in the Union Navy."

14. Lincoln wrote this letter to Andrew Johnson, then governor of Tennessee. Quoted in Basler, *Collected Works of Abraham Lincoln*, 149–50.

15. Carnes, *Secret Ritual and Manhood in Victorian America*.

16. Mitchell, *Vacant Chair*, 153, 154.

17. Horton and Horton, *In Hope of Liberty*, 269–70.

18. Horton, "Freedom's Yoke," 51–54.

19. *Repository of Religion and Literature and of Science and Art* (1863–1864) microfilm, 24.

20. Scott, "Gender: A Useful Category of Historical Analysis." On the changing nature of gender roles during the war, see Faust, *Mothers of Invention*, 135–38; Whites and Long, *Occupied Women*, 6–8.

21. Quoted in Adams, *On the Altar of Freedom*, 3–4.
22. Berlin, Reidy, and Rowland, *Freedom*, 94–95.
23. Brown, *Negro in the American Rebellion*, 144–56.
24. Quoted in Horton and Horton, "Violence, Protest, and Identity," 83.
25. Quoted in Williams, *American Negro from 1776 to 1876*, 24–25.
26. See Montgomery, *Beyond Equality*.
27. Sergeant Morgan W. Carter to "Friend Charles," December 3, 1864, manuscript from a private collection, Fort Ward Museum and Historical Site.
28. McPherson, *Struggle for Equality*, 61–65.
29. Sattira Douglass to Robert Hamilton, *Weekly Anglo-African*, July 4, 1864; quoted in Ripley, *Black Abolitionist Papers*, vol. 3, 284–86.
30. Ripley, *Black Abolitionist Papers*, vol. 3, 124.
31. *Christian Recorder*, February 20, 1864.
32. *Weekly Anglo-African*, June 20, 1863.
33. *Weekly Anglo-African*, June 20, 1863.
34. Foner, *Story of American Freedom*, 95–100.
35. Blight, *Frederick Douglass' Civil War*, 157–60.
36. Blight, *Frederick Douglass' Civil War*, 157–60.
37. Walker, *Rock in a Weary Land*, 30–45; McPherson, *Struggle for Equality*, 61–65.
38. McPherson, *Negro's Civil War*, 175–79.
39. Quoted in Foner, *Frederick Douglass*, 530.
40. Blassingame, Hinks, and McKivigan, *Frederick Douglass Papers*, 565–66.
41. Kerber, *No Constitutional Right to Be Ladies*, 242–43.
42. Quoted in Andrews, *Oxford Frederick Douglass Reader*, 224.
43. McPherson, *Negro's Civil War*, 101–12.
44. Quoted in Foner, *Story of American Freedom*, 37.
45. Redkey, "Black Chaplains in the Union Army," 334.
46. *Christian Recorder*, September 17, 1864.
47. Garland H. White to E. M. Stanton, May 7, 1862, W-561 1862, Letters Received, Records of the Office of the Secretary of War.
48. Blassingame, "Negro Chaplains in the Civil War," 23–24.
49. State of Indiana, Office of the Adjutant General, *Report of the Adjutant General of the State of Indiana, 1861–1865*, vol. 1, 79–81. The adjutant general continued: "The state of public feeling in the West was not altogether favorable to the employment of that class of [black] persons as soldiers . . . to those citizens whose political importance has always been subservient to the slavepowers."
50. Smith, "Camp-in-the-Field, VA," to "My Dear Parents," February 22, 1865, Smith Family Papers.
51. Garland H. White to Secretary Stanton, May 18, 1864. White, Compiled Service Record, Records of the Adjutant General's Office.

52. *Indianapolis Daily Journal*, December 12, 1863. In 1865, Indianapolis's leaders offered $375 each to black men who volunteered on behalf of the city.

53. Garland White, Terra [*sic*] Haute, to Governor Oliver Morton, Indianapolis, November 28, 1863, Anna Wright Papers.

54. *Indianapolis Daily State Sentinel*, December 9, 1864.

55. Salmon Hall Papers, #S572.

56. Like so many men of his day, Richard Yates opposed the spread of slavery into the West, but his desire to see the destruction of slavery in the United States was only lukewarm. See Krenkel, *Richard Yates*, 97–108.

57. *Indianapolis Daily Journal* February 27, 1863.

58. Line officers were commissioned to lead combat units. One hundred African American men received commissions as officers. Of that group, eight were surgeons commissioned as majors. Twenty-one black men were awarded the Congressional Medal of Honor. On honors that black soldiers received, see Trudeau, *Like Men of War*, 455–69.

59. *Christian Recorder*, May 21, 1864.

60. James C. Vanderbilt, Oxford, Mississippi, to "Mother," December 15, 1862, James C. Vanderbilt Letters. Vanderbilt was a member of Company K of the Twenty-Third Indiana Volunteer Infantry Regiment.

61. "Soldiers of a Massachusetts Black Regiment to the President," Folly Island, South Carolina, to President Abraham Lincoln, July 16, 1864. Quoted in Berlin, Reidy, and Rowland, *Freedom*, 401.

62. National Archives and Records Service, *Negro in the Military Service of the United States, 1639–1886*, roll 2, 1818. Delany wrote this letter from Chicago, Illinois, on December 15, 1863, to the Honorable Secretary of War Stanton. For a discussion of Delany's career, see Ullman, *Martin Delany*.

63. Thomas is credited with adding seventy-six thousand men (white and black) to the Union army during his career. See United States War Department, *War of the Rebellion Official Records*, ser. 3, vol. 3, 100–101.

64. Quoted in French, *Life, Speeches, State Papers and Public Services of Governor Oliver P. Morton*, 352.

65. Westwood, *Black Troops, White Commanders, and Freedmen*.

66. Berry, *Military Necessity and Civil Rights Policy*, 43–52.

67. Blight, "Meaning or the Fight," 145.

68. Berry, *Military Necessity and Civil Rights Policy*.

69. National Archives and Records Service, *Negro in the Military Service of the United States, 1639–1886*, roll 3, 2352. Apparently taken from the *Congressional Globe*, no date or speaker given.

70. Frederick Douglass, "Negroes and the National War Effort" (address, Philadelphia, Pennsylvania, July 6, 1863); quoted Blassingame, Hinks, and McKivigan, *Frederick Douglass Papers*, 592–95.

71. For Illinois, see Hicken, *Illinois in the Civil War*, 136. For Indiana, see Thornbrough, *Indiana in the Civil War Era*, 139.
72. Hicken, *Illinois in the Civil War*, 137–38.
73. *Christian Recorder*, March 29, 1864.
74. Spotswood Rice to Kittey Diggs, September 3, 1864, enclosed in F. W. Diggs to Genl. Rosecrans, September 10, 1864, Letters Received, Records of the United States Army Continental Commands.
75. William J. Brown to the Secretary of War, April 27, 1864, Letters Received, Colored Troops Division.
76. Redkey, *Grand Army of Black Men*, 235. This "Massachusetts Soldier" wrote his letter from Morris Island, South Carolina, in December 1863, to Theodore Tilton of the *Boston Journal*.
77. Roediger, *Wages of Whiteness*, 55.
78. Nelson, *National Manhood*, xi.
79. Horton, "Freedom's Yoke."
80. Quoted in Miller, "Garland H. White," 209.
81. Quoted in Adams, *On the Altar of Freedom*, 119.
82. *Indianapolis Daily Journal*, October 2, 1865.

5. Black Women's Wartime Political Culture

1. See, generally, Carby, "On the Threshold of Woman's Era"; Hall, "Mind That Burns in Each Body"; Hine, "Rape and the Inner Lives of Black Women in the Middle West."
2. Berlin, Reidy, and Rowland, *Freedom*, 29–32.
3. On nation building and the role of work, see Jones, *Labor of Love, Labor of Sorrow*.
4. Sterling, *We Are Your Sisters*, 3–23; Yellin and Van Horne, *Abolitionist Sisterhood*, 91–158.
5. Hunter, *Bound in Wedlock*; Berlin and Rowland, *Families and Freedom*, 88–93.
6. Stevenson, "Us Never Had No Big Funerals or Weddin's on de Place."
7. James Fry to Lorenzo Thomas, April 9, 1865, Letters of Lorenzo Thomas.
8. Lorenzo Thomas to Secretary Stanton, Final Report, Louisville, Kentucky, October 3, 1865, Letters of Lorenzo Thomas. See also Meier, "Lorenzo Thomas and the Recruitment of Blacks in the Mississippi Valley."
9. The 1860 census reported 3,819 "free colored females" in Illinois and 5,637 in Indiana. (That includes female children.) The number of free black males from ages one to nineteen was 3,076 in Indiana and 276 in Illinois. U.S. Bureau of the Census, 1860 U.S. Census, Population Schedule.
10. H. G. Mosee, according to the 1860 census, was a twenty-three-year-old porter who had been born in Kentucky.

11. H. G. Mosee to Secretary Stanton, New Albany, Indiana, April 1, 1865, M-248 1865, Letters Received, Colored Troops Division.

12. Taylor, *Black Woman's Civil War Memoirs.*

13. Berlin and Rowland, *Families and Freedom*, 3.

14. Mrs. John W. Wilson to Hon. E. M. Stanton, Detroit, Michigan, May 27, 1865, Letters Received, Colored Troops Division.

15. Willie Ann Grey to Philip Grey, April 7, 1866, Registered Letters Received, ser. 4239, Richmond, VA, Supt. 3rd District, Bureau of Refugees, Freedmen, and Abandoned Lands, National Archives and Records Administration. Churches often took up collections for widows' families. In 1862, for instance, the Indiana Conference of the AME Church collected $412.13 for "the support of widows." *Christian Recorder*, August 30, 1862.

16. Rosanna Henson to Abraham Lincoln, Mt. Holly, New Jersey, 11 July 1864, Letters Received, Records of the Paymaster General.

17. Rachel Ann Wicker to Mr. President Andrew, Miami, Ohio, September 12, 1864, Letters Received, Colored Troops Division. Governor Andrew of Massachusetts forwarded the letter to Lincoln, assuming that Wicker had confused the president and the governor.

18. Jane Welcome to Abraham Lincoln, Carlisle, Pennsylvania, November 21, 1864, Letters Received, Colored Troops Division.

19. John Turner to Michigan Militia Agent, Alexandria, Virginia, July 20, 1865, Letters Received, Colored Troops Division. Turner stated that he enlisted in Detroit, Michigan, but he did not mention his state of residence or birth.

20. Ann to My Dear Husband, Paris, Missouri, January 19, 1864, enclosed in letter from Brig. Genl. William A. Pile to Maj. O. D. Greene, February 11, 1864, Letters Received, Records of the United States Army Continental Commands.

21. George G. Freeman to Chief Justice of the United States Supreme Court, "General Hospital," Beaufort, South Carolina, June 25, 1865, Letters Received, Colored Troops Division.

22. Warren D. Hamelton to the Secretary of War, Fort Jefferson, Tortugas, Florida, May 1865, Letters Received, Colored Troops Division.

23. Berlin, Fields, and Reidy, "Fighting on Two Fronts."

24. Lucy Bailey to the Secretary of War, Detroit, Michigan, May 11, 1865, Letters Received, Colored Troops Division.

25. Berlin, Durrill, Miller, Rowland, and Schwalm, "To Canvass the Nation."

26. Hannah Johnson to President Lincoln, Buffalo, New York, July 31, 1863, Letters Received, Colored Troops Division.

27. Eberhart, "Reminiscences of the Civil War."

28. Catherine Massey to the Secretary of War, Hampton, Fortress Monroe, Virginia, July 10, 1865, Letters Received, Colored Troops Division.

29. Hine and Thompson, *Shining Thread of Hope*, 126.

30. Fahs, "Feminized Civil War," 1461.

31. *Christian Recorder*, March 12, 1964.

32. Carlson, "Black Community in the Rural North," 13.

33. Peterson, *"Doers of the Word,"* 8–9.

34. Jones, *Labor of Love*, 284.

35. Taylor, *Race and the City*.

36. McCaul, *Black Struggle for Public Schooling in Nineteenth-Century Illinois*, 18–19.

37. Fisher, "Negro Churches," 553.

38. Washington, *Frustrated Fellowship*, 28–29.

39. Washington, *Frustrated Fellowship*, 30. See also Fitts, *History of Black Baptists*, 65–66.

40. Brand, *Illinois Baptists: A History*, 142. See also George, "Widening the Circle," 79–82.

41. Washington, *Frustrated Fellowship*, 30–31.

42. Magee, *Night of Affliction and Morning of Recovery*.

43. Jones, *All Bound Up Together*, 166–77.

44. Quoted in Blanchard, *Discovery and Conquests of the North-West*, 297.

45. Chapman, *That Men Know So Little of Men*, 7–10.

46. Quoted in Blanchard, *Discovery and Conquests of the North-West*, 299–300.

47. Quoted in Blanchard, *Discovery and Conquests of the North-West*, 312.

48. Quoted in Blanchard, *Discovery and Conquests of the North-West*, 312.

49. *Christian Recorder*, September 14, 1861.

50. Sattira "Sattie" Douglas was married to H. Ford Douglas. She used her nickname when she wrote letters, but her contemporaries also referred to her as "Satie" or "Statie."

51. *Christian Recorder*, October 24, 1863.

52. Hine, "Lifting the Veil, Shattering the Silence," 228.

53. *Christian Recorder*, April 16, 1864.

54. Yee, *Black Women Abolitionists*, 74.

55. *Christian Recorder*, June 8, 1861.

56. *Provincial Freeman*, September 9, 1854.

57. *Christian Recorder*, November 21, 1863.

58. *Christian Recorder*, March 12, 1864.

59. *Christian Recorder*, December 12, 1863.

60. Downs, *Sick from Freedom*.

61. Women's Central Association of Relief, *Report Concerning the W.C.A.R.*, 6–9. Between fifty and sixty white women attended the meeting.

62. United States Sanitary Commission, *Documents of the United States Sanitary Commission, 1861–1866*, doc. no. 32.

63. Attie, "Warwork and the Crisis of Domesticity in the North," 248.

64. Schultz, *Women at the Front*.

65. Peterson, "United States Sanitary Commission"; Parrish, "Western Sanitary Commission."
66. Attie, *Patriotic Toil*, 93.
67. *Christian Recorder*, December 12, 1863.
68. Quoted in Parsons, *Memoir of Emily Elizabeth Parsons*, 138–39.
69. Quinn Chapel A.M.E. Church Papers, 1847–1967.
70. Williams, *Christian Recorder*, 103–6, 119–24.
71. *Christian Recorder*, July 30, 1864.
72. *Christian Recorder*, December 17, 1864.
73. *Christian Recorder*, July 30, 1864.
74. *Christian Recorder*, June 3, 1865.
75. *Christian Recorder*, June 24, 1865.
76. United States Christian Commission, Minutes of the Executive Committee. See also "Christian Commission, including Letters Sent to the Central Office, 1862–1865 (15 vols.)" and "Record of Ladies Auxiliary Christian Commissions" (record groups 94.49 and 94.59, respectively).
77. *Christian Recorder*, November 7, 1863.
78. *Christian Recorder*, December 31, 1864.
79. *Christian Recorder*, January 16, 1864.
80. *Christian Recorder*, March 12, 1864.
81. *Christian Recorder*, October 3, 1863.
82. *Christian Recorder*, November 21, 1863.
83. There is also some indication that Chicago's black women activists formed another smaller group called the Ladies Loyal League.
84. Venet, "Emergence of a Suffragist."
85. *Christian Recorder*, October 29, 1863.
86. *Chicago Tribune*, June 15, 1865.
87. *Christian Recorder*, March 22, 1865.
88. *Christian Recorder*, May 3, 1865.
89. Giesberg, *Civil War Sisterhood*, 49–52.
90. Dedmon, *Fabulous Chicago*.
91. *New York Times*, July 15, 1865.
92. Ann P. Hosmer Papers.
93. *Christian Recorder*, December 17, 1864.
94. *Christian Recorder*, December 17, 1864.
95. Department of War, *Order of the Secretary of War*.
96. Newberry, *U.S. Sanitary Commission in the Valley of the Mississippi*.
97. On the illusionary trope of "separate spheres," see Kerber, "Separate Spheres, Female Worlds, Woman's Place."
98. *Christian Recorder*, December 12, 1863.
99. *Chicago Tribune*, August 24, 1841.

100. Yee, *Black Women Abolitionists*, 46–52.
101. Griffler, *Front Line of Freedom*, 83, 114.
102. Quoted in Blanchard, *Discovery and Conquests of the North-West*, 300.
103. Jones, *Black Laws of Illinois*, 3.
104. Jones, "Second Proclamation to the Free People of Color, Chicago."
105. Brown, "Negotiating and Transforming the Public Sphere," 124. Brown makes a distinction between the "external political arena" and the "internal community institutions" of the black community in post-emancipation Richmond, Virginia.

Conclusion

1. *Harpel's Scrapbook*, "Obituaries, up to 1884: John Jones."
2. Thornbrough, *Negro in Indiana*, 235.
3. Lindsey, *Colored No More*, 9.
4. Peterson, *"Doers of the Word,"* 8–9.
5. Hendricks, *Gender, Race, and Politics in the Midwest*.
6. Berkeley, "Colored Ladies Also Contributed," 186.
7. Cott, *Bonds of Womanhood*; Welter, "Cult of True Womanhood."
8. Stetson, "Black Feminism in Indiana," 295.

Bibliography

Newspapers

Anti-Slavery Bugle
Belleville Advocate
Chicago Daily Journal
Chicago Defender
Chicago Democrat
Chicago Tribune
Christian Recorder
Daily Pantagraph
Douglass' Monthly
Fort Wayne Daily Gazette
Frederick Douglass' Paper
Galesburg Republican
Harpel's Scrapbook
Harper's Weekly
Illinois State Journal
Illinois State Register
Indiana Free Democrat
Indianapolis Daily Journal
Indianapolis Daily State Sentinel
Liberator
Louisville Daily Courier
Marion County Clarion
New Albany Daily Ledger
New York Times
Pantagraph
Provincial Freeman
Rocky Mountain News
Voice of the Fair
Voice of the Fugitive
Weekly Chicago Democrat
Weekly Pantagraph
Western Citizen

Primary Sources

An Act to Prevent the Immigration of Free Negroes into the State. *Statutes of Illinois*, 1853.

Annual Report of the Colored Vigilant Committee of Detroit. (Delivered at Detroit City Hall, Michigan, 10 January 1843). Manuscripts Division, Charles H. Wright Museum of African American History, Detroit, Michigan.

Basler, Roy P. ed. *The Collected Works of Abraham Lincoln.* 9 vols. New Brunswick, NJ: Rutgers University Press, 1953–1955.

Bell, Howard Holman, ed. *Minutes of the Proceedings of the National Negro Conventions, 1830–1864.* New York: Arno 1969.

Bibb, Henry. *The Narrative of the Life of Henry Bibb, an American Slave.* 1850. Reprint, Miami: Mnemosyne, 1969.

Blanchard, Rufus. *Discovery and Conquests of the North-West, with a History of Chicago, 1898–1900.* 2 vols. Wheaton, IL: published by the author, 1900.

Blassingame, John W., Peter P. Hinks, and John R. McKivigan, eds. *The Frederick Douglass Papers.* Ser. 1, *Speeches, Debates, and Interviews.* New Haven: Yale University Press, 1985.

Brand, Edward P. *Illinois Baptists: A History.* Bloomington, IL: Pantagraph, 1930. Internet Archive. https://archive.org/details/illinoisbaptists00bran/page/n13/mode/2up.

Brown, William Wells. *The Negro in the American Rebellion, His Heroism, and His Fidelity.* Boston: Lee & Shepard, 1867.

Broyles, Moses. *The History of the Second Baptist Church.* Indianapolis: Printing and Publishing House, 1876.

City Directory, Rockford, Illinois, 1858. Illinois State Historical Library, Springfield, Illinois.

Coffin, Levi. *Reminiscences of Levi Coffin, the Reputed President of the Underground Railroad.* Cincinnati: Robert Clarke, 1880.

Cole, A. C., ed. *The Constitutional Debates of 1847.* Springfield: Illinois State Historical Library, 1919.

Constitution of the State of Illinois, 1818.

Constitution of the State of Indiana, 1816.

Davis, Elizabeth Lindsay. *The Story of the Illinois Federation of Colored Women's Clubs, 1900–1922.* Chicago: n.p., 1922.

Delany, Martin. *The Condition, Elevation, and Emigration of the Colored People of the United States.* 1852. Reprint, New York: Arno Press, 1968.

Department of War. *Order of the Secretary of War, Approved by the President, Appointing the Sanitary Commission,* June 9, 1861, National Archives and Records Administration, Washington, DC.

Eastman, Zebina. *The Black Code of Illinois.* [Chicago, 1883?].

———. Collection. Manuscripts Division, Chicago History Museum Chicago, Illinois.

———. "History of the Anti-slavery Agitation, and the Growth of the Liberty and Republican Parties in the State of Illinois." In *Discovery and Conquests of the North-West, with a History of Chicago,* by Rufus Blanchard. 2 vols. Wheaton, IL: published by the author, 1900.

Eberhart, Lovicy Ann. "Reminiscences of the Civil War, 1861–1865." Unpublished manuscript. Manuscripts Division, Lincoln Presidential Library, Springfield, Illinois.

Edwards, George. Papers. Illinois Historical Society Library, Springfield, Illinois.

Foner, Philip S., ed. *Frederick Douglass: Selected Speeches and Writings.* Chicago: Lawrence Hill Books, 1950.

Foner, Philip S., and George E. Walker, eds. *Proceedings of the Black State Conventions, 1840–1865.* Vol. 2. Philadelphia: Temple University Press, 1980.

Forman, J. G. *The Western Sanitary Commission; A Sketch of Its Origins, History, Labors for the Sick and Wounded of the Western Armies and Aid Given to Freedmen and Union Refugees, with Incidents of Hospital Life.* St. Louis: R. P. Studley & Company, 1864.

French, William M., ed. *Life, Speeches, State Papers and Public Services of Governor Oliver P. Morton.* Cincinnati: Moore, Wilstach & Baldwin, 1864.

Goebes, Alan. *History of the Second Baptist Church.* 1889. Special Collections, Indiana Historical Society, Indianapolis, Indiana.

Hall, Salmon. Papers. Manuscript Section, Indiana State Library, Indianapolis, Indiana.

Hamilton, Allen. Papers. Manuscript Section, Indiana State Library.

History of Gallatin, Saline, Hamilton, Franklin and Williamson Counties, Illinois. Chicago: Goodspeed Publishing, 1887. Manuscripts Division, Chicago History Museum.

Holcombe, John W., and Hubert M. Skinner. *Life and Public Services of Thomas A. Hendricks, with Selected Speeches and Writings.* Indianapolis, 1886.

Hosmer, Ann P. Papers. Manuscript Division, Chicago History Museum.

Indiana House Journal, 1829–1830. Indianapolis: Smith and Bolton, 1829.

Jones, John. *The Black Laws of Illinois and a Few Reasons Why They Should Be Repealed.* Chicago: Tribute Book and Job Office, 1864.

———. Collection. Chicago History Museum.

———. "Second Proclamation to the Free People of Color, Chicago, 1862." John Jones Collection, Chicago History Museum.

Jones, Mary Richardson. "An Interview with Mary Jones." By Rufus Blanchard. In *Discovery and Conquests of the North-West, with a History of Chicago, 1898–1900,* by Rufus Blanchard. 2 vols. Wheaton, IL: published by the author, 1900.

Journal of the Convention of the People of the State of Indiana to Amend the Constitution, Assembled at Indianapolis, October, 1850. Fort Wayne, IN: Fort Wayne Printing, 1936. State Library of Des Moines, Des Moines, Iowa.

Journal of the Senate of the State of Indiana, 1863, during the Forty-Third Session of the General Assembly. Indianapolis: Joseph J. Bingham, State Printer, 1863.

The Laws of Indiana Territory, 1853. Springfield, IL: Jefferson Printing and Stationery, 1931. Illinois State Historical Library.

Letters of Lorenzo Thomas, General's Papers and Books. Record Group 94, Records of the Adjutant General's Office, 1780s–1917. National Archives and Records Administration.

Letters Received, Colored Troops Division. Ser. 360, Record Group 94. National Archives and Records Administration.

Letters Received, Records of the Office of the Secretary of War. Record Group 107 [L-160]. National Archives and Records Administration.

Letters Received, Records of the Paymaster General. Ser. 7, Record Group 99. National Archives and Records Administration.

Letters Received, Records of the United States Army Continental Commands, 1821–1920, Department of the Missouri. Ser. 2593, Record Group 393. National Archives and Records Administration.

Lucas, Sarah Ann. "Proof of Freedom," Miscellaneous Court Records of Floyd County, Indiana, Book of Indentures. Stuart B. Wrege Indiana History Room, New Albany–Floyd County Public Library.

Lusk, D. W. *Eighty Years of Illinois: Politics and Politicians, Anecdotes and Incidents; A Succinct History of the State, 1809–1889.* Springfield, 1889.

Magee, Henry. *Night of Affliction and Morning of Recovery: An Autobiography.* Cincinnati: published by the author, 1873. Illinois State Library, Springfield, Illinois.

Mann, Charles. *The Chicago Common Council and the Fugitive Slave Law of 1850; An Address Read before the Chicago Historical Society, January 29th, 1903.* Chicago: Chicago Historical Society, n.d., 55–86.

Miller, Stephen. Collection. Indiana Division, Indiana State Library.

Minutes of the Annual Session of the Wood River Baptist Sunday School Convention and Its Auxiliaries. Chicago: Baptist Observer, 1842. Church History Documents Collection, University of Chicago Library, Chicago, Illinois.

Minutes of the Committee of the Indiana Yearly Meeting of Friends on the Concerns of People of Color. 1824. Records of the Economy Anti-Slavery Society, Indiana Historical Society.

Minutes of the Henry County Female Anti-Slavery Society. Indiana Division, Indiana State Library.

"Minutes of the Illinois Baptist State Convention." 1848. Edited by Francis Philbrick. University of Missouri, St. Louis.

"Mount Zion Baptist Church Souvenir Program: Indianapolis, Indiana, Sunday, September 29, 1968." Manuscripts Division, Indiana Historical Society.

National Archives and Records Service, *The Negro in the Military Service of the United States, 1639–1886.* Washington, DC: General Services Administration, 1973. Microfilm.

"Negro in Illinois Papers." Illinois Writers Project. Vivian G. Harsh Research Collection of Afro-American History and Literature, Carter G. Woodson Regional Library, Chicago Public Library.

Newberry, J. S. *The U.S. Sanitary Commission in the Valley of the Mississippi during the War of the Rebellion, 1861–1866.* Cleveland, OH: Fairbanks & Benedict, 1871.

"Obituary: Death of Ex-County Commissioner John Jones." *Chicago Tribune,* May 22, 1879.

Parsons, Theophilus, ed. *Memoir of Emily Elizabeth Parsons.* Boston: Little, Brown, 1880.

Payne, Daniel Alexander. *History of the African Methodist Episcopal Church.* Nashville: Publishing House of the A.M.E. Church Sunday-School Union, 1891. Reprint, Arno, 1969.

Petersburg Women's Club, "A History of Pike County." Pike County Historical Material. N.d. Manuscripts Section, Indiana State Library.

Petition of 52 Colored Citizens of Illinois, 18th General Assembly, 1st Session, 1853. Folder 820. Illinois State Archives, Springfield, Illinois.

Proceedings of the Colored National Convention Held in Rochester, July 1853. Rochester, NY: 1853.

Proceedings of the Illinois Anti-Slavery Convention: Held at Upper Alton on the Twenty-Sixth, Twenty-Seventh, and Twenty-Eighth, October 1837. Alton, IL: Parks and Breath, 1838. Lincoln Collection, Special Collections, University of Chicago Library.

Proceedings of the State Convention of Colored Citizens of the State of Illinois, Held in the City of Alton, November 13th, 14th, and 15th, 1856. Chicago: Hays and Thompson, 1856.

Quinn Chapel A.M.E. Church. Papers, 1847–1967. Manuscripts Division, Chicago History Museum.

Reconstruction and Negro Suffrage, Indiana and the War. Vol. 2, no. 15. Adjutant General's Office. Indiana State Library.

Regional History Pamphlet Collection, Vincennes University, Vincennes, Indiana.

Registered Letters Received, ser. 4239, Richmond VA Supt. 3rd District. Bureau of Refugees, Freedmen, and Abandoned Lands, National Archives and Records Administration.

Report of the Debates and Proceedings of the Convention for the Revision of the Constitution of the State of Indiana, 1850–1851. Indianapolis: W. B. Burford, 1935. Indiana State Library.

Report of the Debates and Proceedings of the Convention for the Revision of the Constitution of the State of Indiana. Indianapolis: A. H. Brown, 1850. Indiana State Library.

Repository of Religion and Literature and of Science and Art. Indianapolis: Published for the Literary Societies under the Baltimore, Indiana, and Missouri Conferences of the African Methodist Episcopal Church. Vol. 3 (1863–1864). Microfilm. Indiana Division, Indiana State Library.

Rollin, Frank A. *Life and Public Studies of Martin R. Delany: Sub-assistant Commissioner Bureau Relief of Refugees, Freedmen [. . .] and Late Major 104th U.S. Colored Troops.* Boston: Lee and Shepard, 1868.

Shadd Cary, Mary Ann. "Speeches." Black Abolitionist Archives, University of Detroit Mercy, Detroit, Michigan.

Siebert, William H. *The Underground Railroad from Slavery to Freedom.* New York, 1898.

Smith Family Papers. Manuscript Division, Indiana Historical Society.

South Cavalry Baptist Church Centennial Souvenir Booklet: God's Lighthouse for All Ages—a Century with the Lord, 1875–1975. Manuscript Division, Indiana Historical Society.

Souvenir Program: "The Sixty-Fifth Anniversary of the Olivet Baptist Church, 27th and Dearborn Streets, Sunday, August 15th, 1915." Manuscripts Division, Chicago History Museum.

State of Indiana, Office of the Adjutant General. *Report of the Adjutant General of the State of Indiana, 1861–1865, Containing Indiana in the War of the Rebellion and Statistics and Documents.* 7 vols. Indianapolis, Indiana.

Taylor, Susie King. *A Black Woman's Civil War Memoirs.* Edited by Patricia W. Romero. 1902. Reprint, New York: Marcus Weiner, 1988.

Thornbrough, Gayle, and Dorothy Riker, eds. *Journals of the General Assembly, 1805–1815.* Vol. 2. Indianapolis: Indiana Historical Collections, 1950. Manuscript Division, Indiana State Library.

Tucker, Ebenezer. *History of Randolph County, Indiana.* Chicago: 1882.

United States Bureau of the Census. 1840. Sixth Census of Population, States of Illinois and Indiana. Digital Images. Retrieved from *Historical Census Browser, University of Virginia Library,* 2015.

United States Bureau of the Census. 1850. Seventh Census of Population, State of Illinois. Digital Images. Retrieved from *Historical Census Browser, University of Virginia Library,* 2015.

United States Bureau of the Census. 1860. Eighth Census of Population, States of Illinois and Indiana. Digital Images. Retrieved from *Historical Census Browser, University of Virginia Library,* 2015.

United States Bureau of the Census. 1870. Ninth Census of Population, State of Illinois. Digital Images. Retrieved from *Historical Census Browser, University of Virginia Library,* 2015.

United States Christian Commission. Minutes of the Executive Committee, 1861–1865. Record Group 94.51, National Archives and Records Administration.

United States Sanitary Commission. *Documents of the United States Sanitary Commission, 1861–1866.* 3 vols. New York: Government Printing Office, 1866–1871.

United States Sanitary Commission. Records. Special Collections Division, New York Public Library, New York, New York.

United States War Department. *The War of the Rebellion: A Compilation of the Official Records of the Union and Confederate Armies.* 128 Vols. Washington, DC: Government Printing Office, 1880–1901.

Vanderbilt, James C. Letters. Indiana State Library.

Votaw, Anna M. "Andrew Hampton, Pioneer Nurseryman of Indiana." In *Transactions for the Indiana Horticultural Society for the Year 1908*, 270–78. Indianapolis: Wm. B. Burford, 1909.

Weaver, Elisha. "Knowledge." *Repository of Religion and Literature and of Science and Art*. Vol. 1. 1858.

White, Garland A. Compiled Service Record, Records of the Adjutant General's Office, Record Group 94, National Archives and Records Administration.

Women's Central Association of Relief. *Report Concerning the W.C.A.R.* New York: William C. Bryant, 1861.

Woodward v. the State of Indiana (1855). Supreme Court Papers, No. 879. Box 242. Indiana State Library.

Wright, Anna. Papers. Indiana State Library.

Secondary Sources

Adams, Catherine, and Elizabeth H. Peck. *Love of Freedom: Black Women in Colonial and Revolutionary New England*. New York: Oxford University Press. 2010.

Adams, Virginia Matzke, ed. *On the Altar of Freedom: A Black Soldier's Civil War Letters from the Front—Corporal James Henry Gooding*. Amherst: University of Massachusetts Press, 1991.

Adeleke, Tunde. *UnAfrican Americans: Nineteenth-Century Black Nationalists and the Civilizing Mission*. Lexington: University Press of Kentucky, 1998.

Aldrich, O. W. "Slavery or Involuntary Servitude in Illinois prior to and after Its Admission as a State." *Journal of the Illinois State Historical Society* 9 (July 1916): 117–32.

Andrews, William L., ed. *The Oxford Frederick Douglass Reader*. New York: Oxford University Press, 1996.

Aptheker, Herbert. "The Negro in the Union Navy." *Journal of Negro History* 32 (April 1947): 169–200.

Attie, Jeannie. *Patriotic Toil: Northern Women and the American Civil War*. Ithaca, NY: Cornell University Press, 1998.

———. "Warwork and the Crisis of Domesticity in the North." In *Divided Houses: Gender and the Civil War*, edited by Catherine Clinton and Nina Silber, 247–59. New York: Oxford University Press, 1992.

Auer, Jeffery, ed. *Antislavery and Disunion, 1858–1861*. New York: Harper & Row, 1963.

Baker, Paula. "The Domestication of Politics: Women and American Political Society, 1780–1920." *American Historical Review* 89 (June 1984): 620–47.

Banks, William L. *A History of Black Baptists in the United States*. Haverford, PA: Infinity, 2005.

Bell, Howard Holman. "The National Negro Convention, 1848." *Ohio Historical Quarterly* 68 (October): 357–68.

———. "Some Reform Interests of the Negro during the 1850s as Reflected in State Conventions." *Phylon* 21 (Summer 1960): 173–82.

Bell, Karen Cook. "Self-Emancipating Women, Civil War, and the Union Army in Southern Louisiana and Lowcountry Georgia, 1861–1865." *Journal of African American History* 101 (Winter–Spring 2016): 1–22.

Bensel, Richard F. *Yankee Leviathan: The Origins of the Central State Authority, 1859–1877.* New York: Cambridge University Press, 1990.

Berkeley, Kathleen C. "'Colored Ladies Also Contributed': Black Women's Activities from Benevolence to Social Welfare, 1866–1896." In *The Web of Southern Social Relations: Women, Family, and Education*, edited by Walter J. Fraser Jr., R. Frank Saunders Jr., and Jon L. Wakelyn. Athens: University of Georgia Press, 1985.

———. "'Like a Plague of Locusts': Immigration and Social Change in Memphis, Tennessee, 1850–1896." PhD diss., University of California, Los Angeles, 1980.

———. *The Women's Liberation Movement in America.* Westport, CT: Greenwood, 1999.

Berlin, Ira, Wayne Durrill, Steven F. Miller, Leslie S. Rowland, and Leslie Schwalm. "'To Canvass the Nation': The War for the Union Becomes a War for Freedom." *Prologue: Quarterly of the National Archives* (Winter 1988): 227–47.

Berlin, Ira, Barbara Fields, and Joseph P. Reidy. "Fighting on Two Fronts: The Struggle for Equal Pay." *Prologue: Quarterly of the National Archives* 14 (Fall 1982): 131–39.

Berlin, Ira, Joseph P. Reidy, and Leslie S. Rowland, eds. *Freedom: A Documentary History of Emancipation, 1861–1867.* Ser. 2, *The Black Military Experience.* Cambridge: Cambridge University Press, 1982.

Berlin, Ira, and Leslie S. Rowland, eds. *Families and Freedom: A Documentary History of African-American Kinship in the Civil War Era.* New York: New Press, 1997.

Berry, Mary F. *Military Necessity and Civil Rights Policy: Black Citizenship and the Constitution, 1861–1868.* Port Washington, NY: 1977.

Berwanger, Eugene. *The Frontier against Slavery: Western Anti-Negro Prejudice and the Slavery Extension Controversy.* Champaign: University of Illinois Press, 1971.

———. "Western Prejudice and the Extension of Slavery." *Civil War History* 12 (1966): 197–212.

Bethel, Elizabeth Rauh. *Promiseland: A Century of Life in a Negro Community.* Columbia: University of South Carolina Press, 1997.

Bigham, Darrel E. *We Ask Only a Fair Trial: A History of the Black Community of Evansville, Indiana.* Bloomington: Indiana University Press, 1987.

Billingsley, Andrew. *Mighty like a River: The Black Church and Social Reform.* New York: Oxford University Press, 1999.

Blackett, R. J. H. "'Freeman to the Rescue!' Resistance to the Fugitive Slave Law of 1850." In *Passages to Freedom: The Underground Railroad in History and Memory*, edited by David Blight. Washington, DC: Smithsonian Books in Association with the National Underground Railroad Freedom Center, 2004.

Blackmore, Jacqueline Yvonne. "African-Americans and Race Relations in Gallatin County, Illinois, from the Eighteenth Century to 1870." PhD diss., Northern Illinois University, 1996.

Blassingame, John W. "Negro Chaplains in the Civil War." *Negro History Bulletin* 27 (October 1963): 1–26.

Blight, David W. *Frederick Douglass' Civil War: Keeping Faith in the Jubilee.* Baton Rouge: Louisiana State University Press, 1989.

——. "The Meaning or the Fight: Frederick Douglass and the Memory of the Fifty-Fourth Massachusetts." *Massachusetts Review* (Spring 1995): 144–53.

Blight, David W., and Jim Downs, eds. *Beyond Freedom: Disrupting the History of Emancipation.* Athens: University of Georgia Press, 2017.

Blocker, Jack. *A Little More Freedom: African Americans Enter the Urban Midwest, 1860–1930.* Columbus: Ohio State University Press, 2008.

Blockson, Charles L. *The Underground Railroad: Dramatic Firsthand Accounts of Daring Escapes to Freedom.* New York: Berkeley Books, 1987.

Bond, Beverly. "Every Duty Incumbent upon Them: African-American Women in Nineteenth Century Memphis." In *Trial and Triumph: Essays in Tennessee's African-American History*, edited by Carroll Van West, 203–26. Knoxville: University of Tennessee Press, 2002.

Bontemps, Arna, and Jack Conroy. *They Seek a City.* American Century Series. New York: Hill and Wang, 1945.

Bordewich, Fergus. *Bound for Canaan: The Epic Story of the Underground Railroad: America's First Civil Rights Movement.* New York: HarperCollins, 2006.

Boris, Eileen. "Black and White Activist Women Redefine the 'Political.'" In *Mothers of a New World: Maternalist Politics and the Origins of Welfare States*, edited by Seth Coven and Sonia Michel, 213–45. London: Routledge, 1993.

——. "The Power of Motherhood: Black and White Activist Women Redefine the Political." *Yale Journal of Law and Feminism* 2, no. 1 (1989): 25–50.

Boyd, Melba Joyce. *Discarded Legacy: Politics and Poetics in the Life of Frances E. W. Harper, 1825–1911.* Detroit: Wayne State University Press, 1994.

Brand, Edward P. *History of the Baptists of Illinois*, chapter 42. Scanned and formatted by Jim Duvall for Baptist History Homepage, accessed January 29, 2020, http://baptisthistoryhomepage.com/illinois.baptist.hist.42.html.

Brooks, Walter H. "The Evolution of the Negro Baptist Church." *Journal of Negro History* 7, no. 1 (January 1922): 11–22.

Brown, Elsa Barkley. "Negotiating and Transforming the Public Sphere: African-American Political Life in the Transition from Slavery to Freedom." *Public Culture* 7 (1994): 107–46.

Brown, Kathleen. *Good Wives, Nasty Wenches, and Anxious Patriarchs: Gender, Race, and Power in Colonial Virginia.* Chapel Hill: University of North Carolina Press, 1996.

Brush, Paula Stewart. "The Influence of Social Movements on Articulations of Race and Gender in Black Women's Autobiographies." *Gender and Society* 13, no. 1 (1999): 120–37.

Burin, Eric. *Slavery and the Peculiar Solution: A History of the American Colonization Society.* Gainesville: University Press of Florida, 2005.

Bynum, Victoria Elizabeth. *Unruly Women: The Politics of Social and Sexual Control in the Old South.* Chapel Hill: University of North Carolina Press, 1992.

Cadbury, Henry C. "Negro Membership in the Society of Friends." *Journal of Negro History* 21 (1936): 151–213.

Campbell, James T. *Songs of Zion: The African Methodist Episcopal Church in the United States and South Africa.* New York: Oxford University Press, 1995.

Carby, Hazel V. "'On the Threshold of Woman's Era': Lynching, Empire, and Sexuality in Black Feminist Theory." *Critical Inquiry* 12, no. 1 (1985): 262–77.

Carlson, Shirley Jean Motley. "The Black Community in the Rural North: Pulaski County, Illinois, 1860–1900." PhD diss., Washington University, 1982.

Carnes, Mark. *Secret Ritual and Manhood in Victorian America.* New Haven, CT: Yale University Press, 1989.

Cashin, Joan. "Black Families in the Old Northwest." *Journal of the Early Republic* 15 (Fall 1995): 450–62.

Cayton, Andrew R. L., and Susan E. Grey, eds. *The American Midwest: Essays on Regional History.* Bloomington: Indiana University Press, 2001.

Centennial History of Illinois. Springfield, IL: Centennial Commission, 1920.

Cha-Jua, Sundiata Keita. *America's First Black Town: Brooklyn, Illinois: 1830–1915.* Urbana: University of Illinois Press, 2000.

Chapman, Barbara. *That Men Know So Little of Men: A History of the Negro in Rockford, Illinois, 1834–1973* (Developed by Special Project III, "Service to the Disadvantaged"). Rockford, IL: Rockford Public Library, 1987.

Charles, C. E. "The Economy-Cabin Creek Short Branch and Some of Its Operatives: A Description of One Section of the Underground Railroad System." N.d. Clippings File, Indiana Division, Indiana State Library.

Claeys, Gregory. *Citizens and Saints: Politics and Anti-politics in Early British Socialism.* New York: Cambridge University Press, 2002.

Clegg, Claude A., III. *The Price of Liberty: African Americans and the Making of Liberia.* Chapel Hill: University North Carolina Press, 2004.

Cole, Arthur C. *The Centennial History of Illinois.* Vol. 3, *The Era of the Civil War, 1848–1870.* Springfield: Illinois Centennial Commission, 1919.

Cooper, Zachary. *Black Settlers in Rural Wisconsin.* Madison: Wisconsin State Historical Society, 1977.

Cord, Xenia. "Black Rural Settlements in Indiana before 1860." In *Indiana's African-American Heritage: Essays from Black History News and Notes,* edited by Wilma L. Gibbs, 99–110. Indianapolis: Indiana Historical Society, 1993.

Cott, Nancy F. *The Bonds of Womanhood: "Woman's Sphere" in New England, 1780–1835.* New Haven, CT: Yale University Press, 1997.

Cox, Anna-Lisa. *A Stronger Kinship: One Town's Extraordinary Story of Hope and Faith.* Lincoln: University of Nebraska Press, 2006.

Crenshaw, Gwendolyn. *Bury Me in a Free Land: The Abolitionist Movement in Indiana, 1816–1865.* Indianapolis: Indiana Historical Bureau, 1988.

———. "One Ran to Freedom, Another Caught and Bonded—the Case of Caroline, a Fugitive Slave, and Luther A. Donnell." *Black History News and Notes,* no. 78 (November 1999): 3–5.

Cromie, Robert. *A Short History of Chicago.* San Francisco: Lexikos, 1984.

Curry, Leonard. *The Free Black in Urban America, 1800–1850: The Shadow of the Dream.* Chicago: University of Chicago Press, 1981.

Davidson, John Nelson. *Negro Slavery in Wisconsin and the Underground Railroad.* Milwaukee: Parkman Club Publications, 1897.

Dedmon, Emmett. *Fabulous Chicago: A Great City's History and People.* New York: Random House, 1953.

DePauw, Linda Grant. *Battle Cries and Lullabies: Women in War from Prehistory to the Present.* Norman: University of Oklahoma Press, 2000.

Dickerson, O. M. "The Illinois Constitutional Convention of 1862," *University of Illinois: The University Studies* 1, no. 9 (1905): 15–31.

Dickson, Reverend Moses. *Manual of the International Order of Twelve of Knights and Daughters of Tabor (Containing General Laws, Regulations, Ceremonies, Drill and Landmarks).* Glasgow, MO: Moses Dickson, 1891.

Dixon, Chris. *African America and Haiti: Emigration and Black Nationalism.* London: Greenwood, 2000.

Dobak, William A. *Freedom by the Sword: The U.S. Colored Troops, 1862–1867.* Washington, DC: Center of Military History, 2011.

Downs, Jim. *Sick from Freedom: African American Illness and Suffering during the Civil War and Reconstruction.* Oxford: Oxford University Press, 2012.

Doyle, Don Harrison. *The Social Order of the Frontier Community: Jacksonville, Illinois, 1825–1870.* Urbana: University of Illinois Press, 1983.

Drake, St. Clair. *Churches and Voluntary Organizations in the Chicago Negro Community*. Report. Conducted under the Auspices of the Works Progress Administration, 1940.

Drinkard, Dorothy L. *Illinois Freedom Fighters: A Civil War Saga of the 29th Infantry, United States Colored Troops*. Needham Heights, MA: Simon & Schuster Custom, 1998.

Dunn, Jacob Piatt, ed. *Slavery Petitions and Papers*. Indianapolis: Bowes-Merrill, 1894.

Dunbar, Erica Armstrong. *A Fragile Freedom: African American Women and Emancipation in the Antebellum City*. New Haven, CT: Yale University Press, 2008.

Dykstra, Robert. *Bright Radical Star: Black Freedom and White Supremacy on the Hawkeye Frontier*. Ames: Iowa State University Press, 1997.

Edwards, Laura F. *Gendered Strife and Confusion: The Political Culture of Reconstruction*. Urbana: University of Illinois Press, 1997.

Egerton, Douglas. *Thunder at the Gates: The Black Civil War Regiments That Redeemed America*. New York: Basic Books, 2016.

Eicher, David J. *The Civil War in Books: An Analytical Biography*. Urbana: University of Illinois Press, 1997.

Esarey, Logan. "Internal Improvements in Early Indiana." Indiana Historical Society Publications. Vol. 5, no. 2. Indianapolis: Edward J. Hecker, 1912.

Etcheson, Nicole. *The Emerging Midwest: Upland Southerners and the Political Culture of the Northwest, 1787–1861*. Bloomington: Indiana University Press, 1996.

———. *A Generation at War: The Civil War Era in a Northern Community*. Lawrence: University Press of Kansas, 2011.

Fahs, Alice. "The Feminized Civil War: Gender, Northern Popular Literature, and the Memory of the War, 1861–1900." *Journal of American History* 85, no. 4 (March 1999): 1461–94.

Farnam, Henry W. *Chapters in the History of Social Legislation in the United States to 1860*. Washington, DC: Carnegie Institution, 1938.

Faust, Drew Gilpin. *Mothers of Invention: Women of the Slaveholding South in the American Civil War*. Chapel Hill: University of North Carolina Press, 1996.

———. *This Republic of Suffering: Death and the American Civil War*. New York: Alfred A. Knopf, 2008.

Federal Writers' Project of the Works Project Administration for the State of Illinois. *Illinois: A Descriptive and Historical Guide*. Chicago: A. C. McClurg, 1939.

Fehrenbacher, Don E. *Sectional Crises and Southern Constitutionalism*. Baton Rouge: Louisiana State University Press, 1995.

———. *Slavery, Law, and Politics: The Dred Scott Case in Historical Perspective*. New York: Oxford University Press, 1981.

Finkelman, Paul. "Evading the Ordinance: The Persistence of Bondage in Indiana and Illinois." Chap. 3 in *Slavery and the Founders: Race and Liberty in the Age of Jefferson*. Armonk, NY: M. E. Sharpe, 2001.

———. "The Northwest Ordinance: A Constitution for an Empire of Liberty." In *Pathways to the Old Northwest: An Observance of the Bicentennial of the Northwest Ordinance; Proceedings of a Conference Held at Franklin College of Indiana, July 10–11, 1987*, 1–18. Indianapolis: Indiana Historical Society, 1987.

———. "Slavery and the Northwest Ordinance: A Study in Ambiguity." *Journal of the Early Republic* 6 (Winter 1986): 342–70.

Fisher, Miles Mark. "The History of the Olivet Baptist Church of Chicago." PhD diss., University of Chicago, 1922.

———. "Negro Churches in Illinois: A Fragmentary History with Emphasis on Chicago." *Journal of the Illinois State Historical Society* 56 (Autumn 1963): 552–69.

Fitts, Leroy. *A History of Black Baptists*. Nashville: Broadman, 1985.

Foner, Eric. *Free Soil, Free Labor, Free Men: The Ideology of the Republican War before the Civil War*. New York: Oxford University Press, 1970.

———. *Reconstruction: America's Unfinished Revolution, 1863–1877*. New York: Harper & Row, 1988.

———. *The Story of American Freedom*. New York: W. W. Norton, 1998.

Foner, Jack D. *Blacks and the Military in American History: A New Perspective*. New York: Praeger, 1974.

Fought, Leigh. *Women in the World of Frederick Douglass*. New York: Oxford University Press, 2017.

Frankel, Noralee. *Freedom's Women: Black Women and Families in Civil War Era Mississippi*. Bloomington: Indiana University Press, 1999.

Frazier, E. Franklin. *The Negro Family in Chicago*. Chicago: University of Chicago Press, 1932.

Frederickson, George M. *The Black Image in the White Mind: The Debate on Afro-African Character and Destiny, 1817–1914*. Middletown, CT: Wesleyan Press, 1987.

Gaines, Kevin K. *Uplifting the Race: Black Leadership, Politics, and Culture in the Twentieth Century*. Chapel Hill: University of North Carolina Press, 1996.

Giddings, Paula J. *When and Where I Enter: The Impact of Black Women on Race and Sex in* in America. New York: W. Morrow, 1984.

Giesberg, Judith Ann. *Army at Home: Women and the Civil War on the Northern Home Front*. Chapel Hill: University of North Carolina Press, 2009.

———. *Civil War Sisterhood: The U.S. Sanitary Commission and Women's Politics in Transition*. Boston: Northeastern University Press, 2000.

George, Carol V. R. *Segregated Sabbaths: Richard Allen and the Emergence of Independent Black Churches, 1760–1840*. New York: Oxford University Press, 1973.

———. "Widening the Circle: The Black Church and the Abolitionist Crusade, 1830–1860." In *African-American Religion: Interpretive Essays in History and*

Culture, edited by Timothy E. Fulop and Albert J. Raboteau, 153–76. New York: Routledge, 1997.

Gertz, Elmer. "The Black Laws of Illinois." *Journal of the Illinois State Historical Society* 56 (Autumn 1963): 454–73.

Gillespie, J. "Settlement in Illinois." In *Discovery and Conquests of the North-West with the History of Chicago*, by Rufus Blanchard. Wheaton, IL: published by the author, 1900.

Ginzberg, Lori. *Untidy Origins: A Story of Women's Rights in Antebellum New York*. Chapel Hill: University of North Carolina Press, 2005.

———. *Women and the Work of Benevolence: Morality, Politics, and Class in the Nineteenth-Century United States*. New Haven: Yale University Press, 1990.

Glatthaar Joseph T. *Forged in Battle: The Civil War Alliance of Black Soldiers and White Officers*. New York: Free Press, 1990.

Gliozzo, Charles A. "John Jones: A Study of a Black Chicagoan." *Illinois Historical Journal* 80 (Autumn 1987): 177–88.

———. "John Jones and the Black Convention Movement, 1848–1856." *Journal of Black Studies* 3 (1972): 227–36.

Glymph, Thaviola. "Black Women and Children in the Civil War: Archive Notes." In *Beyond Freedom: Disrupting the History of Emancipation*, edited David W. Blight and Jim Downs, 121–35. Athens: University of Georgia Press, 2017.

Gosnell, Harold Foote. *Negro Politicians*. Chicago: University of Chicago Press, 1969.

Green, William D. *Degrees of Freedom: The Origins of the Civil Rights Movement in Minnesota, 1865–1912*. Minneapolis: University of Minnesota Press, 2015.

Gregg, Howard D. *History of the African Methodist Episcopal Church*. Nashville: African Methodist Episcopal Church, 1980.

Griffin, Paul R. "A Brief Account of the Development and Work of African Methodism in Ohio and Indiana, 1830–1865." *Black History News and Notes* 23 (November 1985): 1–21.

Griffler, Keith P. *Front Line of Freedom: African Americans and the Forging of the Underground Railroad in the Ohio Valley*. Lexington: University Press of Kentucky, 2004.

Grimshaw, William H. *Official History of Freemasonry among the Colored People in North America*. New York: 1903.

Grossman, Lawrence. "'In His Veins Coursed No Bootlicking Blood': The Career of Peter H. Clark." *Ohio History* (Spring 1977): 79–85.

Gutman, Herbert G. *The Black Family in Slavery and Freedom, 1750–1925*. New York: Pantheon Books, 1976.

Guy-Sheftall, Beverly. "Black Women's Studies: The Interface of Women's Studies and Black Studies." *Phylon* 49 (Spring–Summer 1992): 33–41.

Hahn, Steven. *A Nation without Borders: The United States and Its World in an Age of Civil Wars: 1830–1910.* New York: Viking Books, 2016.

Hall, Jacquelyn Dowd. "'The Mind That Burns in Each Body': Women, Rape, and Racial Violence." In *Powers of Desire: The Politics of Sexuality*, edited by Ann Snitow, Christine Stansell, and Sharon Thompson, 328–49. New York: Monthly Review Press, 1983.

Hamm, Thomas D., et al. "Moral Choices: Two Indiana Quaker Communities and the Abolitionist Movement." *Indiana Magazine of History* 87 (June 1991): 117–54.

Hammond, John Craig. *Slavery, Freedom, and Expansion in the Early American West.* Charlottesville: University of Virginia Press, 2007.

Hammond, John Craig, and Matthew Mason, eds. *Contesting Slavery: The Politics of Bondage and Freedom in the New American Nation.* Charlottesville: University of Virginia Press, 2011.

Handy, Reverend James A. *Scraps of African Methodist Episcopal History.* Philadelphia: A.M.E. Book Concern, n.d. Reprint, University Microfilms, 1972.

Hanley, Sarah. "The Family, the State, and the Law in Seventeenth- and Eighteenth-Century France: The Political Ideology of Male Right versus an Early Theory of Natural Rights." *Journal of Modern History* 78 (June 2006): 289–332.

Hansen, Debra Gold. *Strained Sisterhood: Gender and Class in the Boston Female Anti-Slavery Society.* Amherst: University of Massachusetts Press, 1993.

Harding, Vincent. *There Is a River: The Black Struggle for Freedom in America.* New York: Harcourt Brace Jovanovich, 1981.

Harris, Leslie M. *In the Shadow of Slavery: African-Americans in New York City, 1626–1863.* Chicago: University of Chicago Press, 2003.

Harris, N. Dwight. *The History of Negro Servitude in Illinois and of the Slavery Agitation in That State, 1719–1864.* Chicago: A. C. McClurg, 1904. Reprint, Negro Universities Press, 1969.

Harris, Robert L. "H. Ford Douglas: Afro-American Antislavery Emigrationist." *Journal of Negro History* 62, no. 3 (July 1977): 217–34.

Harrold, Stanley. *Border War: Fighting over Slavery before the Civil War.* Chapel Hill: University of North Carolina Press, 2010.

Heinl, Frank J. "An Epitome of Jacksonville History to 1875." Jacksonville: Illinois Centennial Commission, Committee on Historical Publications, 1925.

———. "Jacksonville and Morgan County—a Historical Review." *Journal of the Illinois State Historical Society* 18, no. 1 (April 1925): 1–25.

Heller, Herbert. "Colored People, Settlements, Temperance, Churches, Biography." *Indiana Negro History Society Bulletin*, January 1944, 119–35.

———. "History of Terre Haute, Indiana." *Indiana Negro History Society Bulletin*, January 1944, 1–43.

Hendrick, George, and Willene Hendrick. *Fleeing for Freedom: Stories of the Underground Railroad as Told by Levi Coffin and William Still.* Chicago: Ivan R. Dee, 2004.

Hendricks, Wanda A. *Gender, Race, and Politics in the Midwest: Black Club Women in Illinois.* Bloomington: Indiana University Press, 1998.

Hewitt, Nancy. *Women's Activism and Social Change: Rochester, New York, 1822–1872.* Ithaca, NY: Cornell University Press, 1984.

Hicken, Victor. *Illinois in the Civil War.* Champaign: University of Illinois Press, 1991.

———. "The Record of Illinois Negro Soldiers in the Civil War." *Journal of the Illinois State Historical Society* 56 (1963): 529–51.

Higginbotham, Evelyn Brooks. *Righteous Discontent: The Women's Movement in the Black Baptist Church, 1880–1920.* Cambridge, MA: Harvard University Press, 1993.

Hine, Darlene Clark. "Lifting the Veil, Shattering the Silence: Black Women's History in Slavery and Freedom." In *The State of Afro-American History: Past, Present, and Future.* Baton Rouge: Louisiana State University Press, 1986.

———. "Rape and the Inner Lives of Black Women in the Middle West: The Culture of Dissemblance." *Signs* 14, no. 4 (Summer 1989): 912–20.

Hine, Darlene Clark, and Patrick Kay Bidelman. *The Black Women in the Middle West Project: A Comprehensive Resource Guide, Illinois and Indiana.* West Lafayette: Purdue Research Foundation, 1986.

Hine, Darlene Clark, and Kathleen Thompson. *A Shining Thread of Hope: The History of Black Women in America.* New York: Broadway Books, 1998.

Hitchcock, Orville, and Otta T. Reynolds. "Frederick Douglass' Fourth of July Oration, 1860." In *Antislavery and Disunion, 1858–1861: Studies in the Rhetoric of Compromise and Conflict,* edited by J. Jeffrey Auer. Gloucester, MA: Peter Smith, 1968.

Hite, Roger W. "Voice of a Fugitive: Henry Bibb and Ante-bellum Black Separatism." *Journal of Black Studies* 4 (March 1974): 269–84.

Holt, Michael F. *The Fate of their Country: Politics, Slavery Extension, and the Coming of the Civil War.* New York: Hill and Wang, 2005.

Holt, Thomas C. *Black over White: Negro Political Leadership in South Carolina during Reconstruction.* Urbana: University of Illinois Press, 1977.

———. "Reconstruction in United States History Textbooks." *Journal of American History* 81, no. 4 (1995): 1641–51.

hooks, bell. *Feminist Theory: From Margin to Center.* 2nd ed. London: Pluto, 2000.

Horton, James Oliver. "Freedom's Yoke: Gender Conventions among Free Blacks." *Feminist Studies* vol. 12, no. 1 (1986): 51–76.

———. "Violence, Protest, and Identity: Black Manhood in Antebellum America." In *Free People of Color: Inside the African-American Community,* 80–97. Washington, DC: Smithsonian Institution Press, 1993.

Horton, James Oliver, and Lois E. Horton. *In Hope of Liberty: Community, Culture, and Protest among Northern Free Blacks, 1700–1860*. Chapel Hill: University of North Carolina Press, 1998.

Hubbart, Henry C. *The Older Middle West, 1840–1880: Its Social, Economic, and Political Life and Sectional Tendencies before, during, and after the Civil War*. New York: Russell & Russell, 1963.

Hunter, Lloyd, ed. *Pathways to the Old Northwest*. Indianapolis: Indiana Historical Society, 1988.

Hunter, Tera W. *Bound in Wedlock: Slave and Free Black Marriage in the Nineteenth Century*. Cambridge, MA: Harvard University Press, 2017.

Huston, James L. *Calculating the Value of the Union: Slavery, Property Rights, and the Economic Origins of the Civil War*. Chapel Hill: University of North Carolina Press, 2003.

Jeffrey, Julie Roy. *The Great Silent Army of Abolitionism: Ordinary Women in the Antislavery Movement*. Chapel Hill: University of North Carolina Press, 1988.

Johannsen, Robert W. *The Frontier, the Union, and Stephen A. Douglas*. Urbana: University of Illinois Press, 1989.

Johnson, Franklin. *The Development of State Legislation concerning the Free Negro*. New York: Arbor, 1918.

Johnson, Karen. *Uplifting the Women and the Race: The Lives, Educational Philosophies, and Social Activism of Anna Julia Cooper and Nannie Helen Burroughs*. New York: Garland, 2000.

Johnson, Michael P. *Abraham Lincoln, Slavery, and the Civil War: Selected Writings and Speeches*. Boston: Bedford/St. Martin's, 2001.

———. "Out of Egypt: The Migration of Former Slaves to the Midwest during the 1860s in Comparative Perspective." In *Crossing Boundaries: Comparative History of Black People in Diaspora*, edited by Darlene Clark Hine and Jacqueline McLeod, 223–45. Bloomington: Indiana University Press, 1999.

Jones, Jacqueline. *American Work: Four Centuries of Black and White Labor*. New York: W. W. Norton, 1998.

———. *Labor of Love, Labor of Sorrow: Black Women, Work, and the Family from Slavery to the Present*. New York: Basic Books, 1985.

Jones, Martha. *All Bound Up Together: The Woman Question in African American Public Culture, 1830–1900*. Chapel Hill: University of North Carolina Press, 2007.

Julian, George W. *Speeches on Political Questions*. Westport, CT: Negro Universities Press, 1970.

Kann, Mark E. *A Republic of Men: The American Founders, Gendered Language, and Patriarchal Politics*. New York: New York University Press, 1998.

Kantrowitz, Stephen. *More than Freedom: Fighting for Black Citizenship in a White Republic, 1829–1889*. New York: Penguin, 2012.

Karamanski, Theodore J. *Rally 'Round the Flag: Chicago and the Civil War.* Chicago: Nelson-Hall, 1993.

Keegan, John. *A History of Warfare.* New York: Random House, 1993.

Kerber, Linda K. *No Constitutional Right to Be Ladies: Women and the Obligations of Citizenship.* New York: Hill and Wang, 1998.

———. "Separate Spheres, Female Worlds, Woman's Place: The Rhetoric of Women's History," *Journal of American History* 75 (1988): 9–39.

Kettleborough, Charles. *Constitution Making in Indiana.* 3 vols. Indianapolis: Indiana Historical Commission, 1917.

Kotlowski, Dean J. "'The Jordan Is a Hard Road to Travel': Hoosier Responses to Fugitive Slave Cases, 1850–1860." *International Social Science Review* (Fall–Winter 2003): 1–20.

Krenkel, John H., ed. *Richard Yates: Civil War Governor.* Danville, IL: Interstate, 1966.

Kugler, Israel. *From Ladies to Women: The Organized Struggle for Women's Rights in the Reconstruction Era.* New York: Greenwood, 1987.

Landon, Fred. "The Negro Migration to Canada after the Passing of the Fugitive Slave Act." *Journal of Negro History* 5 (January 1920): 22–36.

Lapsansky, Emma Jones. "'Since They Got Those Separate Churches': Afro-Americans and Racism in Jacksonian Philadelphia." *American Quarterly* 32 (Spring 1980): 54–78.

LaRoche, Cheryl Janifer. *Free Black Communities and the Underground Railroad: The Geography of Resistance.* Urbana: University of Illinois Press, 2014.

Lebsock, Suzanne. *The Free Women of Petersburg: Status and Culture in a Southern Town, 1784–1860.* New York: W. W. Norton, 1984.

Leonard, Elizabeth. *Yankee Women: Gender Battles in the Civil War.* New York: W. W. Norton, 1994.

Levine, Robert S., ed. *Martin R. Delany: A Documentary Reader.* Chapel Hill: University of North Carolina Press, 2003.

Lewis, Earl. *In Their Own Interests: Race, Class, and Power in Twentieth-Century Norfolk, Virginia.* Berkeley: University of California Press, 2001.

Lincoln, C. Eric, and Lawrence H. Mamiya. *The Black Church in the African-American Experience.* Durham, NC: Duke University Press, 1990.

Lindsey, Treva B. *Colored No More: Reinventing Black Womanhood in Washington, D.C.* Urbana: University of Illinois Press, 2017.

Litwack, Leon F. *North of Slavery: The Negro in the Free States, 1790–1860.* Chicago: University of Chicago Press, 1961.

Litwack, Leon F., and August Meier, eds. *Black Leaders of the Nineteenth Century.* Urbana: University of Illinois Press, 1988.

Logan, Rayford. *The Negro in American Life and Thought: The Nadir, 1877–1901.* New York: Dial, 1954.

Logan, Shirley Wilson. *"We Are Coming": The Persuasive Discourse of Nineteenth-Century Black Women*. Carbondale: Southern Illinois University Press, 1999.

Long, E. B. Foreword. *Illinois in the Civil War*, edited by Victor Hicken. Chicago: University of Illinois, 1991.

Longstreet, Stephen. *Chicago: 1860–1919*. New York: David McKay, 1973.

Mahoney, Olivia. "Black Abolitionists." *Chicago History* (Spring–Summer, 1991): 22–37.

Mangione, Jerry. *The Dream and the Deal: The Federal Writers' Project, 1935–1972*. Syracuse, NY: Syracuse University Press, 1996.

Manning, Chandra. *What This Cruel War Was Over: Soldiers, Slavery, and the Civil War*. New York: Vintage, 2007.

Martin, Bonnie. "Neighbor-to-Neighbor Capitalism: Local Credit Networks and the Mortgaging of Slaves." In *Slavery's Capitalism: A New History of American Economic Development*, ed. Sven Beckert and Seth Rockman, 107–21. Philadelphia: University of Pennsylvania Press.

Masur, Kate. "The Problem of Equality in the Age of Emancipation." In *Beyond Freedom: Disrupting the History of Emancipation*, ed. David W. Blight and Jim Downs, 77–89. Athens: University of Georgia Press, 2017.

Maxwell, William Quentin. *Lincoln's Fifth Wheel: The Political History of the United States Sanitary Commission*. New York: Longmans, Green, 1956.

McCaul, Robert L. *The Black Struggle for Public Schooling in Nineteenth-Century Illinois*. Carbondale: Southern Illinois University Press, 1987.

McCurry, Stephanie. *Masters of Small Worlds: Yeoman Households, Gender Relations, and the Political Culture of the Antebellum South Carolina Low Country*. New York: Oxford University Press, 1995.

McDonald, Lois. "Negro Migration into Indiana, 1800–1860." MA thesis, Indiana University, 1945.

McHenry, Elizabeth. *Forgotten Readers: Recovering the Lost History of African-American Literary Societies*. Durham, NC: Duke University Press, 2002.

McManus, Michael J. *Political Abolitionism in Wisconsin, 1840–1861*. Kent, OH: Kent State University Press, 1998.

McPherson, James M. *Battle Cry of Freedom*. New York: Oxford University Press, 1988.

———. *The Negro's Civil War: How American Blacks Felt and Acted During the War for the Union*. New York: Ballantine Books, 1965.

———. *Ordeal by Fire: The Civil War and Reconstruction*. New York: Alfred A. Knopf, 1982.

———. *The Struggle for Equality: Abolitionists and the Negro in the Civil War and Reconstruction*. Princeton, NJ: Princeton University Press, 1964.

Mehlinger, Louis R. "The Attitude of Free Negroes toward African Colonization." *Journal of Negro History* 1 (1916): 293–322.

Meier, Michael T. "Lorenzo Thomas and the Recruitment of Blacks in the Mississippi Valley, 1863–1865." In *Black Soldiers in Blue: African American Troops in the Civil War Era*, edited by John David Smith, 249–75. Chapel Hill: University of North Carolina Press, 2002.

Middleton, Stephen. *The Black Laws in the Old Northwest: A Documentary History.* Westport, CT: Greenwood, 1993.

Miller, Edward A., Jr. *The Black Civil War Soldiers of Illinois: The Story of the Twenty-Ninth U.S. Colored Infantry.* Columbia: University of South Carolina Press, 1998.

———. "Garland H. White, Black Army Chaplain." *Civil War History* 43 (1997): 201–18.

Miller, Floyd John. *The Search for Black Nationality: Black Emigration and Colonization, 1787–1863.* Chicago: University of Illinois Press, 1979.

Mitchell, Reid. *The Vacant Chair: The Northern Soldier Leaves Home.* New York: Oxford University Press, 1993.

Money, Charles H. "Fugitive Slave Law of 1850 of Indiana." *Indiana Magazine of History* 17, no. 2 (June 1921): 159–98.

Montgomery, David. *Beyond Equality: Labor and the Radical Republicans, 1862–1872.* New York: Alfred A. Knopf, 1967.

Moore, Lamire Holden. *Southern Baptists in Illinois.* Nashville: Benson, 1957.

Morris, Aldon D. *The Origins of the Civil Rights Movement.* New York: Free Press, 1984.

Morrison, Michael. *Slavery and the American West: The Eclipse of Manifest Destiny and the Coming of the Civil War.* Chapel Hill: University of North Carolina Press, 1997.

Muelder, Hermann R. *Fighters for Freedom: The History of Anti-slavery Activities of Men and Women Associated with Knox College.* New York: Columbia University Press, 1959.

———. *A Hero Home from the War: Among the Black Citizens of Galesburg, Illinois.* Galesburg: Knox College Library, 1987.

Muirhead, John W. *A History of African-Americans in McLean County, Illinois, 1835.* Bloomington, IL: Bloomington-Normal Black History Project, McClean County Historical Society, 1998.

Myers, Amrita Chakrabarti. *Forging Freedom: Black Women and the Pursuit of Liberty in Antebellum Charleston.* Chapel Hill: University of North Carolina Press, 2001.

Nelson, Dana D. *National Manhood: Capitalist Citizenship and the Imagined Fraternity of White Men.* Durham, NC: Duke University Press, 1998.

Norton, Herman A. *Struggling for Recognition: The United States Army Chaplaincy, 1791–1865.* Washington, DC: Office of the Chief of Chaplains, Department of the Army, 1977.

Onuf, Peter S. *Statehood and Union: A History of the Northwest Ordinance.* Bloomington: Indiana University Press, 1987.

Orleck, Annalise. *Storming Caesar's Palace: How Black Mothers Fought Their Own War on Poverty.* Boston: Beacon, 2005.

Ostler, Jeffrey. *The Plains Sioux and U.S. Colonialism from Lewis and Clark to Wounded Knee.* New York: Cambridge University Press, 2004.

Owens, Deirdre Cooper. *Medical Bondage: Race, Gender, and the Origins of American Gynecology.* Athens: University of Georgia Press, 2017.

Parrish, William E. "The Western Sanitary Commission." *Civil War History* 36 (March 1990): 17–35.

Payne, Ethel. "Unearth Tale of 'Forgotten Man,'" *Chicago Defender,* July 12, 1951, 13.

Peters, Pamela R. *The Underground Railroad in Floyd Country, Indiana.* Jefferson, NC: McFarland, 2001.

Peterson, Carla. *"Doers of the Word": African-American Women Speakers and Writers in the North (1830–1880).* New Brunswick, NJ: Rutgers University Press, 1995.

Peterson, Richard H. "The United States Sanitary Commission and Thomas Starr King in California, 1861–1864." *California History* (Winter 1993–1994): 325–38.

Phillips, Christopher. *The Rivers Ran Backward: The Civil War and the Remaking of the American Middle Border.* New York: Oxford University Press, 2016.

Pierce, Bessie Louise. *A History of Chicago.* Vol. 2, *From Town to City, 1848–1871.* New York: Alfred A. Knopf, 1940.

Pierce, Richard B. "Negotiated Freedoms: African Americans in Indiana." In *The State of Indiana History 2000: Papers Presented at the Indiana Historical Society's Grand Opening,* edited by Robert M. Taylor Jr., 319–41. Indianapolis: Indiana Historical Society, 2001.

Pierson, Michael D. *Free Hearts and Free Homes: Gender and American Antislavery Politics.* Chapel Hill: University of North Carolina Press, 2003.

Pierson, William D. *Black Yankees: The Development of an Afro-American Subculture in Eighteenth-Century New England.* Amherst: University of Massachusetts, 1988.

Potter, David. *The Impending Crisis, 1848–1861.* New York: Harper & Row, 1976.

Pratt, Mildred, ed. *We the People Tell Our Story: Bloomington-Normal Black History Project.* Normal: Illinois State University, 1987.

Pryor, Elizabeth. *Colored Travelers: Mobility and the Fight for Citizenship before the Civil War.* Chapel Hill: University of North Carolina Press, 2016.

Quinn Chapel. *110th Anniversary, 1847–1947.* Chicago: African Methodist Episcopal Church, 1957.

———. *120th Anniversary, 1847–1967.* Chicago: African Methodist Episcopal Church, 1967.

Raboteau, Albert J. *Canaan Land: A Religious History of African Americans.* Oxford: Oxford University Press, 2001.

Rael, Patrick. *Black Identity and Black Protest in the Antebellum North.* Chapel Hill: University of North Carolina Press, 2002.

———. "Black Theodicy: African Americans and Nationalism in the Antebellum North." *North Star: A Journal of African-American Religious History* 3, no. 2 (Spring 2000): 1–24.

Redkey, Edwin S. "Black Chaplains in the Union Army." *Civil War History* 33 (December 1987): 334–64.

———. *A Grand Army of Black Men: Letters from African-American Soldiers in the Union Army, 1861–1865.* Cambridge: Cambridge University Press, 1992.

Reed, Christopher Robert. *Chicago's Black Century.* Vol. 1, *1833–1900.* Columbia: University of Missouri Press, 2005.

Reed, Harry. *Platform for Change: The Foundations of the Northern Free Black Community, 1775–1865.* East Lansing: Michigan State University, 1994.

Rhodes, Jane. *Mary Ann Shadd Cary: The Black Press and Protest in the Nineteenth Century.* Bloomington: Indiana University Press, 1998.

Richardson, Marilyn. *Maria W. Stewart: America's First Black Woman Political Writer: Essays and Speeches.* Bloomington: Indiana University Press, 1987.

Richter, Daniel K. *Facing East from Indian Country: A Native History of Early America.* Cambridge, MA: Harvard University Press, 2001.

Ripley, C. Peter. *The Black Abolitionist Papers.* Vol. 3, *The United States, 1830–1846.* Chapel Hill: University of North Carolina Press, 1991.

———. *The Black Abolitionist Papers.* Vol. 5, *The United States, 1859–1865.* Chapel Hill: University of North Carolina Press, 1992.

Robb, Dale. "Progress in Attaining Liberty and Justice for Negroes in Morgan County, Illinois, 1823 to 1967." Jacksonville, IL: Morgan County Historical Society, 1967.

Robertson, Stacey M. *Hearts Beating for Liberty: Women Abolitionists in the Old Northwest.* Chapel Hill: University of North Carolina Press, 2010.

Roediger, David. *The Wages of Whiteness: Race and the Making of the American Working Class.* New York: Verso, 1999.

Rojas, Fabio. "Social Movement Tactics, Organizational Change, and the Spread of African-American Studies." *Social Forces* 84, no. 4 (2006): 2147–66.

Romeo, Sharon. *Gender and the Jubilee: Black Freedom and the Reconstruction of Citizenship in Civil War Missouri.* Athens: University of Georgia Press, 2016.

Rothman, Adam. *Beyond Freedom's Reach: A Kidnapping in the Twilight of Slavery.* Cambridge, MA: Harvard University Press, 2015.

Ryan, Mary P. *Women in Public: Between Banners and Ballots, 1825–1880.* Baltimore: Johns Hopkins University Press, 1990.

Salafia, Matthew. *Slavery's Borderland: Freedom and Bondage along the Ohio River.* Philadelphia: University of Pennsylvania Press, 2018.

Saline County Historical Society. *Saline County, a Century of History, 1847–1947.* Harrisburg, PA, 1974. Northwestern University Library, Rare Books Collection, Evanston, Illinois.

Schultz, Jane. *Women at the Front: Hospital Workers in Civil War America*. Chapel Hill: University of North Carolina Press, 2007.

Schwalm, Leslie A. *Emancipation's Diaspora: Race and Reconstruction in the Upper Midwest*. Chapel Hill: University of North Carolina Press, 2009.

———. *A Hard Fight for We: Women's Transition from Slavery to Freedom in South Carolina*. Champaign: University of Illinois Press, 1997.

———. "'Overrun with Free Negroes': Emancipation and Wartime Migration in the Upper Midwest." *Civil War History* 50 (June 2014): 145–74.

Scott, Anne Firor. "Most Invisible of All: Black Women's Voluntary Associations." *Journal of Southern History* 56, no. 1 (1990): 3–22.

———. "Women's Voluntary Associations: From Charity to Reform." In *Lady Bountiful Revisited: Women, Philanthropy, and Power*, edited by Kathleen D. McCarthy, 35–54. New Brunswick: Rutgers University Press, 1990.

Scott, Joan Wallach. "Gender: A Useful Category of Analysis." *Gender and the Politics of History*, 28–50. New York: Columbia University Press, 1988.

Scudder, Horace E. *American Commonwealth: Indiana*. New York: Houghton Mifflin, 1899.

Seigel, Peggy Brase. "Moral Champions and Public Pathfinders: Antebellum Quaker Women in Eastcentral Indiana." *Quaker History* 81, no. 2 (Fall 1992): 87–106.

Shepard, Merle B. *A History of the Negro Schools in Vigo County*. MA thesis, Indiana State Teachers College, 1948.

Silber, Nina. *Daughters of the Union: Northern Women Fight the Civil War*. Cambridge, MA: Harvard University Press, 2005.

Silverman, Jason H., and Donna J. Gillie. "'The Pursuit of Knowledge under Difficulties': Education and the Fugitive Slave in Canada." *Ontario History* 74 (June 1982): 95–112.

Simeone, James. *Democracy and Slavery in Frontier Illinois: The Bottomland Republic*. DeKalb: Northern Illinois University Press, 2000.

Simmons, William J. *Men of Mark: Eminent, Progressive, and Rising*. Cleveland: George M. Rewell, 1887.

Sinha, Manisha. *The Slave's Cause: A History of Abolition*. New Haven: Yale University Press, 2016.

Smith, Charles Spencer. *A History of the African Methodist Episcopal Church*. Philadelphia: Book Concern of the A.M.E. Church, 1922.

Sorensen, Kathy Owen. *Illinois Women: 75 Years of the Right to Vote*. Chicago: Chicago *Sun-Times* Features, 1996.

Stampp, Kenneth M. *Indiana Politics during the Civil War*. Indianapolis: Indiana University Press, 1978.

Sterling, Dorothy, ed. *Speak Out in Thunder Tones: Letter and Other Writings by Black Northerners, 1787–1865*. New York: De Capo, 1998.

————, ed. *We Are Your Sisters: Black Women in the Nineteenth Century.* New York: W. W. Norton, 1997.

Stetson, Erlene. "Black Feminism in Indiana, 1893–1933." *Phylon* 44 (1983): 292–98.

Stevenson, Brenda E. "'Us Never Had No Big Funerals or Weddin's on de Place': Ritualizing Black Marriage in the Wake of Freedom." In *Beyond Freedom: Disrupting the History of Emancipation*, edited by David W. Blight and Jim Downs, 39–59. Athens: University of Georgia Press, 2017.

Stewart, James Brewer. "The Emergence of Racial Identity and the Rise of the White North, 1790–1840." *Journal of the Early Republic* 18 (Spring 1998): 181–217.

Taylor, Henry Louis. *Race and the City: Work, Community, and Protest in Cincinnati, 1820–1970.* Champaign: University of Illinois Press, 1993.

Taylor, Nikki M. *America's First Black Socialist: The Radical Life of Peter H. Clark.* Lexington: University Press of Kentucky, 2013.

————. *Frontiers of Freedom: Cincinnati's Black Community, 1802–1868.* Athens: Ohio University Press, 2005.

Taylor, Robert M., Jr., ed. *The State of Indiana History 2000: Papers Presented at the Indiana Historical Society's Grand Opening.* Indianapolis: Indiana Historical Society, 2001.

Thompson, William C. "Eleutherian Institute: A Sketch of the Unique Step in the Educational History of Indiana." *Indiana Magazine of History* 19 (June 1923): 100–127.

Thornbrough, Emma Lou. "Indiana and Fugitive Slave Legislation." *Indiana Magazine of History* 50 (September 1954): 210–28.

————. *Indiana in the Civil War Era, 1850–1880.* Indianapolis: Indiana Historical Society, 1995.

————. *The Negro in Indiana before 1900: A Study of a Minority.* Bloomington: Indiana University Press, 1993.

————. "The Race Issue in Indiana Politics during the Civil War." *Indiana Magazine of History* 47 (1951): 171–194.

————. *Since Emancipation: A Short History of Indian Negroes, 1863–1963.* Indianapolis: Indiana Division, American Negro Emancipation Centennial Authority, 1963.

Trotter, Joe William. *River Jordan: African American Urban Life in the Ohio Valley.* Lexington: University Press of Kentucky, 1998.

Trudeau, Noah Andre. *Like Men of War: Black Troops in The Civil War, 1862–1865.* Boston: Little, Brown, 1998.

Turner, Glennette Tiley. *The Underground Railroad in Illinois.* Glen Ellyn, IL: Newman Educational Publishing, 2001.

Ullman, Victor. *Martin Delany: The Beginnings of Black Nationalism.* Boston: Beacon, 1971.

VanderVelde, Lea. *Mrs. Dred Scott: A Life on Slavery's Frontier.* New York: Oxford University Press, 2009.

VanderVelde, Lea, and Sandhya Subramanian. "Mrs. Dred Scott." *Yale Law Journal* 106 (January 1997): 1033–122.

Van West, Carroll, ed. *Trial and Triumph: Essays in Tennessee's African American History.* Knoxville: University of Tennessee Press, 2002.

Venet, Wendy Hamand. "The Emergence of a Suffragist: Mary Livermore, Civil War Activism, and the Moral Power of Women." *Civil War History* 48 (June 2002): 143–64.

Vincent, Stephen. *Southern Seed, Northern Soil: African-American Farm Communities in the Midwest, 1765–1900.* Bloomington: Indiana University Press, 1999.

Voegeli, V. Jacque. *Free but Not Equal: The Midwest and the Negro during the Civil War.* Chicago: University of Chicago Press, 1967.

———. "The Northwest and the Race Issue, 1861–1862." *Mississippi Valley Historical Review* 50 (September 1963): 235–51.

Walker, Clarence E. *A Rock in a Weary Land: The African Methodist Episcopal Church during the Civil War and Reconstruction.* Baton Rouge: Louisiana State University Press, 1982.

Walker, Juliet E. K. *Free Frank: A Black Pioneer on the Antebellum Frontier.* Lexington: University Press of Kentucky, 1983.

Washington, James Melvin. *Frustrated Fellowship: The Black Baptist Quest for Social Power.* Macon, GA: Mercer University Press, 1986.

Watkins, Sylvestre C., Sr. "Some of Early Illinois' Free Negroes." *Journal of the Illinois State Historical Society* 56, no. 3 (Autumn 1963): 495–507.

Welter, Barbara. "The Cult of True Womanhood: 1820–1860." *American Quarterly* 18, no. 2 (1966): 151–74.

Westwood, Howard C. *Black Troops, White Commanders, and Freedmen during the Civil War.* Carbondale: Southern Illinois University Press, 1992.

White, Deborah Gray. *Ar'n't I a Woman? Female Slaves in the Plantation South.* New York: W. W. Norton, 1999.

———. "Simple Truths: Antebellum Slavery in Black and White." In *The Underground Railroad in History and Memory,* edited by David W. Blight. Washington, DC: Smithsonian Books, 2004.

———. *Too Heavy a Load: Black Women in Defense of Themselves, 1894–1994.* New York: W. W. Norton, 1999.

White, Shane. *Prince of Darkness: The Untold Story of Jeremiah Hamilton, Wall Street's First Black Millionaire.* New York: St. Martin's, 2016.

Whites, LeeAnn, and Alecia P. Long. *Occupied Women: Gender, Military Occupation, and the American Civil War.* Baton Rouge: Louisiana State University Press, 2009.

Williams, George Washington. *The American Negro, from 1776 to 1876: Oration Delivered July 4, 1876, at Avondale, Ohio.* Cincinnati: Robert Clark, 1876.

Williams, Gilbert Anthony. *The Christian Recorder, Newspaper of the African Methodist Episcopal Church: History of a Forum for Ideas, 1854–1902.* Jefferson, NC: McFarland, 1996.

Williamson, Joel. *After Slavery: The Negro in South Carolina during Reconstruction, 1861–1877.* Chapel Hill: University of North Carolina Press, 1965.

Wilson, Muriel Braxton. "Center City Origins of the South Side Black Community of Chicago, 1860–1890." MA thesis, Roosevelt University, 1984.

Woodson, Carter G. *A Century of Negro Migration.* 1918. Reprint, New York: AMS Press, 1970.

———. *The History of the Negro Church.* 2nd ed. Washington, DC: Associated Publishers.

Woodward, C. Vann. *Origins of the New South: 1877–1913.* Baton Rouge: Louisiana State University Press, 1951.

———. *Reunion and Reaction: The Compromise of 1877 and the End of Reconstruction.* Garden City, NY: Doubleday, 1956.

———. *The Strange Career of Jim Crow.* New York: Oxford University Press, 1955.

Wright, Richard, ed. *Centennial Encyclopaedia of the African Methodist Episcopal Church.* Philadelphia: Book Concern of the A.M.E. Church, 1916.

Yancy, George. *Black Bodies, White Gazes: The Continuing Significance of Race in America.* Lanham, MD: Rowman & Littlefield, 2016.

Yannessa, Mary Ann. *Levi Coffin, Quaker: Breaking the Bonds of Slavery in Ohio and Indiana.* Richmond, IN: Friends United Press, 2001.

Yee, Shirley J. *Black Women Abolitionists: A Study in Activism, 1828–1860.* Knoxville: University of Tennessee Press, 1992.

Yellin, Jean Fagan, and John C. Van Horne. *The Abolitionist Sisterhood: Women's Political Culture in Antebellum America.* Ithaca, NY: Cornell University Press, 1994.

Zilversmit, Arthur, ed. *Lincoln on Black and White: A Documentary History.* Belmont, CA: Wadsworth Publishing Company, 1971.

Index

Page locators in italics refer to illustrations.

Jennifer R. Harbour is an associate professor of black studies and women's and gender studies at the University of Nebraska Omaha. She teaches courses on African American history, modern African history, and international human rights.